CLOSER AND CLOSER APART

CLOSER & CLOSER APART

JEALOUSY IN LITERATURE

ROSEMARY LLOYD

Cornell University Press   ITHACA AND LONDON

First published 1995 by Cornell University Press

Printed in the United States of America

⊗ The paper in this book meets the minimum requirements
of the American National Standard for Information Sciences—
Permanence of Paper for Printed Library Materials, ANSI Z39.48–1984

Library of Congress Cataloging-in-Publication Data

Lloyd, Rosemary.
    Closer and closer apart : jealousy in literature / Rosemary Lloyd.
        p.   cm.
    Includes bibliographical references and index.
    ISBN 0-8014-3151-4 (alk. paper)
    1. Jealousy in literature.   2. Literature—History and criticism.   I. Title.
PN56.J43L56   1995   95-19545
809'.93353—dc20

You cannot build bridges between the wandering islands;
The Mind has no neighbors, and the unteachable heart
Announces its armistice time after time, but spends
Its love to draw them closer and closer apart.

A. D. Hope, *The Wandering Islands*

Contents

Foretext

And each man kills the thing he loves.
                    Oscar Wilde, "The Ballad of Reading Gaol"

Deep in the bowels of the Palais de Justice, in a cell whose darkness and piercing cold prefigure those of the grave, the priest Claude Frollo, whose given name encapsulates the idea of enclosure, narrates to Esmeralda the story of how she unwittingly and unwillingly seduced him, transforming his dominant characteristic from zealotry to jealousy. Condemned to death for a presumed murder, an attack perpetrated in fact by the insanely jealous Frollo, Esmeralda is also condemned to listen in silence to his narration:

> "Before I met you, young lady, I was happy . . ."
> "So was I!" she sighed listlessly.
> "Don't interrupt me."[1]

Power, in Victor Hugo's claustrophobic society, which metaphorically models jealousy, lies with the one whose tale is heard; authority lies with the one who enforces authorship. Jealousy is a passion so powerful that it destroys communication, just as tyrannical political power in Hugo's novel attempts to destroy the printing presses, breaking down the very relationship with the Other that gives that relationship birth.

1. Victor Hugo, *Notre-Dame de Paris* (Paris: Garnier-Flammarion, 1967), 342.

Frollo's tale reinforces these images of silencing and static, while the architectural space in which he narrates it, and the space in which the event narrated took place, both emblematize male power structures. High in his cell in Notre-Dame, the priest was lost in a book when his reading was interrupted by the sound of Esmeralda's tambourine, drawing his gaze down to the square, as his soul is to plunge into torment, and as Esmeralda herself is to tumble into the depths of justice. The static that has disrupted his reading has also ripped apart his interpretation of existence, his role as innocent intellectual, and his vows of celibacy. Esmeralda is the uninvited, unwelcome, and unintentional guest at the feast of purity and knowledge, just as Frollo himself, peering through the spy hole as Phoebus seduces Esmeralda, is the unintended reader at the feast of love. These images of the invasive, penetrating gaze, repeated obsessively throughout the text, together with the depiction of events interrupted in their normal course by the unexpected arrival of a third party, reproduce the very fabric of jealousy, and Frollo's equally obsessive narrating of events, real or imaginary, reveals an archetypal response to that passion. His silencing of her reaction ("Don't interrupt me!") offers a *mise en abyme* of his solution to the predicament in which he finds himself: his attempt on Phoebus's life (an attempt to silence the rival), his refusal to tell Esmeralda that Phoebus survived the attack (an attempt to silence rival interpretations of events),[2] and his determination to have Esmeralda hanged in order to still the voice of his own sexuality—all reflect the jealous lover's refusal to countenance the irruption of other voices, the rival's or the beloved's. Furthermore, readings of the text that focus on the political forces at work in Hugo's society—the obscurantist desires of the alchemists, the anarchy of the thieves and beggars, the egalitarian visions of those who support the press, and so forth—also reveal the extent to which sexual jealousy acts as a metaphor for the struggle for political power.

Whereas Frollo's story shows jealousy at its most destruc-

2. Ibid., 353: "It would have been too painful for him to give the woman he loved good news about his rival. Any man in his place would have acted in just the same way."

tive, other explorations bring into focus its power to create, the ways in which it stimulates the imagination, its tendency to transform space and time. Thus, the sultan Schahriar, conjuring jealousy by executing each new wife on the day following their wedding, is outwitted by Scheherazade, who replaces the image of death at dawn with that of her younger sister, substitutes continuity for completion, and provides through an unending series of narratives the image of the constant renewal of sexual desire. Here, the jealous lover's compulsion to silence the other is overridden by a compulsion to listen to the other, while the obsessive and painful narration of what the other might be doing is replaced by the pleasure of listening to the other narrate. The narrative frame is firmly based on stereotypes: the male's concept of power as the imposition of death, the female assumption of power through the life-giving force that creates children, stories, and, ultimately, love itself.

Although modern colloquial usage tends to elide the differences between the concepts of jealousy and envy, the exploration of those boundless possibilities of the imagination demands at least a working definition of each. Where envy concerns what one would like to have but does not possess, jealousy centers on what one has and does not wish to lose. When that "possession" is another person, whose freedom of mind, if not of body, cannot be controlled by the jealous individual, jealousy unleashes passions that shed a powerful and disturbing light on concepts of self, other, gender, and society. Cognate with *zealous*, the term connotes the close relationships between love and hatred, creation and destruction, what reason craves and what imagination fears.

In reading texts that concern jealousy, we find ourselves constantly sharing in the voyeuristic gaze, participating in the endless narrating of the possible, present as the third party between lovers, and also incessantly open to the disruptive static that comes between us and the text when we escape the jealous text's vigilance in order to indulge our own narrations. Because jealousy is figured as watching and interpreting, as telling and silencing, it also acts as a trope for both consuming and creating art and literature. Indeed, it is my argument that the act of reading and decoding the other that lies at the very heart of jealousy encapsulates both the creation and the deciphering of texts, that jealousy in literature is not merely a theme but also, and more vitally, a strategy, both readerly and writerly.

As Richard Terdiman memorably puts it in his exploration of memory, "the object of any study must be distinguished from the remainder of the world's endless flux."[3] Many people have helped me distinguish the exemplifications of jealousy I explore in the following pages, and to all of them I am grateful. To those whose suggestions I was unable to use, and to readers who feel that essential examples have been willfully neglected, I can only apologize.

To Larry Porter, who asked me about this project as he was about to give a lecture at Bloomington, and who came out of the lecture saying: "Does it matter whether jealousy is justified?" I offer admiration and thanks. Jeanne Peters and Catherine Bernard recommended novels that enriched my images of jealousy. Robert Lethbridge, Susan Nelson, Moya Andrews, and Lana Ruegamer were unfailingly supportive. Stephen Noreiko helped me with etymologies and shared his vast knowledge of the implications of colors in French mythology and imagination. Members of the French and Italian brown-bag discussion group, and audiences at Lawrence, Kansas, and at Louisville, Kentucky, asked suggestive questions and further added to my reading list. I am grateful to Indiana University for the award of a faculty fellowship for the summer of 1993 and to the department of French and Italian for additional financial assistance. Julie Starr collected a range of inspiring and often depressing visual representations of jealousy that helped sharpen my thinking.

To Matei Calinescu and Margot Gray, who both commented on sections of the first draft and who, in very different ways, encouraged and inspired me, I owe my warmest thanks. It will be clear to anyone reading this how much I owe to the percep-

---

3. Richard Terdiman, *Present Past: Modernity and the Memory Crisis* (Ithaca: Cornell University Press, 1993), 7.

tions, humanity, and sheer good sense of Ross Chambers: I hope it is equally clear how grateful I am to him.

The epigraph of the book is from A. D. Hope, *the Wandering Islands*, in his *Collected Poems*. HarperCollins Publishers has graciously granted permission to reprint it here.

Sections of chapters 2 and 3 appeared in an earlier form in "Mirroring Difference, Figuring Frames" in *Nineteenth-Century French Studies* (Spring 1991), and I would like to thank the editor for permission to reprint them here.

As always, my greatest debt, although not for any knowledge of jealousy, is to Paul.

ROSEMARY LLOYD

Bloomington, Indiana

CLOSER AND CLOSER APART

Introduction

I have gone into a certain amount of detail, because in these
moments of jealousy one generally loses one's head.
                                        Stendhal, *De l'amour*

"Sexual jealousy," suggests Harold Bloom in an introduction
to Proust, "is the most novelistic of circumstances, just as incest, according to Shelley, is the most poetic of circumstances."[1] So dogmatic an assertion, demanding, as it does, a
leap of faith on the part of the reader, is likely to set in train
not readerly compliance, but the kind of resistance and revolt
that comes from the reader suddenly hearing other voices on
the line,[2] raising questions that throw into doubt the critic's
maxim. Why should jealousy be ranked highest among novelistic circumstances? Why should its analysis and exploration
be limited to the novel, when so many plays and poems focus
on jealousy? And why bring in Shelley and incest when the
latter, far from being intrinsically poetic, is more likely to con-
jure up in the modern mind not the forbidden love between
brother and sister, but distinctly more sordid images of adults
seducing their prepubescent or adolescent children?
    This kind of static on the line, the interference that comes

1. Harold Bloom, "Introduction to Proust," in *Dilemmas du roman: Essays in
Honor of Georges May*, ed. Catherine Lafarge (Saratoga, Calif.: Anma Libri,
1990), 311.
2. The metaphor is borrowed from Michel Serres, *Le Parasite* (Paris: Grasset,
1980).

I

between writer and reader when what is said breaks the pattern of direct communication to allow a chaotic influx of other voices, offers a fertile paradigm for the nature of sexual jealousy itself. What attracts me to the exploration of jealousy in literature is not merely the dramatic interest of the subject, or the psychological insights offered, but above all the light such investigations shed on the relationship between writer, reader, and text, between speaker, listener, and discourse.[3] The circumstances of jealousy, indeed, are often trivial and superficial, "trifles light as air."[4] *Othello*'s center of interest, for instance, is surely not the puerile, mindless jealousy aroused in the Moor, but the chilling portrayal of the domination of Othello's mind by Iago, the perturbing study of those strategies that best transform sexual and political insecurity into the key to a man's destruction.

Indeed, what seizes the attention in such explorations of jealousy is very often the manipulation of literary strategies, the exploration of gender through the lens of jealousy, and the creation of a universe of suspicion in which time, place, and language are distorted in such a way as to replicate the contours of the passion itself. Jealousy, in other words, becomes a metaphor for all the forces of chaos that threaten to disrupt what we take for normality and reality, the chaos that gives power to the shapes and patterns of fiction.

Lovers wrenched apart by an upsurge of jealousy may indeed feel not only that communication between them has become dysfunctional, but that they no longer speak the same language. In a similar way, it is important to be sure that we know what we mean when we talk of jealousy. Even though my purpose is not to dictate to others how the term should be used, I do want to clarify that here *jealousy* has its more limited meaning. Because the term has so complex a history, and is used so loosely in contemporary speech, it is worthwhile exploring its definitions and etymology. Peter Van Sommers's compassionate psychological analysis of the emotion offers a

3. For interesting discussions of the differences between listener and reader, see Jean Rousset, *Le Lecteur intime: De Balzac au Journal* (Paris: Corti, 1986), 1–35.
4. Shakespeare, *Othello*, 3.3.

sharp and helpful distinction between envy and jealousy, two words frequently employed interchangeably: "envy concerns what you would like to have but don't possess, jealousy [. . .] concerns what you have and do not wish to lose."[5] Hanna Segal, pithily summarizing Melanie Klein's *Envy and Gratitude*, further distinguishes between the two in noting that envy is one of the earliest emotions individuals experience, with jealousy coming somewhat later:

> Jealousy is based on love and aims at the possession of the loved object and the removal of the rival. It pertains to a triangular relationship and therefore to a time of life when objects are clearly recognized and differentiated from one another. Envy, on the other hand, is a two-part relation in which the subject envies the object for some possession or quality; no other live object need enter into it. Jealousy is necessarily a whole-object relationship, whilst envy is essentially experienced in terms of part-objects, though its persists into whole-object relationships.[6]

These distinctions are both suggestive and serviceable, helping to explain, for instance, why envy is one of the seven deadly sins, while jealousy is not. La Rochefoucauld, confronting the same question, asserted: "Jealousy is, to some extent, fitting and reasonable, since it tends merely to preserve property that belongs to us or that we believe belongs to us, whereas envy is a rage which cannot bear that others should own property."[7] Finally, James Joyce supplies a witty and parodistic differentiation in the Ithaca section of *Ulysses*, when he lists Bloom's sentiments, on thinking of Molly and Blazes Boylan, as "envy, jealousy, abnegation, equanimity" and adds the following qualifications:

> Envy?
> Of a bodily and mental male organism specially adapted for the superincumbent posture of energetic human copulation

5. Peter Van Sommers, *Jealousy* (Harmondsworth: Penguin, 1988), 1.
6. Hanna Segal, *Introduction to the Work of Melanie Klein* (London: Hogarth Press, 1973), 40.
7. François de La Rochefoucauld, *Maximes* (Paris: Larousse, 1975), 28.

and energetic piston and cylinder movement necessary for the complete satisfaction of a constant but not acute concupiscence resident in a bodily and mental female organism, passive but not obtuse.

Jealousy?
Because a nature full and volatile in its free state, was alternately the agent and reagent of attraction. Because action between agents and reagents at all instants varied, with inverse proportion of increase and decrease, with incessant circular extension and radial reentrance. Because the controlled contemplation of the fluctuation of attraction produced, if desired, a fluctuation of pleasure.[8]

The terms are used indiscriminately in such popular "feel-good" books as Nancy Friday's *Jealousy*, where the expression "jealousy" applies to a broad range of passions, from envy to lust and greed. While this kind of usage blurs the boundaries between categories that are intellectually valuable and psychologically justifiable, such confusion is understandable in that historical explorations of the term indicate that these boundaries have long posed problems. Margot Grzywacz's fascinating etymological survey of the word in Romance and Germanic languages asserts, indeed, that the concept was one of those that proved to be the most difficult to express in language and was therefore among the last to find an unambiguous term.[9] Classical Latin used *invidia*, without strictly differentiating between envy and jealousy. It was not until the postclassical era that Latin borrowed the late and poetic Greek word *zelotypia* and the associated adjective *zelosus*. It is from this adjective that are derived French *jaloux*, Provençal *gelos*, Italian *geloso*, and Spanish *celoso*. Grzywacz argues that all these terms, like the German word, *Eifersucht*, which appeared in the sixteenth century, do not arise directly from Greco-Roman culture but seem rather to reflect the Biblical term *zelotes*. The fact that jealousy is cognate with zealotry implies a close relationship

8. James Joyce, *Ulysses* (New York: Vintage, 1990), 732.
9. Margot Grzywacz, *"Eifersucht" in den romanischen Sprachen* (Bochum-Langendreer, Germany: H. Pöppinghaus, 1937), 4.

between religious and erotic love. Indeed, she affirms, the whole of the Old Testament portrays the relationship between God and His people in erotic metaphors, as that between a jealous husband and his wife, and portrays the worship of other gods as the equivalent of adultery.

One might note in passing that Grzywacz argues that the spelling of the word in French, Provençal, and Italian suggests contamination with the adjective *giallo* meaning yellow, the color associated with jealousy. Later scholars have contested this reading and have seen it as merely a popular etymology, created after the fact, but in any case the suggestion demonstrates the extent to which yellow is connected in the popular imagination with the idea of jealousy.[10] It is, of course, no accident that yellow also symbolizes cuckoldry.

Dictionary definitions of the word give some hint of the complexity of the emotion and of the metaphorical uses to which it has been put. The nineteenth-century French dictionary compiled by Littré, for instance—he who is reported, when his wife caught him *in flagrante delicto* with another woman, to have responded to her exclamation: "Je suis surprise!" ["I'm surprised!"] by informing her that correctly speaking *he* was the one who was surprised and that she should have described herself as astonished—lists eight main uses of the word. The entry begins with "zealous" and "pain caused by the fact that one cannot obtain or does not possess that which someone else has obtained or possesses" (more precisely covered by the term "envy"), before reaching as its third use the definition: "feeling that arises from being in love and that is produced by the fear that the beloved might prefer someone else." It is under this heading that Littré refers to the "lunettes de jalousie," a device allowing one to look directly at objects that seem to be at right angles to the viewer. The emphasis on spying on others, or alternatively preventing others from seeing, is, as we shall discover, a central element of jealousy, both as emotion and as literary device. The *Oxford English Dic-*

---

10. I am indebted to Stephen Noreiko, of the University of Hull, for his comments on the colors associated with jealousy and envy and for his suggestion that the putative etymological link between yellow and jealousy may reflect the popular imagination (private letter, 26 July 1993).

tionary of 1703, for instance, mentions a "jealous glass," consisting of a translucent pane through which it is impossible to look.

The Littré dictionary's list then continues through a series of further uses that emphasize the ease with which the term acquired metaphorical meanings: the feeling of umbrage inspired in others by the power of a prince or a State; the disquiet aroused in the enemy when an army attacks certain points of its defense; a trellis of wood or iron that allows one to see without being seen; a kind of dance; a marine term referring to a ship being rolled and rocked by stormy seas as a jealous lover is tossed about by the force of jealousy.

Some of the complexities of the emotion itself are suggested in the German term, *Eifersucht*, which combines the word for zeal or passion (*Eifer*) with the expression for illness, mania, addiction (*Sucht*). It gives rise to a complex and typically German pun: "Die Eifersucht ist eine Leidenschaft, die mit Eifer sucht, was Leiden schafft" ["Jealousy is a passion that zealously seeks that which causes suffering"]. Hildegard Baumgart, in her psychological study of jealousy, draws on this elegant play on words to argue that the term evokes the "paradox of the need to torture oneself for the sake of successfully regaining the other in a way that is anything but successful."[11]

Other writers on jealousy have also drawn inspiration from the word's complex etymology. Thus, Roland Barthes plays on the etymological links between jealousy and zealotry when he affirms: "jealousy is ugly and bourgeois: it's unworthy, a kind of *zeal*—and it's that zeal that we spurn."[12] And he exemplifies the obsessive desire for precision and the tendency to repetition that are characteristic of jealousy in his enumeration of the sufferings felt by the jealous lover: "When I'm jealous, I suffer four times over: because I'm jealous, because I criticize myself for being so, because I'm afraid my jealousy will hurt the other person, because I've allowed myself to be dominated by something banal. I suffer because I'm excluded, because I'm

---

11. Hildegard Baumgart, *Jealousy: Experiences and Solutions*, trans. Manfred Jacobson and Evelyn Jacobson (Chicago: University of Chicago Press, 1990), 31.
12. Roland Barthes, *Fragments d'un discours amoureux* (Paris: Seuil, 1977), 172–73.

aggressive, because I'm mad, because I'm cheap."[13] Indeed, jealousy, at least in literary texts, seems to unleash, in response to its tendency to chaos, a relentless analytical tendency that drives the jealous lover not merely to subject the actions of beloved and rival to a microscopic attention, but also to assess his or her own actions with a similarly aggressive and persistent intensity.

This painstaking, indeed zealous, attention to details, real or imaginary, is reflected, or perhaps more accurately mimed, in two nineteenth-century French studies of love which were to have considerable impact on later writers: Stendhal's *De l'amour* and Balzac's *Physiologie du mariage*. In both, textual strategies not merely underpin, but also demonstrate, psychological strategies.

Stendhal's influential and well-known evocation depicts love as crystallization, a process in which the loved person accumulates all those beauties, virtues, and perfections the lover most admires, as a bare branch left in the salt mines gathers hundreds of tiny crystals of salt. But he also implies that jealousy functions in a similar way. The state of mind is identical in love and jealousy, with the lover continuing to project on to the beloved whatever that lover craves or fears, but once jealousy has been aroused, the crystallization process becomes a source, not of delight, but of torment. The essential point here is that neither the crystals of love nor those of jealousy are intrinsic to the individual who has inspired the emotion, but are projections determined by what the lover most desires or most dreads.

Stendhal's technique in analyzing jealousy and suggesting remedies is, moreover, analogous to the process of crystallization itself, since he accumulates a series of notions, many of them garnered from other writers and allows them to gather and take shape in the reader's mind, rather than attempting to build up a logically constructed argument about a passion that itself is anything but logical.[14] He protects himself in cavalier

---

13. Ibid., 173.
14. Ann Jefferson argues, indeed, that the crystallization process itself is novelistic and that Stendhal's study, far from being a theoretical statement func-

fashion from any possible accusations of plagiarism (a device that, as I shall argue in chapter 4, has much to do with jealousy) by asserting abruptly in a footnote: "The reader will have noticed, without my needing to mark every occurrence, several [...] ideas taken from famous authors. What I'm trying to write is a work of history, and such ideas are historical facts."[15]

For Stendhal, jealousy is the worst of all torments, leading to an extreme unhappiness, poisoned, as he puts it, by "a lingering hope" (123). Yet Stendhal's tone in evoking jealousy fluctuates wittily between sympathy and mockery, in an apparently self-parodic illustration of the jealous person's need to hide his or her hand. Most notably, perhaps, his attention is focused above all on the rival, with the beloved summarily reduced to the appellation of "the love-object" (124). The torment of jealousy, it would seem, stems less from the beloved's rejection of the self than from the dual thought that the rival might be happy and that the "love object" might be a subject. Stendhal's suggestion for an urbane way of challenging the rival without revealing one's own jealousy is, of course, ostensibly comic, but the concomitant reduction of the woman to an object that men take it in turns to possess underlines the extent to which the crystallization process denies the beloved's separate individuality:

> According to the rule that you should never strengthen your enemy's hand, you have to hide your love from your rival, and, under the pretext of vanity and appearing as far removed as possible from being in love, say to him in the deepest secrecy, with all possible courtesy, and with the utmost calm and simplicity: "Sir, I have no idea why public opinion has taken it into its head to give me little so-and-so; people are even kind enough to think I'm in love with her; now if *you* wanted her, I'd hand her over to you with the best will in the world, were it not that I would unfortunately run the risk of appearing ridiculous. In six months, you'll be perfectly wel-

---

tioning as a monologue, offers "un exemple sans pareil du texte multilingue." "*De l'amour* et le roman polyphonique," *Poétique* 13 (April 1983): 162.
15. Stendhal, *De l'amour* (Paris: Garnier-Flammarion, 1965), 130.

come to take her, but today the honor that is for some reason attached to such matters forces me to tell you, to my very great regret, that if per chance you were not sufficiently well-mannered to wait your turn, it would be necessary for one of us to die." (123)

While part of this reaction is a narcissistic desire to protect the ego, its comic trappings should not blind us to its explicit re-ification and belittling of woman. Moreover, as previous critics have pointed out, the implication that jealousy is above all an affair between men is central to many texts, both thematically and structurally, whether or not they carry with them the ho-mosexual suggestions Freud perceived in Tolstoy's *Kreutzer Sonata*.[16]

The first section of Stendhal's study of jealousy is devoted to that felt by men, yet he does also raise the questions of how a woman feels when she realizes her lover is jealous and of the nature of jealousy inspired in women. The first discussion is presented as mere speculation—"I do not know what effect a man's jealousy has on the heart of the woman he loves."[17] Yet while Stendhal denies knowledge of how the woman may feel as the object, innocent or not, of jealousy, when it comes to what it feels like to be a woman racked by jealousy, he no longer has any doubts and is unabashed in his acceptance of double standards: "A woman feels sullied by jealousy; it makes her look as if she is running after a man; she believes she is her lover's laughing-stock and that he is particularly amused by her most tender transports; she is forced to behave somewhat cruelly, and yet she cannot legally kill her rival" (130). In other words, woman as mere catalyst is seen as non-threatening and therefore not particularly interesting, whereas a woman who actively experiences so powerful an emotion is perceived as menacing and therefore must be ridiculed, not merely by her lover, but by the narrator himself. Furthermore, that narrator attempts to convince us that "[t]he difference be-

---

16. See René Girard, *Mensonge romantique et vérité romanesque* (Paris: Gras-set, 1961), and Sigmund Freud's reading of the Tolstoy tale in *Gesammelte Werke*, vol. 13 (London: Imago, 1940).
17. Stendhal, *De l'amour*, 128.

tween female infidelity and male infidelity is so substantial that a passionate woman can forgive an infidelity, which is something a man can never do" (131). This kind of argument by wish-fulfillment is very much part of the logic of jealousy: the jealous person convinces himself or herself that what they want to be true must therefore be true.

Moreover, Stendhal embeds into his argument yet another aspect of jealousy, when he recommends as perhaps the sole remedy for the pain of jealousy a very close observation of the rival's happiness (123). While the text argues that such espionage will reveal the paucity of that happiness, the compulsion to watch, as numerous literary texts and works of art, as well as psychological studies, reveal, is a central element of jealousy itself.

In what initially appears to be a fairly light-hearted analysis, therefore, Stendhal's technical strategies achieve a remarkably accurate textual mimicry of central characteristics of jealousy: the argument by wish-fulfillment, the reduction of the beloved to object, and the compulsion to spy.

Balzac's cynical study of marriage, *La Physiologie du mariage*, although completely different in tone from Stendhal's book, also uses textual strategies, in addition to analysis, to re-create through mimicry the oppressive, monomaniacal nature of jealousy. This appears on first reading to be presented as very much an affair between men, with the implied reader firmly designated as masculine, and women invoked as objects to be controlled, manipulated, and dominated: "[W]oman is a delicious instrument of pleasure, but you have to know the trembling chords, study the placements, learn the timid keyboard, get by heart the changing and capricious fingering."[18] The narrative focus itself is one of constant oppression, apparently leaving the reader, or at least the *narrataire* implied in the text, no room for negotiation. Questions are always rhetorical; the aphorism is the natural mode of expression; conviction, when not taken merely for granted, is assumed to be carried by the numerical weight of arguments that accumulate in list form, just as Balzac's husband figure, being always jealous, entertains

18. Honoré de Balzac, *Physiologie du mariage* (Paris: Flammarion, 1968), 82.

no questions about his wife's possible infidelity and takes it as a given that faithlessness is part of her nature.

The relationship of husband to wife in this study is, therefore, also that of narrator to implied reader, making the art of marriage analogous to the art of writing. One of the aphorisms in the conjugal catechism suggests this link with particular force: "a husband's genius lies in the skill with which he can capture the nuances of pleasure, develop them, give them a new style, an original expression" (87). We are, of course, implicitly invited to see that these elements also constitute the genius of the writer. Elsewhere Balzac demands of his reader the same kind of response needed to react to *La Comédie humaine*—"In this book we will try always to paint frescoes, and leave the miniatures up to you" (122)—or urges husbands to follow the example of modern authors who write more prefaces than books.

One further aspect of the self-referential nature of Balzac's treatise should be stressed, since it exploits a metaphor frequently encountered in evocations of jealousy: that of the beloved as text, to be deciphered by a lover who has conscientiously studied the art of breaking the code.

Yet what is remarkable about the *Physiologie* is that it is precisely these links between reader and jealous lover, these invitations to enlarge, embellish, and decode that lead us back into the text's intricate ironies, just when we felt we were forever designated by Balzac as passive, compliant, nonresisting. Ironically, it is that very designation that sparks the revolt against authorial dictatorship and leads to a questioning of the image of the husband's tyranny as justifiable. In the terms of W. S. Gilbert's *Utopia Limited*, Balzac implies, and invites his reader to share, a preference for despotism tempered by dynamite.[19]

Balzac's analysis of jealousy is not merely more multilayered but also far more cynical, more slippery, and infinitely more down to earth than Stendhal's. Briefly, according to the *Physiologie*, jealousy is nonsensical unless used as a weapon. For

---

19. W. S. Gilbert, *Utopia Limited*, in *Original Plays* (London: Chatto and Windus, 1923), third series, 409.

a woman, so the argument runs, a husband's obvious jealousy is useful, because it justifies her adulterous behavior and because it is beneficial to her to appear in the eyes of society as a victim. Jealousy, moreover, offers women almost their only means of holding power over men. For men, however, Balzac's witty and satirical narrator continues, feelings of jealousy are neither more nor less than flaws in reasoning: "Either we're loved or we're not: given those two extremes, jealousy is a sentiment that serves a man no purpose" (204).

Despite—or because of—its surface misogyny, the *Physiologie du mariage* is an extremely fertile exploration of what society, or at least literature, constitutes as male and female. Its slippery and unpredictable irony ensures that "nothing is but what is not," and makes of his prima facie intransigence "a real moral kaleidoscope, with its thousands of different patterns" (169).

Some of those thousand different patterns can be found reflected in those aphorisms scattered through Proust's *A la recherche du temps perdu* that concern the nature and function of love and of jealousy.[20] While Stendhal and Balzac were writing in the aftermath of Napoleon's failure both to continue the Revolution and to establish a permanent Empire Proust wrote as he witnessed the collapse of the very society he was describing: for all three, the attraction of jealousy as subject clearly lies in more than the superficially sexual, offering in addition the possibility of exploring the destructive nature of a passion that seeks exclusive control of an individual and therefore can metonymically suggest the cankers that destroy a society. The central importance of jealousy to Proust's great work can in part be perceived through the fact that his initial choice of title, for the section ultimately called "Sodome et Gomorrhe," was "Une Jalousie."[21] Moreover, Balzac's image of jealousy as kaleidoscope is one Proust himself uses, but transforms, in exploring the nature of the relationship between jealousy and

20. See also Christie McDonald, "Republications," trans. G. Smolenski, in *Reading Plus*, ed. Mary Ann Caws and Eugene Nicole (New York: Peter Lang, 1990), 197–222.
21. Marcel Proust, *A la recherche du temps perdu* (Paris: Pléiade, 1954), 2: 1173. A section of this part of the work was published under the title "Jalousie."

knowledge: "from the moment we wish to know, as the jealous person wishes to know, everything becomes a vertiginous kaleidoscope in which we can no longer detect anything."[22] The influence of Stendhal's metaphor of crystallization is also evident here, even if Proust tends to prefer the term "irradiation."[23]

For Marcel, as for Swann before him, love and jealousy are states of mind that have little to do with the external reality of another person—and everything to do with the nature and situation of the individual. Because Marcel's childhood love of his mother has taught him to associate love with anxiety, he need only feel anxious to convince himself that he loves the person who has caused that anxiety. Once we know love's song, as Swann puts it, we have merely to meet someone singing that song and we'll join in at whatever verse they have reached, whether or not we really want to sing at all. Love and jealousy are portrayed as latent within each individual, ready to be released, in the most arbitrary fashion, through the most illogical of circumstances. As long as Marcel feels certain that he knows where Albertine is, the thought of her bores him: it is only when he believes that he can read between the lines of her letters or interpret undertones in her telephone conversations, in ways that make him believe he has uncovered indications of pleasures and acquaintances unknown to him, that it is possible for him to love her. Even then, such agitation may simply fade, without attaching itself to the cause of agitation in the form of desire: "I was utterly shaken by the painful longing to know what she could have been doing, by that latent love we always carry within ourselves; for a moment I even believed that love would bind me to Albertine, but it merely trembled on the spot and its final rumblings died away, before it even set out" (2, 798). Jealousy operates in the same way, lured as if by a bait, attracted as if by a magnet, to suspicions that are, so to speak, projections of the self, with no necessary connection at all with the other person:

22. Ibid., 3: 519.
23. See, for instance, ibid., 3: 642.

The truth is never anything other than a bait for an unknown on whose path we can never travel very far. It is better not to know, to think as little as possible, not to provide jealousy with the slightest concrete detail. Unfortunately, if external life does not provide them, details can also be supplied by our inner lives; if there were no walks with Albertine, chance thoughts met in the reflections I made all alone sometimes provided me with those small fragments of the truth that attract like a magnet, a little piece of the unknown which, henceforth, becomes painful. (3, 24–25)

In other words, love and jealousy project on to the beloved elements that exist only in the person who loves (or at least who experiences jealousy) (3, 912). Like knowledge, Marcel insists, jealousy is located within, and cannot go beyond, the self: "As there is no knowledge, so one can almost say there is no jealousy, save of oneself" (3, 386).

The solipsistic nature of desire and the inseparability of love and jealousy are both frequently asserted, as in the following statement, in which the creative role of the rival is also made particularly clear: "It would come about, if we were better able to analyze our love affairs, that we would see that often women please us only because of the counterweight of the men from whom we have to win them; once this counterweight disappears, the woman's charm fades away" (3, 413n). Yet, even leaving aside the profound ambiguity of Proust's sexual nature, it would, I think, be a misreading of this passage to assume that jealousy in his writings becomes a matter for men alone, with the female beloved reduced to object. Here it is not so much the rival as sexual individual that seizes the attention: it is, rather, the possible existence of the rival as essence. Proust's point here seems far more to be that solipsism is so intrinsic to the human mind that since love itself is merely a projection of the ego on to a screen provided by another, such love can be maintained only if the ego is stimulated to continue the projection. This stimulation is provided by the presence of a third instance, anxiety, that appears to come between the ego and the screen and is embodied in the text by the rival.

Proust's concept of desire also spotlights the creative power of jealousy, the dynamism that enables a comparison between jealousy and the imagination: "One of jealousy's powers is the ability to reveal to us the extent to which the reality of external facts and human emotions remains an unknown that gives birth to thousands of suspicions" (3, 519). The ways in which jealousy stands as an analogy for the creative powers of artist or writer are made even more central to Proust's work in a passage in which Albertine, because of the jealous curiosity she arouses in Marcel, becomes an avatar of the goddess of Time: "urgently inviting me, in a cruel manner that offered no escape, to search for the past, she was like a great goddess of Time" (3, 386–87). As the very image of jealousy, she inspires that exploration of the past that constitutes Proust's great novel. Moreover, jealousy, like involuntary memory, provides access to past aspects of the self, allows the individual to become again a version of the self that belongs to the past, and thus unites those disparate selves that otherwise would seem forever fragmented from each other.

The richness and complexity of these meditations on jealousy, narrating, and reading suggest the degree to which writers and thinkers have drawn on imagery and structures associated with jealousy in producing their literary and philosophical frameworks. But why limit a study of such explorations to the post-revolutionary period? Although I have included a few texts that predate the nineteenth century, most of the material I explore in this book reflects the conceptual and social structures of the last two centuries. The reasons for this choice concern the radical transformations in the concept of the individual and in relations between the sexes that have been taking place in that period.

Nancy Armstrong, in *Desire and Domestic Fiction*, makes a powerful case for historicizing sexuality and takes to task Ian Watt and Sandra Gilbert and Susan Gubar for failing to foreground the "historical conditions that have confronted women as writers" and for ignoring thereby the "place of women's writing in history" (8). Her argument that "the gendering of human identity provided the metaphysical girders of modern culture" (14) is convincing, but demands a mode of reading that takes for granted the transparency of language and the representative nature of fiction. My analysis is more concerned with exploring some of the ways in which fictional writing manipulates language and refuses to be tied uniquely to the time in which it was written. A historical study of the modes of jealousy cannot be written, I would argue, until more is known about the narratological devices employed and the degree to which sexual jealousy is used to convey a particular political consciousness.[24]

As Charles Taylor argues in his wide-ranging and stimulating study of the evolution and implications of contemporary visions of the individual consciousness, *Sources of the Self*, eighteenth-century Europe experienced profound intellectual changes that brought about a massive shift in concepts of what Taylor terms the modern identity.[25] This shift can be seen first in the value that came to be placed on ordinary life and on the individual, rather than on, say, military heroism and the state. Novels of this period, as Ian Watt points out in *The Rise of the Novel*, explore in close detail the fabric of everyday life and have characters who are no longer archetypes, as they are in *Pilgrim's Progress*. Unlike the allegorical figures in Bunyan's novel, for example, they are known by personal names and demonstrate personal idiosyncrasies.[26] In this shift of focus, and the stylistic changes that went with it, is reflected an alteration in images of the world and of the place of the individual within it: the demise of a vision that conceived of the world as embodiment and archetype, where what dominated was the general, was matched by the triumph of a way of thinking in which the general is reached only by studying the particular. In this atmosphere, the analysis of love and of jealousy turns away from the archetypes of, say, Tristan and Isolde, and allows the focus to settle on individual men and women.

Related to this change was the increased importance the eighteenth century placed on sentimentalism, the relative priv-

24. Nancy Armstrong, *Desire and Domestic Fiction* (Oxford: Oxford University Press, 1987).
25. Charles Taylor, *Sources of the Self: The Making of the Modern Identity* (Cambridge: Harvard University Press, 1985).
26. Ian Watt, *The Rise of the Novel* (London: Chatto and Windus, 1957), chap. 1.

ileging of what was regarded as the feminine, and an idealiza-
tion of mariage and of family life.[27] As Kenneth Clark puts it,
"The new sensibility, of which Watteau was the prophet,
showed itself most of all in a more delicate understanding of
the relations between men and women."[28] The family becomes
the haven in which emotions and feelings can be given free
expression, and it is because of this need for mutual trust that
jealousy becomes less concerned with loyalty to a family name
or with a sense of feudal possession of wife by husband. Instead, jealousy is now centered around the individual as individual, and adultery is seen as a betrayal of personal trust.

Yet, with the coming of the French Revolution, as Madelyn
Gutwirth has recently pointed out in her wonderfully titled
Twilight of the Goddesses, the violence of class struggle spilled
over into relations between the sexes, so that women's bodies
were not merely exploited in political cartoons and other
works of art to present woman as magna mater, succoring the
masses with her multiple breasts and thus reduced to mere
physical function, but also allegorized as the destructive revolution itself, plucking out the entrails of her children.[29] That
intricate duality, which finds a reflection in the ambivalence
of Mozart's Don Giovanni, shows how far, to quote Clark, "the
pursuit of happiness and the pursuit of love, which had once
seemed so simple and life-giving, have become complex and
destructive."[30] It is this complexity, the development from sentimentalism to melancholy, the shift from an awareness of the
individual's value to an obsession with the individual's impor-

27. On this, see Philippe Ariès, *L'Enfant et la vie familiale sous l'Ancien Ré-
gime* (Paris: Seuil, 1973); George Boas, *The Cult of Childhood* (London: Warburg
Institute, 1966); David Hunt, *Parents and Children in History: The Psychology
of Family Life in Early Modern France* (New York: Basic Books, 1973); Linda
Pollock, *Forgotten Children* (Cambridge: Cambridge University Press, 1983);
Martine Segalen, *Love and Power in the Peasant Family: Rural France in the
Nineteenth Century*, trans. Sarah Matthews (Chicago: University of Chicago
Press, 1983); Edward Shorter, *The Making of the Modern Family* (London: Collins, 1976); and my *Land of Lost Content* (Oxford: Clarendon, 1992).
28. Kenneth Clark, *Civilisation* (London: BBC and John Murray, 1969), 235.
29. Madelyn Gutwirth, *The Twilight of the Goddesses: Women and Representation in the French Revolutionary Era* (New Brunswick, N.J.: Rutgers University Press, 1992), 340.
30. Clark, *Civilisation*, 243.

tance, that makes jealousy so central a feature of nineteenth- and twentieth-century literature.

Finally, this period also saw a radical shift in the awareness of time. As Frank Kermode suggests in his series of lectures, *The Sense of an Ending*, the discovery of infinite time became central to the sciences in the nineteenth century and gradually permeated the general consciousness with a questioning of the inevitability of apocalypse.[31] This idea of what Walter Benjamin terms "homogenous, empty time"[32] leads to a change in our conception of the individual, who becomes, in Taylor's terminology, "the disengaged, particular self, whose identity is constituted in memory."[33] Although humanity has always made meaning out of life by telling tales around the campfire, it is the sense that life acquires meaning within homogenous time *only* by its transformation into story that determines the form of modern literature and of modern autobiography.[34]

I do not wish to argue, of course, that the position of women within that overall evolution in the sense of self remained static in the two centuries I explore or that it moved in harmony with the position of men. Nor would anyone argue that it was identical in all the countries on whose literature I draw in the following chapters. The differences in attitude between France and England, to take one example, were both marked and remarkable. Thus, for instance, the desire to belittle and control women that Madelyn Gutwirth sees as central to the revolutionary period in France may well have been primarily political in origin, whereas, so Lawrence Stone tells us, it was the revival of the Puritan religion in England that provoked the resurgence of a vision of male/female relations based on "the enforcement of patriarchy and obedience."[35] Napoleon's public

31. Frank Kermode, *The Sense of an Ending* (New York: Oxford University Press, 1967).
32. Walter Benjamin, *Illuminations*, trans. Harry Zohn (New York: Schocken, 1969), 261.
33. Taylor, *Sources of the Self*, 288.
34. See also Paul J. Eakin, *Fictions in Autobiography: Studies in the Art of Self-Invention* (Princeton: Princeton University Press, 1985).
35. Lawrence Stone, *The Family, Sex, and Marriage in England, 1500–1800* (London: Weidenfeld and Nicolson, 1977), 667. See also Gordon Schochet, *Patriarchalism in Political Thought* (New York: Basic Books, 1975).

puritanism informs the code of laws he drew up, but the tenor of the age was far different from that of Victorian England. Yet throughout the nineteenth century, and well into the twentieth century, the thinking of both continental Europe and insular Britain often focused on the questions of marital tyranny and wifely revolt, of the inability of the two sexes to find common ground, and of the search for harmonious relationships within or outside marriage. It is in that context of a common set of questions, rather than any hypothetical unity in the answers offered, that this exploration is located.

In this book, I shall argue that jealousy is one of the prime instigators of narrative, as the jealous lover weaves stories to fill the lacunae in his or her knowledge of the other and as the object of jealousy narrates events—real or imaginary—to deny, placate, mislead, or reject the emotions of jealousy. Moreover, jealousy creates its own time, a time far removed from that of physics, a time in which linearity is supplanted by circularity or spirality. "Love," argues Proust, and for him love and jealousy are synonymous, "is space and time made perceptible to the heart."[36] As such, jealousy becomes not merely a reason to explore, but more importantly a means of exploring, the forms and time of modern narration.

Many critical studies have investigated the theme of love in monographs or in comparative analyses, but most of them have been thematic or psychoanalytical in focus, and two of the most influential have been rigidly and somewhat repressively androcentric.[37] Denis de Rougemont's *Love in the Western World* traces the evolution of the myth of Tristan and Isolde through Western civilization, noting the transformations and restructuring it has undergone through time and in different cultures. What he reads as literature's opposition between passionate love on the one hand and the companionable love that comes with and in marriage on the other, carries, in his eyes,

36. Proust, *A la recherche*, 3: 385.
37. One further study of jealousy in literature, although useful, is not central to my concerns because its focus is on the literature of an earlier period: Madeleine Berthaud, *Le Thème de la jalousie dans la littérature française à l'époque de Louis XIII* (Geneva: Droz, 1981).

a clear moral message for everyday life. This message is that the passion, as he puts it, "which novels and films have now popularized is nothing else than *a lawless invasion and flowing back* into our lives of a spiritual heresy the key to which we have lost."[38] The transparency of the literary text, its unproblematic mediation of messages directly applicable to the nonfictional world, is never closely questioned in Rougemont's study. Besides, in questions such as "Marrying Iseult?" (283–285), Rougemont consistently posits a male reader, and one, moreover, who is apparently incapable of performing the function that is constantly demanded of female readers and doubtless practiced by the vast majority of male readers, that of migrating from their biological gender to that of a particular fictional character. The question of whether Isolde might wish to marry Tristan is never raised, for reasons made clear by the following statement in Rougemont's study: "Iseult is ever a stranger, the very essence of what is strange in woman and of all that is eternally fugitive, vanishing, and almost hostile in a fellow-being, that which indeed incites to pursuit, and rouses in the heart of a man who has fallen a prey to the myth an avidity for possession so much more delightful than possession itself. She is the woman-from-whom-one-is-parted: to possess her is to lose her" (285). As Leslie Rabine puts it, with forgivable terseness, "in Rougemont's theory, the exclusion of women from membership in humanity flows out of a logic that separates spiritual ideals from social reality."[39]

The reader in Rougemont's study must always read as male, because the spiritual, which is consistently associated with male in this study, is alone assumed to have value. Within such a stifling framework, a study of jealousy would be little more than a study of narcissism.

Besides, Rougemont's preoccupation with the avatars of this particular myth, and especially his desire to uphold marital love, make it impossible for him to respond to shifts in narrative or other fictional techniques whose processes might in-

38. Denis de Rougemont, *Love in the Western World*, trans. Montgomery Belgion (New York: Pantheon, 1956), 137.
39. Leslie Rabine, *Reading the Romantic Heroine: Text, History, Ideology* (Ann Arbor: University of Michigan Press, 1985), 27.

troduce a disruptive or ludic switch of focus. His study must, in other words, focus all but exclusively on the thematic, thrusting aside such literary strategies as serve to question and undermine those very thematics.

René Girard's *Mensonge romantique et vérité romanesque,* as well as his more recent works, propose—and dogmatically promote—a vision of desire in which the subject's central focus is not on the beloved but on the rival, termed the mediator in Girard's lexicon. He draws a sharp distinction, in other words, between the image of love as dual, and the pattern of desire as triangular. All desire, in Girard's thesis, is mimetic and mediated, with the desiring subject constantly basing desire on what an admired other desires: "The mediator's prestige conveys itself to the desired object and confers on it an illusory value."[40] As he puts it elsewhere, "the rival is needed because his desire alone can confer on the girl [*sic*] whatever value she has in the eyes of the subject."[41]

As Toril Moi argues, however, this theory cannot account, indeed is not allowed by Girard himself to account, for female desire: for him, the desiring subject is always male, while the object of that desire is always female. Homosexual desire is posited as aberrant, although the rival with whom the subject longs to share the beloved is of the same sex as the subject: "You're not revealing anything or making anything comprehensible if you reduce triangular desire to a homosexual passion which of necessity is opaque for a heterosexual," he truculently proclaims.[42] That reference to inevitable opacity implies, of course, that female jealousy cannot be the central theme of "true" literature, because it would remain equally opaque to what in computing terms one might describe as the default (i.e., male) reader. Emma Bovary's desire, for instance, has validity in Girard's theory only insofar as it is identified with that of Flaubert.[43]

40. Girard, *Mensonge romantique et vérité romanesque,* 25.
41. René Girard, *"To Double Business Bound": Essays on Literature, Mimesis, and Anthropology* (Baltimore: Johns Hopkins University Press, 1978).
42. Girard, *Mensonge romantique et vérité romanesque,* 52.
43. Ibid., 298. Girard takes it for granted that Flaubert really did assert: "Madame Bovary c'est moi!" Yet there is, of course, no evidence other than hearsay for this exclamation.

The theory of mimetic desire, which Girard claims to be understood and illustrated by the great novelists, therefore presents jealousy as only prima facie triangular: its dominant dynamics is always that of the movement between the two desiring males, indeed, ultimately, as he argues in the concluding chapter of *Mensonge romantique et vérité romanesque*, the only true object of desire, the only valid mediator, is the Christian God.

Girard's study shows, moreover, a revealing imbrication of subject and method. By constantly denouncing and deriding "romantic criticism" and "romantic critics" (never named), Girard designates himself as the Other on whom he implicitly charges his readers to model themselves. In his jealous protection of his theory and in his desire to win his readers over, this critic reveals the mechanisms he himself portrays as central to jealousy and desire. I shall suggest in subsequent chapters that such a twinning of strategy and theme is also common in literary texts that focus on jealousy. Nevertheless, for all its androcentrism, Girard's theory has undeniably played an important role in shaping our thought about the literary representation of passion, and it offers stimulating suggestions for a model of love and jealousy. His focus, his metaphors, and his challenging readings of certain texts, have provided a powerful impetus to studies of the novel.

The same kind of phallocentrism can be seen in Philippe Chardin's *L'Amour dans la haine, ou la jalousie dans la littérature moderne*. This is above all an exploration of the narrative structures employed by five male writers—Dostoevsky, James, Svevo, Proust, and Musil. The opening and closing quotations in Chardin's introduction reveal that not merely the choice of authors, but also the presuppositions that underlie the critical reading of them, are exclusively centered on the male: he opens with a quotation from the psychoanalyst André Green, setting the emotion of jealousy in the concrete of the Oedipal complex—"every man is inescapably touched by jealousy, because he is the product of two parents, one of whom was the object of his desire and the other the obstacle to the satisfaction of that desire"[44]—and closes with Joë Bosquet's

44. André Green, *Un œil en trop*, 111. Quoted in Philippe Chardin, *L'Amour*

comment in a letter: "In the 13th century there were troubadours who travelled from love court to love court, and there were grave discussions of questions like the following: What is preferable? Is it better to see one's lady die, or to know that she is unfaithful?"[45]

Chardin's exploration of modern representations of jealousy leads him to the somewhat familiar conclusion that the consecrated image of the triangle has been displaced by (or indeed has always merely masked) a passion that is above all an affair between men, where what dominates is the fascination exerted not by the beloved but by the rival. Nevertheless, Chardin has twice loaded the dice in his favor. First, he elides the difference between jealousy and hatred in order to open up the meaning of the term and to set aside what he cavalierly refers to as obsolescent "distinguos."[46] Here, to paraphrase Flaubert, one might minimally draw attention to the difference of feelings that are hidden under similar expressions. Second, and most important, Chardin seriously distorts his picture in selecting only male writers to produce what he terms "a modern vision of jealousy."[47]

As Freud and Michel Serres have both argued, in their very different ways, whenever we are two together we are three or four or more: the triangle is little more than a convenient simplification in evocations of jealousy, and, as I shall argue, the role of the rival is far more complex than Chardin admits. Chardin's choice of texts and authors, however much it may have been generated by the arbitrary and external force of a French *aggrégation* syllabus,[48] merely reproduces male power structures and therefore both facilitates and reflects the suppression of the feminine he not surprisingly claims to discover in them. For all its weaknesses, however, Chardin's reading of

---

dans la haine, ou la jalousie dans la littérature moderne (Geneva: Droz, 1990), 7.
45. Joë Bosquet, *Lettres à Marthe*, quoted in Chardin, *L'Amour dans la haine*, 31.
46. See, for instance, Chardin, *L'Amour dans la haine*, 20.
47. Ibid., 11.
48. See, for this suggestion, Dominique Millet-Gerard, "Review of Chardin, *L'Amour dans la haine,*" *Revue d'histoire littéraire de la France* 93, 2 (March–April 1993): 305–6.

jealousy in these texts has much to offer in terms of showing the narrative benefits of that complex passion, its ability to open up, for instance, the domains of art for a Proust or of suffering and therefore purification for a Dostoevsky. Moreover, his focus on structures draws attention to the way in which jealousy causes an eternal return to the initial source of suffering. Yet, because it remains so closed to possibilities of female, lesbian, and homosexual versions of jealousy, Chardin's thesis remains essentially vitiated.

Leslie Rabine's intelligent and forceful study of romantic heroines in both male- and female-authored texts proposes a very different program. Rather than yielding to the potency of the phallocentric social and literary forces at work, for instance, in Rougemont's and Chardin's studies, Rabine has set out to "resist and violate the complicity between author and reader upon which rests so much of the seduction of classic texts."[49] Within this program Rabine focuses on romance and romantic love in the broad sense of those terms: although her subject matter only occasionally coincides with that of this book, her explorations of the disruptive forces released (if we question the readings that the narrative voice appears to impose) offer any study of jealousy useful patterns of resistance and therefore of creation.

One further analysis seems to me to be crucial to any examination of jealousy within literature: Ross Chambers's exploration of what he terms "narrative and other triangles." Chambers urges the study of narrative to break away from its dual model of communication, and to explore models that define the narrative situation as triangulated, "or indeed," he characteristically adds, "quadrangulated."[50] Chambers argues that in many texts emotional triangularity finds a parallel in a "thematics of discursive triangularity," a model that reveals textual discourse itself as "the site of a split subject and a double address" (32). Narrative, in this theory, exists precisely because the direct transfer of a message cannot be controlled, because there is always leakage, interference, static on the ra-

49. Rabine, *Reading the Romantic Heroine*, 19.
50. Ross Chambers, "Narrative and Other Triangles," *Journal of Narrative Technique* 19 (1989): 32.

dio station or a bug on the telephone line, and because the stories themselves, far from trying to exercise rigid control over those irruptions of chaos, exploit them, indeed, as Chambers puts it, "give them a crucial place in the system" (46). Thus, Albertine, fearing Marcel's jealousy, interrupts her direct message to him, when she breaks off a sentence at the words: "me faire casser . . . ," but Marcel, here figuring the resisting reader, opens up the multiple possibilities of her words to arrive at a conclusion, which may not be the correct one, but which does at one level respond to a truth she is conveying to him: her fear, precisely, of his jealousy.[51]

In this book I shall argue that jealousy, in offering a paradigm for such irruptions of chaos, provides both a thematic and a narrative window through which the text can expose and explore its own workings. Even more important, perhaps, as so many readings of jealousy reveal both a sexual and more generally a political reactionism, attempting to control what is uncontrollable in it, as the jealous subject attempts in his or her readings to control the object of jealousy by shifting the focus to the cause of that jealousy, I shall be seeking a narrative model that, in Chambers's words, "would recognize and legitimate the uncontrollability of discourse."[52]

Where my essay differs from previous studies of jealousy, therefore, is primarily its focus on the textual strategies associated with jealousy. Jealousy within literature may well be a very different monster from jealousy in day-to-day existence: this book does not attempt any psychoanalytical extrapolations, nor—more reluctantly—does it stray into the borderline territory of the private diary or letters, where the recording of jealousy may well exploit strategies that recall, although they do not replicate, those of literature. The diaries of Sophia Tolstoy and the correspondence between Violet Trefusis and Vita Sackville-West, for instance, suggest that such an area would yield complex findings that would need to be seen against the background of other such texts and set into different critical methodologies from those I use here. Although I reluctantly

51. Proust, *A la recherche*, 3: 339.
52. Chambers, "Narrative and Other Triangles," 33.

leave aside diaries and letters, I have deliberately made my choice of texts as eclectic as possible within the constraints of Western literature of the last two centuries. My investigation takes as its motto Proust's observation that writers and artists function as mirrors of what surrounds them and that genius consists in "the power of reflection rather than the intrinsic quality of the spectacle that is reflected."[53] What I want to explore in the following chapters is not so much the psychological or moral nature of jealousy insofar as it is reflected in literature, but rather the reflective power afforded by jealousy itself, the ways in which it functions as a lens, capturing, magnifying, and distorting the designs of writing, the strategies of reading, and the uncontrollable interference with messages through which are released literature's most powerful forces.

53. Proust, *A la recherche*, 1: 555.

1 Windows on Jealousy: Interpreting the Other

As he gazed round, some letters caught his eye,
Carved on the trees which cast a grateful shade,
He stopped and stared; at once he knew that by
The hand of his beloved they were made.
            [. . .]

A hundred times the lovers' names are seen,
"Angelica," "Medoro" intertwined.
Each letter is a knife which, sharp and keen,
Pierces his bleeding heart; his tortured mind,
Rejecting what it knows these carvings mean,
A thousand explanations tries to find:
Some other maiden may have left her mark,
Writing "Angelica" upon the bark.

And then he says: "I know this writing well.
I've seen and read it many times of yore.
In fond imagination—who can tell?—
Perhaps she calls me by this name, Medore."
By means of notions so improbable,
And from the truth departing more and more,
Although for comfort he has little scope,
The unhappy Count contrives to build false hope.
                Ariosto, *Orlando Furioso*, Canto XXIII

Interpreting the other on the basis of limited information—
marks cut into a tree in Orlando's case—is frequently troped
in literature through images suggesting limitation and reinforced by the adoption of a restrictive, biased, or distorting

27

narrative focus. Such a focus represents the "jealous glass" described in the *Oxford English Dictionary* or the *lunettes de jalousie* mentioned by Littré.[1] Thus, for example, a man stands in a darkened street, gazing at the one lighted window in an apartment block, attempting to divine what is going on behind the shutters, trying to establish the difference between the window's message now and its message in the past, raging against the suspicion that a world of binary oppositions (inside/outside, male/female, us/others) has been split asunder by the invasive influence of a third pole. Thief or detective, the man is, physically, emotionally, intellectually, an outsider, and because of the particular narrative focus adopted, we, too, stand in the street attempting to shed light on the truth.

> Amidst the darkness of all the windows in the street in which the lights had long been extinguished, he saw a single window from which escaped—through the shutters [*volets*] that squeezed its mysterious, golden pulp—the light that filled the bedroom and which, on so many other evenings, when he saw it from afar as he entered the street, had delighted him and announced to him: "she is there, waiting for you" and which now tormented him by telling him: "she is there with the person she was waiting for." He wanted to know who it was; he crept along the wall until he reached the window, but he could see nothing through the slanting slats [*lames*] of the shutter; he could only hear in the silence of the night the murmuring of a conversation.[2]

The obsessional nature of the emotion is immediately obvious: this light, these voices, that room alone exist in a world where the blackness of night stands for both the blindness of fixation and the darkness of ignorance. Fetishlike, the light in its turn evokes not merely the woman and the room that through its decoration, its knickknacks, and its odors externalizes, if not her personality, at least what her lover wants to know of that personality.

1. See the Introduction to this volume, p. 5.
2. Marcel Proust, *A la recherche du temps perdu* (Paris: Pléiade, 1954), 1: 273.

Knowing the woman, accepting her as she is, acknowledging that her personality exceeds the shapes into which he wants to place her are as impossible for the viewer as it is for him to see into the room through the slanting bars of the shutters: jealousy, as Robbe-Grillet so meticulously and obsessively reveals in his novel, is precisely that which distorts, limits, and perhaps protects vision.

Yet if the shutters offer an icon of a vision restricted by jealousy, so too in this passage does the light evoke the woman metonymically. Squeezing through the shutters in the same way that the woman evades the lover's desire to enclose and imprison her, this light becomes a golden fruit bursting out of its skin, a promise of knowledge, as the fruit in the Garden of Eden promised knowledge, if only the knowledge of exile. And because the light also implies the woman, she too is metamorphosed into fruit, consumable, apparently on offer, but on offer equally to all potential consumers. The movement between images, between the physical and the literary, between realism and myth, that is enabled by the light's ability to link two spheres, also connects inner and outer—the world of the street, implicitly depicted here as the domain of the male, and the world of the interior, that of the female; the world of the mind, and the world of the body.

That slippage also obtains between past and present, the uniformity of memory and the singularity of experience, the time when the light promised the woman's availability and the moment when it seemed to indicate that she was henceforth available only to someone else.

The very mobility of the language draws attention to suggestions embedded in the words themselves, slipping from one meaning to another in a series of polysemantic terms or potential puns. *Volets*, evoking *vol* (flight and theft), *voleur* (thief), *évoluer* (move and develop), the paddle of a water wheel; *lames*, suggesting not merely the bars of the shutter but knives, waves, the slender piece of material that covers over a coarser substance, language itself spread thin over the chaos of emotions: "The word," as Flaubert maintains in *Madame Bovary*, "is a rolling-mill [*laminoir*] that always stretches the emotions out."[3]

As the passage proceeds, it transforms the imagery of light into a metaphor for knowledge, so that the text's onlooker finds the icon of the illicit lovers appearing in his mind's eye as in an illuminated manuscript, the deciphering of which will lead to greater understanding:

> And perhaps what he felt at that moment that was almost pleasurable was something different, too, from the calming of a doubt or a pain: it was a pleasure of the intellect. If, ever since he had fallen in love, things had again assumed for him some of that delicious interest he had formerly found in them, but only in so far as they were illuminated by the memory of Odette, now it was another faculty of his studious youth that was brought back to life by his jealousy, the passion for truth, but this too was a truth placed between him and his mistress, a truth that received its light from her alone, an entirely individual truth, the sole object of which was something of countless value and almost of disinterested beauty, that is, Odette's actions, her relationships, her plans, her past. At every other stage in his life, the little acts and daily gestures of an individual had always struck Swann as having no value: if someone gossiped to him about them, he found such gossip trifling, and the moments he spent listening to it were those in which he felt most mediocre. But in this strange period of love, the individual takes on such depths that the curiosity he felt awakening within him with regard to a woman's slightest occupations was the same curiosity he had felt in the past for History. And everything that would have filled him with shame hitherto, spying at a window, who knows? perhaps, tomorrow, cunningly leading third persons to talk, or bribing servants, or listening at doors, now seemed to him, just like the deciphering of texts, the comparison of evidence, and the interpretation of monuments, merely methods of scholarly investigation possessing a true

3. Gustave Flaubert, *Madame Bovary* (Paris: Garnier, 1971), 239.

intellectual value and perfectly appropriate to a search for the truth.[4]

The metaphor of enlightenment, threaded through this passage in words like *illuminated* and *light*, joins the image of the searcher after truth, wandering through dark subterranean passages, decoding tiny suggestions to reach a truth and a history that have no claim to capital letters.

Deciphering, sifting, interpreting, the jealous lover, in searching for the truth, adapts the techniques of the savant, but brings them to bear on the tawdry details of gossip: the masterful brush strokes of the genre painter turned to the purposes of rhopography.[5] The desire for knowledge, as in *Genesis*, debases the individual, drives us into that archetypally Proustian awareness that the only paradises are those we have lost.

Some of the same images recur when Swann seeks to decipher through its envelop a letter Odette has asked him to mail for her. The delicacy of the paper, together with the firmness of the card it contains, allow him to read both the ostensible *billet de digestion* and the covert *billet doux*, offering him "a fragment of Odette's life, as if in a narrow luminous section cut directly into the unknown."[6] Like the bars of the shutter, the envelop allows only a glimpse of the truth, as if it were a telescope showing only a tiny section of the sky, from which the astronomer were obliged to extrapolate the entire universe. This image of the meager, illuminated section from which the jealous lover projects a massive constellation of doubts, possibilities, fears, and assumptions not only reappears in later sections of *A la recherche*, where it dominates the relationship between Marcel and Albertine, but also becomes a magic casement, drawing on and feeding into much of literature.

Detective and scientist, creative writer and blind person, the jealous lover wanders through a labyrinth whose walls are covered with hieroglyphics, projecting over and over again in his or her mind the image of something half heard or half seen,

4. Proust, *A la recherche*, 1: 273–74.
5. See Norman Bryson, *Looking at the Overlooked: Four Essays on Still-Life Painting* (Cambridge: Harvard University Press, 1990).
6. Proust, *A la recherche*, 1: 283.

rewriting the past, sucking the fruit of experience for every last drop of sensation, never able to leave the boundaries of personality or of the senses.

Part of the force of this depiction of Swann's jealousy, like that of the studies of jealousy in Charlus, and Saint-Loup, lies in the degree to which the lover is excluded from knowledge the narrator shares with the reader: however closely they may be observed, Swann, Charlus and Saint-Loup are seen from the outside, leaving the narrative focus free to shift in order to offer us images and statements that provide apparently incontrovertible proof of guilt, or innocence, in the person under suspicion. The study of Marcel's jealousy, however, is radically different, for whereas the characters of Odette, Rachel, and Morel are presented from the viewpoint of the far-seeing nonlover, Albertine's nature remains enigmatic, beyond our power to determine, since with her we are limited to the blinders of Marcel's jealousy, a focalization that is never capable of illuminating us where she is concerned.

This touches on a further question that I want to raise only briefly here and return to later in my conclusion: that of how important it is to the reader to know whether jealousy is or is not substantiated. Swann's jealousy, associated though it may be with images of light and beauty, can, in the final analysis, appear only tawdry, aroused by a woman whom the reader has been forced to see from the early passages of *Combray* as a demimondaine, someone who is bound to arouse feelings of jealousy in anyone who supposes she belongs to him or her alone. It is the search for knowledge, however, that lifts this emotion from the ridiculous to something approaching the sublime. Musset's *Confession d'un enfant du siècle* of 1836 shows only too clearly how strong the risk is that jealousy's obsessive interpretation of the other, when not accompanied by a character's reasonable doubt and a desire to know the truth, can be equivalent to to mere moodiness, an adolescent inability to accept the other as other, a neurotic iteration of the individual's innocence and the other's guilt.[7] Moreover, while

7. Alfred de Musset, *La Confession d'un enfant du siècle* (Paris: Gallimard, Folio, 1973). Richard Terdiman's brilliant reading of the *Confession* takes as a given the "betrayal" of the Parisian mistress, without questioning the degree of

Proust's study transcends, or perhaps sidesteps, contemporary notions of male and female, Musset's remains debilitatingly anchored to the misogyny of his age, an age, moreover, whose power structures he seeks to deconstruct through the very metaphor of jealousy. In this text, jealousy becomes the force that rails against one form of oppression while justifying another.

Musset's evocation of jealousy, in all its willful banality and impoverishment, is determined by and clearly illustrates the often quoted depiction of the *mal du siècle*, the sufferings of French youth in a society and time that rejects, crushes, and debases their talents, leaving them nothing to do but grow old. The myth that Musset meticulously constructs in his initial chapters of a (male) generation caught in the vast desert between the ruins and fossils of a glorious but irretrievable Napoleonic past and the dawning light of a great future forever just beyond their reach highlights the disillusion, hypocrisy, and wasted gifts of contemporary youth. Prevented by historical accident and social constraints from fulfilling what they believed to be their potential, perverted by the influence of "English" morals (by which is implied a certain sexual hypocrisy), and inoculated with the virus of German romantic melancholy, these sons of Empire and grandsons of revolution, as Musset terms them, have no means of relating to the other: "Friendship consists in lending money; but it's rare to have a friend you can love enough to do that. The value of your kith and kin is measured by what you inherit from them; love is a corporal exercise; the only intellectual pleasure lies in vanity."[8] Forced, then, to accept the denial of their talents (or what they believe to be their talents), these young men have to consent

---

betrayal Octave himself reveals in his treatment of her as object and possession. Both the political oppression and the behavioral oppression Terdiman so interestingly intertwines in his analysis of the text are catastrophic in Octave's view because of their limitation of the individual: but it is still necessary to extrapolate from this male-on-male oppression the more general oppression of women that the text also reveals. See Richard Terdiman, "The Mnemonics of Musset's *Confession*" (*Representations* 26 [1989]: 26–48), and his revision of this article in *Present Past: Modernity and the Memory Crisis* (Ithaca: Cornell University Press, 1993).

8. Musset, *Confession*, 31–32.

to a subordinate situation usually reserved for women, and this renders all the more difficult relations with the opposite sex. Indeed, the need to convince themselves of their own superiority becomes so acute that the possibility that a woman might not accept them creates a situation with which they are incapable of dealing. That the central female figure in the novel draws largely on Musset's perception of the personality of George Sand, who so flagrantly, if so ambivalently, refused the codes of behavior contemporary society attempted to impose on women, reveals the extent to which images of jealousy, for all their timelessness, owe much of their outward form to the historical matrix from which they are drawn.[9]

Musset's first-person narrator, Octave, leads up to his depiction of the experience of jealousy through a series of false starts: the justification for writing at all, which lies, as the first chapter declares, in the conviction, or at least the claim, that the "dreadful moral illness"[10] that attacked him in the first flower of youth is widespread; the long evocation in the second chapter of the causes and nature of this *mal du siècle*; and the explicit statement of narrative drive and purpose that opens the third chapter: "I must tell of the occasion on which I was first struck down by our century's ailment" (38). Like the kind of stuttering repetition of phrases that in social discourse indicates both a reluctance to embark on certain material and a refusal to let anyone else slip a word in, these affirmations of intention, and the way in which they are constantly broadened to implicate contemporary youth, reinforce the narrator's refusal to accept the individuality of those around him. Moreover, the difficulty of penetrating that individuality, of discovering what really lies behind the multiple layers of the surface, is thrust into the foreground as part of the preparation for the moment that is defined as the one that infects Octave with the *mal du siècle*.

The event takes place immediately after a masquerade, and

9. The Sand-Musset affair provoked several novels and countless biographical pieces. For example, Naomi Schor refers to Sand's own fictionalized account of the affair, *Elle et Lui*, as "the paradigmatic French revenge novel." *George Sand and Idealism* (New York: Columbia University Press, 1993), 217 n. 1.

10. Musset, *Confession*, 19.

the implications of pretense, dissimulation, and façade continue in the description of the supper itself, with its richly
dressed guests, its fine food, its images of light and sound and
ephemerality, all leading up to the description of the mistress
as a "superb creature whom [he] idolized" (38). The word
créature is of course heavily loaded, evoking, as Littré crisply
puts it, "a woman of whom one speaks without respect." No
description of this woman, then, except in terms of the young
man's emotions and male society's judgments. She is there
merely to be idolized and consumed, as the following statement makes clear: "My mistress had given me an assignation
for the night, and I lifted my glass to my lips as I gazed at her"
(38).

The sexual parallels between woman and wine glass prepare
the moment when Octave drops his knife, searches for it under
the table, and finds his beloved's legs elastically, if improbably,
wrapped around those of the young man sitting next to her, a
man who is, moreover, a longtime friend of Octave. The erotic
suggestions in the dropped knife and the glass, with their
attendant reifications of lover and beloved, are as blatant as the
woman's duplicity is beyond doubt. Here the intellectual
quest, the transformation of lover to detective, the difficulty of
knowing the truth, and the possibility that suspicion is unjus-
tified, the central elements, in other words, of Proust's depiction of jealousy, are all absent. What the narrator strives to
emphasize in this evocation of disillusionment and despair is
that corruption is dominant and that no question of the woman's innocence can be entertained, however fleetingly. Jealousy
here becomes a political and social topos, figured as the eternal
repetition of failure, part of the metonymical chain of intellectual and revolutionary powerlessness in the post-Napoleonic
era.

Octave's response is presented as typical of his character,
making this seminal episode, too, only one of an endless series.
This is not surprising, for the *mal du siècle* stems largely in
Musset's depiction from a sense of being hopelessly trapped in
a desert of time, a continuous loop in which any action has
already been taken and will be taken again. The point of comparison Octave offers, moreover, reinforces this sense of end-

less mirror repetition as it is taken from Tirso de Molina's play, *El Burlador de Sevilla y convidado de piedra* that inspired not only Molière's *Dom Juan* but also numerous other avatars: "Now, at every point in my life when I have come to believe for a long time and in all confidence either in a friend or in a mistress and have suddenly discovered that I was mistaken, I can convey the effect this revelation had on me only by making a comparison with the statue's hand. It is truly the impression of marble, as if reality in all its mortal iciness had frozen me with a kiss; it is the touch of the man of stone" (41). Yet what is perhaps most striking about this comparison is its blatant inappropriateness, because the original marble handshake metes out punishment not to the victim of deceit and betrayal, but to the perpetrator. While the text trumpets Octave's innocence, therefore, the subtext implies guilt and invites punishment. Jealousy, in this case, appears not as the instigating force behind a desire to know, but as the most powerful manifestation of a sense of inadequacy: there can be no doubt about the infidelity of the other, precisely because the self defines itself in terms of its inability to succeed—in work, in friendship, in love. The violent hatred directed at the object of jealousy, then, is merely one facet of the loathing felt for the self. The inability to deal with the independence of the other, moreover, externalizes and clarifies the individual's failure to accept his own identity.

However different these two cases of jealousy may be, they have at least one common factor, crucial to our reading of them: in these passages the narrative focus is strictly limited to the mind of the jealous lover. This internal focalization, taken to such claustrophobic extremes in Robbe-Grillet's novel, *La Jalousie*, is a central means by which the reader is compelled to participate in the protagonist's suffering, without being provided space to mock, despise, or even pity the emotion of jealousy.

A twist in the narrative viewpoint, an opening up of the space needed for compassion and judgment can shed an entirely different light on depictions of jealousy: one thinks of the scene in *La Traviata* where Alfredo strikes Violetta in a fit of jealousy dependent on his not knowing what we know as the reason why she left him; or, in a very different mode, of Karenin's ice-cold fury when Anna faints at the race course, in a physical revelation of her love for Vronsky. While the narrative retains an external point of view, its contrasting presentations of Anna and her husband make it difficult for the reader to interpret Karenin's response as other than despicable, as being based on a sense of propriety and property rather than love. Moreover, twists in the focalization often reflect far more than a narrative experiment, suggesting social and historical change or indicating a tightening or loosening of censorship laws. All through the narrative works of nineteenth-century France such exploration grows out of a rapidly changing society whose class structure, moral values, and personal ambitions were experiencing radical shifts.

Experimentation with the novel in general, and with narrative perspective in particular, combined in several nineteenth- or early-twentieth-century works, with a growing interest in the challenge of exploring the minds of children, to produce works of limited focalization, where jealousy between adults is presented through the observations of the uncomprehending child, a technique that Henry James, for instance, exploits in *What Maisie Knew* and that such recent writers as Nadine Gordimer in *My Son's Story* and Roddy Doyle in *Paddy Clarke, Ha Ha Ha* manipulate with such power and pathos. While there is always a sense of the adult writer manipulating the child's presumed innocence or the adolescent's loss of innocence, this kind of representation of sexual jealousy highlights the often bizarre nature of social conventions and personal drives and permits a degree of suggested eroticism or even obscenity that would be hard to imagine in other nineteenth-century works written with that particular audience in mind.

In Jules Vallès's innovative and experimental *L'Enfant*, the chapter entitled "Un Drame" presents through the narrow window of the child-narrator's comprehension just such a scene of adult jealousy between husband and wife, sparked off by a seductive female neighbor. Vallès's love of puns and onomatopoeia combines with a colloquial use of the term "make music/ love" already present in Flaubert's *Madame Bovary* and exploited again with reference to Vinteuil's daughter in *A la recherche du temps perdu* . The neighbor, Madame Brignolin, is described in the following idiosyncratic way: "She's a plump little creature, lively and with eyes full of fire; she is wonderfully merry and it's a delight to watch her trotting about, giggling, flirting, leaning back to laugh [. . .] and she has a way of shivering that seems curious even to my father, for he blushes, grows pale, loses his voice and knocks chairs over."[11] As if this misreading of his father's response were not enough to provide a wink between adults over the child-narrator's head, Jacques goes on to describe Madame Brignolin's musical evenings: "In the evenings she gets out a fresh dressing gown and makes a bit of music in front of the old grand piano [*piano à queue*]; at the end of each piece, she extracts from it a deep 'boom' from somewhere in the deep notes and a flute-like 'ee' from among the high notes" (183).

The reference to the *queue*, ostensibly the tail of the grand piano, together with the sounds produced, suggests that Madame Brignolin's kind of music is indeed likely to cause disturbance in the neighboring households. Her husband, a chemist, is rarely at home: "il est toujours dans les *cornues*" [he is always in his retorts (literally "horned ones")], Jacques explains, adding an extra nudge to the slow when he says: "I've even noticed that people laughed when they said that word" (184). Hardly surprising then that the friendship between the two families rapidly disintegrates and that the relationship between Vingtras père and Madame Brignolin leads to deep, and for the child incomprehensible, depression in his mother: "I hardly understand anything, but it seems to me that Mme Brignolin has a hand in this black melancholy that's visited our house, in my mother's white rage" (190). With its puns (as in the preceding quotation with its allusion to the piano's black-and-white notes), its onomatopoeia, and its experimental, if somewhat heavy-handed, doubling of child voice and adult whisper, this passage is a vital part of Vallès's corrosive depiction of the family and thereby of society in general, but it is also, for all its brevity, a remarkable addition to evocations of jealousy. Here the narrow window through which jealousy is

11. Jules Vallès, *L'Enfant* (Paris: Livre de Poche, 1985), 183.

viewed transforms the emotion into a metonymical image of the incomprehensibility of the adult word for a child and more generally of the other's world for each individual.

Although the decision to use the child as focus gives a particularly clear-cut example of jealousy's limited and limiting vision, other forms of narrative experimentation permit more subtle, and frequently more disquieting, effects. In *La Cousine Bette*, for instance, Balzac, writing toward the end of Louis-Philippe's July Monarchy, at a time of significant social change and profound political instability, seizes on the possibilities of shifting and blurring focalizations to present his picture of woman as deceiver and to do so in ways that transform the powerful female protagonist, Valérie, into an image of the writer, constantly and ingeniously revising and transforming her text for the benefit of a range of different readers, as those who wanted to succeed either socially or politically were obliged to do. As Vautrin, the counterfeit forger, represents the writer's satanic power to re-create the world, so Valérie, as teller of tales, is able to spin versions of reality that enable each of her lovers to see himself as hero. It is by this false transformation of the bourgeois male into Romantic hero and military strategist that the apparently weaker woman, like the apparently marginalized writer, succeeds in gaining control over a society unaware that it has lost its power.

By way of illustration, take the passage in which the Brazilian Montès finds Valérie at a dinner party attended by her husband and two lovers. Here the dual questions of "who sees" and "who speaks" and the vital dichotomy between them lie at the center of our response and point to hidden political truths. Narrative omniscience, together with pronounced narrative partiality, refuse any sense of tragedy here, and emphasize instead the comic aspects of male malleability at the mercy of female fabrications. Moreover, the passage is preceded by a typical Balzacian aside: "Let's at least acknowledge this immutable fact: in Paris, life is too full for malevolent people to do evil instinctively; all they do is protect themselves against attack by means of vice."[12] The deliberately alienating

12. Honoré de Balzac, *La Cousine Bette* (Paris: Folio, 1972), 202.

effect of this insistence on the novelist's often-claimed role as observer is reinforced by the witty or informative chapter titles, which also serve to present the characters as representatives rather than individuals: Montès is "Un revenant à revenu" [a phantom with finance], and Hulot's predicament is depicted as part of a study of behavioral patterns through the title "The Age at which a Ladies' Man Grows Jealous."

Other techniques in this passage intervene to control and guide the reader, particularly in terms of the tempo Balzac provides. Where Musset evokes the emotion of jealousy through an unrelenting sense of progression and Proust intermingles an apparently destructive forward movement with resurgent memories of the past, the passage in *La Cousine Bette* balances narration with description, suddenly stopping the flow to insist on an image, as, indeed, the jealous mind may constantly return to particular images, shunning progression in favor of circularity.

Movement dominates the Brazilian baron's arrival: the games of whist are in full swing and the room is crowded with Mme Marneffe's "faithful" when the valet announces his arrival, thus inflicting on his mistress "a violent shock" and forcing her to rush to the door, greeting him as "her cousin" and whispering in his ear that unless he accepts this description all is over between them. To play Valérie's game, in other words, a jealous lover has to acknowledge and adhere to whatever narrative she tells about him. This burst of energetic movement is then frozen to allow for a lengthy, lovingly detailed depiction of Montès, whose physical beauty is matched by the expensive clothing that stamps him immediately as "a true Brazilian millionaire" (202). While, in the eyes of Valérie's other lovers, he all too obviously promises her bountiful amounts of "l'or et le plaisir" [money and pleasure], those motive forces of Balzacian society, other aspects of his personality are conveyed through comparisons with animals, a technique typical of Balzac in general, of course, and of this novel in particular, but acquiring here an unusual degree of intensity and ferocity, as the following quotation suggests: "His brow, hooked like that of a satyr, which is a sign of stubbornness in passion, was topped by hair the color of jet, as thick as a virgin forest, under which glittered light-colored eyes, so tawny that you'd have thought the baron's mother, when she was pregnant with him, had been frightened by a jaguar" (203). His uniqueness reduces Valérie's two middle-aged, hitherto placid lovers to twin images of jealousy, from whom the narrative voice distances both itself and the reader by indicating them as objects, not of pity or fear, but of amusement, objects, moreover, that the discerning eye can easily read:

> The Brazilian's arrival, his pose, his air provoked two movements of curiosity mingled with anxiety, two movements that were perfectly identical and came from Crevel and the Baron. In each of them there was the same expression and the same presentiment.
>
> As a result, the maneuver inspired in these two real passions became so comical through the simultaneity of the exercise that it brought a smile to the lips of those sharp enough to read in it a revelation. (203)

A moment of punning dialogue not only shifts the tempo from these two descriptions, but also focuses on polysemantic possibilities, as Marneffe, in apparent reference to the card game, asserts: "*You've got hearts* and you've just reneged." But again the rhythm changes as Balzac introduces a passage of close description of Valérie which parallels that of the Brazilian; but where he was presented as an active and potentially threatening subject, she is offered as a comestible and consumable object:

> Her white breast glittered in its tight lace whose russet tones showed off the matte satin of those beautiful shoulders, for Parisian women (how they do it, I do not know!) are able to have beautiful flesh and yet stay slim. Clad in a black velvet dress that at every moment seemed on the point of slipping off her shoulders, she wore a lace headdress interwoven with clusters of flowers. Her arms, at once delicate and plump, appeared from puff sleeves lined with lace. She looked like one of those lovely pieces of fruit seductively arranged on a beau-

tiful plate [*assiette*] that set the steel [*acier*] blade of the knife
a-quiver. (204)

Valérie is thus presented as objet d'art, lovingly created by herself ("how they do it, I do not know!," exclaims the otherwise
omniscient narrator), constantly promising more than she is
currently giving, framed by lace in which the flower embel-
lishments speak of the ephemeral nature of beauty and pleasure, and finally equated with the beautiful fruit that the knife
longs to penetrate. All this clearly labels her as available, but
only to the highest bidders. The phonetic chain that produces
"acier" from "assiette" combines with the controlled violence
detected in Montès to suggest "assassin," and the knife, with
all its obvious phallicity, also belongs to a set of images evoking the savagery of desire and the destructive nature of jealousy.

The implicit suggestions of close affinities between sex, jealousy, and death are reinforced by a series of images linking love
and war, a familiar and apparently timeless trope, after all, and
one also exploited by writers as different as Stendhal and
Proust.[13] What is less usual is that here the emblematic figure
of Napoleon evokes, not the male lovers, but Valérie: "Between
those three absolute passions [...] Madame Marneffe remained calm and clear-headed, like General Bonaparte when,
at the siege of Mantua, he had to react to two armies while
continuing to besiege the town."[14] There is, of course, an
evident sense of blatant narrative satisfaction in this neat numerical parallel, reinforced by the use of titles for both protagonists. Moreover, it sets the scene for a false parallel, in which
an individual's self-perception collides with the text's irony,
conveyed both by a distinct lessening in narrative sympathy
directed toward him and by the ludicrous exaggeration in the
points of comparison: "Jealousy, as it played over Hulot's face,
made him as terrible as the late marshal Montcornet setting
out on a charge against a Russian unit. In his capacity as a
handsome man, this Senior Member of the Council of State

13. See the Introduction for links between jealousy and war suggested in the
dictionary definitions.
14. Balzac, *La Cousine Bette*, 205.

had never known jealousy, just as Murat had never experienced fear" (205). There is, moreover, a hint of the cuckold's horns [*cornes*] in the name *Montcornet*, and a certain, no doubt deliberate, awkwardness in the bracketing of fear and jealousy, in the assumption that analogy provides incontrovertible proof of authenticity. Besides, the comparison continues through a passing reference to Mirabeau, only to collide against the supercilious glance of Montès, for whom Hulot is no more than a "fat Chinese vase" (206).

The multiple readings of the other provided by this passage, enriched by metaphors of consumption and destruction, reveal not only how jealousy's distorting lens reduces both lover and beloved to objects, but also how fragile and vulnerable the jealous individual then becomes. Balzac drives this point home in a subsequent episode in which Valérie convinces her four lovers that each is the father of the child she is expecting, secure in the knowledge that her cynical husband will happily accept the child as a stepping-stone for his ambitions. Refusing to dress this awareness in metaphor, the text is pointedly and bitterly lapidary here: "Thanks to this strategy based on the vanity of each of her lovers, Valérie had at her table four men, each joyful, animated, charmed, and believing himself adored, men whom Marneffe, in a joking aside to Lisbeth, termed the five—for he included himself—fathers of the Church" (280–81).

Jealousy, in this novel, is seen both as a potent force and as something debasing, allowing Crevel and Hulot to accept what they know to be lies merely in order to retain possession not only of Valérie's favors, but also, and more importantly, of their own self-images. For Montès, however, there is no such compromise: once he is sure of Valérie's deceit, he does not hesitate to destroy her, aware that failure to do so will result in self-destruction, if not physically, at least in terms of what he perceives as his honor. There are obvious political analogies, at a time when the bourgeoisie increasingly faced the need to decide between accepting debasing compromise or overthrowing the state and incurring the loss of all they possessed.

Reading and interpreting the other are central in these passages, where individuals play and replay in their minds actions and words that seem to contain garbled clues to a hidden truth.

The young Balzac of *La Physiologie du mariage* may have been optimistic, in a tongue-in-cheek manner, when he asserted: "The slightest movement of the lips, the most imperceptible contraction of the nostrils, the most unnoticeable shades of the eyes, a change in the voice, and those indefinable clouds that envelop the features, or those flames that illuminate them, all is language for you."[15] Yet not only are the characters of his novels deprived of this ability to render the physical an instant and accurate guide to the psychological, but even within *La Physiologie* the legibility of female features becomes increasingly questionable. "Once women have reached the stage where they seek a degree of deceit, their faces become as impenetrable as the void" (249), he asserts, not without ambivalence, and he finesses his earlier claims by confessing: "Up to the age of thirty, a woman's face is a book written in a foreign language, a language one can still translate, despite the difficulties of all the idiosyncrasies of the idiom; but, once she has turned forty, a woman becomes an indecipherable scrawl, and if anyone can make out an old woman, it's another old woman" (264). In order to achieve any kind of deciphering, it seems, Balzacian characters are forced to reduce the other, both the beloved and the intruder, to some kind of icon. Simplified and reified, the other would be more easily controlled. Searching for enlightenment in such instances is always ambiguously presented: as with Oedipus, knowledge may be worse than ignorance, darkness better than illumination.

That desire for illumination—the longing to find a window, or a jealous glass, allowing access into the other's mind—is intimately bound up not merely with a desire for political control, as Balzac's metaphors suggest, but also, and perhaps especially in such repressively conformist societies as Victorian England, in a sense of entrapment within the self that gives rise within studies of jealousy to a series of spatial metaphors. Such entrapment, for instance, is oppressively explored by Trollope in his novella *Kept in the Dark*. In it he teases out many of the metaphorical suggestions we have already encountered in other depictions of moments of jealous suspicion,

15. Honoré de Balzac, *Physiologie du mariage* (Paris: Flammarion, 1968), 171.

and he does so in a narrative that re-creates with particular intensity the feeling of claustrophobia experienced both by the jealous husband, subjugated by the rigid bands of his image of marriage, and by the unwilling cause of his rage.

From the arresting opening sentence of this narrative: "There came an episode in the life of Cecilia Holt which it is essential should first be told,"[16] with its relentless rhythms and its complex time frame, Cecilia's life, in both senses of the word, is forever colored by a single event. This determined simplification of an existence presented, and in turn seen, as dominated by one circumstance, is part of the very essence of jealousy, characteristic of both the inability or refusal to see incidents in context and a tendency to read into them an importance damaging both for lover and beloved. But it is also central to the art of the storyteller: the aptitude for convincing the reader that shapes and patterns can be extracted from what, for most existences, appears to lack both form and direction. Moreover, where the guilty individual, a Valérie Marneffe, for instance, tells many versions of a single episode, the jealous person can only recount the same story, the one that causes most pain. Multiplicity, one might argue in this context, is the privilege of the happy few.

The episode in question concerns an aborted engagement between Cecilia and the profligate and selfish Sir Francis Geraldine. When her future husband, George Western, tells her of his own broken engagement, which not only followed a very similar pattern but ended with the fiancée's announcement that she had agreed to marry Geraldine's cousin, Cecilia finds it impossible to recount her own tale. Two acknowledged reasons prevent her: first, the sense of duplication, the fear that he might imagine she tells her tale only in order to gain his sympathy or, worse, to mock him; second, the fact that where their tales differ is in the response of others: "It was said truly of him, that the girl had jilted him, but falsely of her that she had been jilted" (35). There is, it seems, a possible third reason, and that is that a previous engagement ought to be disclosed

16. Anthony Trollope, *Kept in the Dark* (Oxford: Oxford University Press, 1991), 1.

because sexual freedoms were permitted to engaged women that made them less pristine than would otherwise have been the case.

Nevertheless, what may be most at issue here is not so much retrospective jealousy, a concept difficult to grasp unless one pictures love as competition, but more a jealous clinging to a particular image of the other and thereby, of course, of the self. There is, in other words, the sense of an intellectual betrayal, of a desire to know, frustrated by a determination on the other's part to keep some matters secret. Speaking of his former fiancée, Western argues: "I had loved a girl whose existence I had imagined, and of whom I had seen merely the outward form, and had known nothing of the inner self. What is it that we love? [. . .] Is it merely the colored doll, soft to touch and pleasant to kiss? Or is it some inner nature which we hope to discover, and of which we have found the outside so attractive? I had found no inner self which it had been possible that I could love" (34). The problem for both Western and Cecilia lies partly in the fact that this statement, although its ostensible audience is Cecilia, addresses itself to a male "we"—as indicated by the reference to the colored doll, the softness, and so on—and partly in that it demands a knowledge Western is unwilling to seek out and in no way able to accept. Multiply addressed, it rejects the possibility that its ostensible recipient might also be multiple and above all that that recipient might be other than a mirror reflecting the speaker. To discover the "inner nature" Western claims to covet, he would have to be willing to accept both the otherness of women and a woman's right to a personality and a past or, in other words, to her own story.

Speaking to him of what had happened is made impossible by his self-inflating ego: "He was so full of affairs which were his own, which were so soon to become her own, that there was not a moment for her in which she could tell the story" (46). Time here is the domain of the man, conceived of in spatial terms as expanding to crush the woman's time in the same way that his personality swells to crush hers. His current (indeed recurrent) need for her to make him happy is made so evident to her that she cannot bring herself to tell what will undoubtedly make him, if only temporarily, unhappy: "The time came when he was alone with her, sitting with his arm around her waist, telling her of all the things she should do for him to make his life blessed;—and how he too would endeavor to do some little things for her in order that her life might be happy. She would not tell it then" (46). The very submission demanded of women, the very fact that a man expects a woman to fall silent when he wishes to speak, renders it impossible for Cecilia to say here what needs to be said.

Moreover, it proves equally beyond her to tell him in a letter, for "when the letter was completed, she found it to be one which she could not send."[17] One reason for this impossibility lies in the way in which something she wants to portray as a brief and unimportant episode nevertheless swells in the telling to fill "various sheets of paper" (40). Herein lies one of the central aspects of jealousy, brilliantly caught by Trollope in this fleeting allusion: like the contents of Pandora's box, the image that lies at the heart of jealousy cannot be contained in space or time but constantly swells to fill both, stifling both sufferer and victim. Jealousy is nothing if not a tale that grows longer in the telling.

Furthermore, just as the jealous mind obsessively replays suspicions or events, so the structure of Trollope's novella is based on repetition—not just in the mirroring of the two broken engagements (further reflected, but in a degraded form, in the abortive engagement of Francis Geraldine and Francesca Altifiorla) but in the fact that whereas Cecilia's letter remains unsent, Western does learn of her past through a letter sent by Francis Geraldine. Here again both the woman's voice and her right to silence are thrust under by the belligerent power of male speech. Besides, the whole theme of reading and interpreting the other, which is so central to the depiction of jealousy, is repeatedly stressed through allusions to letters and through metaphorical depictions of the individual as an open or sealed letter. Lady Grant makes this parallel explicit, referring allusively to the ancient wish that minds be open to the

17. Ibid., 41. The Dover edition of *Kept in the Dark*, which reproduces the original serial publication in *Good Words*, includes a wonderfully melodramatic illustration of this event that brings home the degree of mental anguish Cecilia feels.

gaze,[18] when she remarks: "a man expects to see every thought in the breast of the woman to whose love he trusts, as though it were all written there for him in the clear light, but written in letters which no one else shall read."[19] The impossibility of such openness, together with the duplicity of both spoken and written word, are what lie at the heart of this evocation of jealousy. The static hum of both the other's never fully knowable past and the other's always partly unknowable alterity breaks the idealized contact between lover and beloved.

If letters are central to the theme of jealousy, they are also a means of rewriting truth, or the individual's perception of truth, in ways that can alter that individual's sense of the external world as well as of inner landscapes. The creation of physical correlatives for the mood of jealousy is, indeed, one of the most arresting features of depictions of jealousy. In *Kept in the Dark*, the image of whose title runs through the entire novella and prepares the sudden change of Western's mood, the arrival of Geraldine's letter telling him of Cecilia's previous engagement, recreates the world for him: "It can seldom be the case that a man shall receive a letter by which he is so absolutely lifted out of his own world of ordinary contentment into another absolutely different. And the world into which he was lifted was one black with unintelligible storms and clouds. It was as though everything were suddenly changed for him" (95). The storms and clouds of this depiction, the blackness that ironically overcomes him now that he is no longer "kept in the dark," suggest a landscape of the emotion of jealousy, a landscape whose bleakness has nothing to do with the jealous lover's geographical situation. Western's flight to Italy sets in train a sharp dichotomy between the brilliance of sun and sky that Romanticism attributed to the South, and the inescapable blackness of the Englishman's mental horizons. Such emo-

18. "The Greek god Momus, critic of his fellow gods and of created reality, is said to have blamed Vulcan because in the human form, which he had made of clay, he had not placed a window in the breast, by which whatever was felt or thought there might easily be brought to light" (Dorrit Cohn, *Transparent Minds* [Princeton: Princeton University Press, 1978], 3). See Cohn's book more generally for a stimulating exploration of the narratological implications and extensions of this image.
19. Trollope, *Kept in the Dark*, 75.

tional landscapes, as in many techniques associated with jealousy, reveal that what seems timeless and universal is frequently deployed in ways that are both personally and politically specific. Thus, to provide a brief example, Shirley Hazzard's *The Transit of Venus* charts a universal landscape of jealousy, but adapts it from rural to urban and in particular notes the way in which a sudden awareness of loss focuses attention on minute and meaningless details from which the suffering mind struggles to extract significance. Ted Tice, told that the woman he loves is about to marry another man, finds himself staring with tormented intensity at the clothes of the person who has conveyed this information to him: "The cicatrice of stitching on her gloves was an imprint on his brain. Earrings of pearl stared, white-eyed as fish. There was a streak of flowered scarf, inane, and the collar blue. Grief had a painter's eye, assigning arbitrary meaning at random—like God."[20] That intensity of vision that comes with the pain of jealousy and separation leads to a particular reading of external space when Ted moves from a department store into the street: "The claustrophobic building had provided shelter of a kind, with its avenues resembling city planning, its racks and trays overflowing with daily life, its suburbs named Millinery and Haberdashery in memory of childhood. In the open street Ted Tice was grappled, and experienced bodily lightness of a sort that accompanies physical peril. He would get through these moments as a duty in preparation for the next phase, the realization that was to take him and maul him."[21] The transformation of self and ambient space through jealousy has rarely been so powerfully and concisely realized as in this luminous passage.

Both the emotional universality and the political specificity of the bleak and catastrophic terrain of jealousy are given an especially pungent savor in Choromanski's extraordinary novel, *Jealousy and Medicine*, written in 1932, in the partic-

20. Shirley Hazzard, *The Transit of Venus* (Harmondsworth: Penguin, 1980), 197.
21. Ibid., 197–98. Even though it could be argued that the main emotion here is of loss, it is that sense of loss that is necessary to spark off jealousy, and Hazzard's presentation of an external world that alters to become the reflection of suffering is too sharply realized an example to be omitted.

ularly dark days of a Poland in the grip of a brutal military dictatorship and a bleak economic depression.[22] Moreover, whereas other writers, perhaps most notably Proust, have elaborated a series of parallels between love and illness or jealousy and disease, *Jealousy and Medicine* not only does so with ferocious and unremitting intensity but also sets that extended metaphor in the framework of a landscape and a climate that re-create to the full the physical experience of jealousy. Here, in other words, both the focalization and the context of the narration combine to force the reader to confront the nature of jealousy. That climate, moreover, is what most powerfully determines the ways in which the other is interpreted, acting as a form of external, irrational commentary on the possibilities of deceit and the suspicions of jealousy. What is more, the inescapable nature of the emotional climate is stressed in this novel by the circularity of its structure, a circularity that also, of course, emphasizes the obsessional nature of the passion. And throughout, the lover's desire to read and thereby control the other, the implacable inhumanity of urban existence, narrating a story unframed for the individual, and the claustrophobic nature of sexual desire telling of its own obsessive fall— all suggest powerful political metaphors.

The narration begins with the story's end, presented to us in a series of initially incomprehensible, half-glimpsed fragments that reproduce the jealous mind's sense of things not understood together with its desire to impose on such fragmentary knowledge some kind of significance and order, however arbitrary, to create a meaningful narration that would imply knowledge. The overall circularity implied by such an *entrée en matière* further represents the jealous hero's constant replaying of the past in his drive to extract meaning from it and is reinforced, and the sense of claustrophobia intensified, by repetition throughout the novel of a narrow range of images. In addition, the entire narrative is colored by the initial irony

22. Summarily and short-sightedly dismissed as "une œuvre violente et loufoque" by Philippe Chardin, *L'Amour dans la haine, ou la jalousie dans la littérature moderne* (Geneva: Droz, 1990), 18, this novel is more sympathetically but briefly treated by Sydney Schultze, "Choromanski's *Jealousy and Medicine*," *International Fiction Review* 10, 1 (Winter 1983): 15–18.

embedded in the fact that just when Widmar expects finally to be enlightened about his wife's conduct, the lights go out all over the city. The blackness that surges over Western when he is enlightened, in other words, reappears in this physical assertion of the impossibility of ever discovering the full truth about another person. Moreover, it carries with it a suggestion that apparent illumination might still leave one blinded and in the dark, as Swann, on discovering that the lighted window is not Odette's, realizes that some forms of knowledge still leave one out in the dark street.

Choromanski provides a further sly turn to the screw when Widmar's watch appears to have stopped working: "The hand—damn it!—had not moved even a hairsbreadth."[23] Not merely landscape and weather, but time itself, are reforged by jealousy's manipulative narration. As if to underscore this point, the age of the characters, even when presented with numerical precision, seems to bear no relationship to their appearance, particularly in the case of the tailor, Gold, who, either because he is to die so soon or to bolster his image as the ageless wandering Jew, is described as being thirty-eight but appears far older (6).

The narrative is set in autumn, not merely justifying thereby the hot and clammy windstorm that tears at the city, as jealousy itself buffets Widmar, and the colored leaves, whose multiple suggestions the text so tyrannically teases out, but also setting off the ironic echoes of hackneyed images connecting the season with a sense of loss, the passing of youth and vigor, the coming of death. Those deliberately clichéd associations gain further resonances, moreover, through the interweaving into the narration of popular songs. These songs remind the reader of the overworked nature of a theme treated in this case with such arresting originality and enrich the many other echoes to previous depictions of jealousy. Among these allusions, there is a further, barely suggested irony in that the opening and closing scenes take place on a Friday, with its

---

23. Michal Choromanski, *Jealousy and Medicine*, trans. Eileen Arthurton-Barker (Norfolk, Conn.: New Directions Books, 1964), 1–2, 212.

manifold reverberations for both Christian and Greco-Roman mythology.

Just as such allusions emphasize both the timeless nature of jealousy and the power that passion has to manipulate the individual's awareness of time, that is, to replace chronological time with phenomenological time, so also is jealousy presented as an emotion affecting all the senses. Vision, predictably, remains of dominant importance: the desire to see and the inability to do so are both depicted as part of the very fabric of jealousy, and, therefore, central to what drives the narrative onward. The darkness of the stormy autumnal nights, a darkness so enveloping and horrible that the doctor, Tamten, describes it at one point as producing "a sensation of total psychophysical disorientation" (55), not only makes it impossible to see but comes to stand, in this richly symbolic universe, for the impossibility of any kind of complete knowledge at all. The desire to see and the limitations on vision are also represented, here as in other studies of jealousy, through the many references to windows, which, while they seem to offer further vistas, nonetheless limit and mediate those vistas.

There is a close link between windows and the surgical intervention that reveals to Tamten and his colleague something hidden within Rebecca's body, providing, in other words, a window on her life. This connection is suggested when Widmar, lost in thought concerning the eighth minute in his wife's operation, the minute about which he has so far discovered nothing, is unaware of the tailor's presence:

> "This damned business hasn't been quite solved yet, you understand. What's the meaning of the eighth minute?"
> "Eighth minute?" asked the tailor. "Eighth . . . ? But I wanted to tell you something else, sir."
> "Ah?" cried Widmar, as if he had suddenly come to himself. He understood in a flash what it was about. "The window."
> (63)

The reference here is to the window through which Gold's epileptic son claims to have seen a woman, taken for Rebecca, but it is Widmar's subconscious connection that opens the image up for us.

Nevertheless, vision in this novel seems always to be hampered. Rubinski, the hospital orderly present at the operation, could see nothing of the patient during those critical minutes. While further information is offered by Sophia Dubilanska's diary, it is insinuated that this presents a distorted view, not merely because she is myopic, but because, as Widmar's former long-term mistress, she is jealous of Rebecca. When she describes seeing Rebecca faint on the dance floor, she gives a detailed and precise account of Rebecca's face: "I distinctly saw her face. She was terribly pale, with the clayey pallor of the dying. I realized she was suffering physically and seemed to be tortured with pain" (122), but she is unable to recognize her own surgeon, Tamten, relying on her companion to tell her who he is. Her description of her emotion on learning his identity offers a curious transposition of causes:

"Who is that man?" I asked my companion, and sat down again at the table with an air of perfect indifference.
"Doctor Tamten," he told me.
This saddened me a little, as always when I'm reminded of my nearsightedness. (122)

Obviously the sadness arises less from myopia than from the realization of Rebecca's power to attract men. Of the others who may have seen damning evidence against Rebecca, Gold's view of the couple he observes in the rented room is restricted, since he peers in from outside, and the child Baruch not only cannot interpret what he sees—the woman and her naked breast—but also suffers an epileptic fit immediately afterward, suggesting that he may merely have been hallucinating. Even mirrors show less the physical object standing before them than the emotion of the person reflected: "The mirror misted over, I could see our dark shapes and the blobs of our faces" (115).

The inadequacy of vision for interpreting the outside world is reinforced by images suggesting the difficulty or indeed impossibility of reading: Tamten wears red glasses to read x-rays, glasses that transform his eyes into "bleeding holes" (43); Rebecca at one stage seems to be poring over a book, but Widmar notices the book is upside down.

The centrality of vision, but also its ultimate unreliability, is underpinned by the numerous, highly varied references to color. The tawny gold of the doctor's eyes, of brandy, of the autumn leaves; the lemon yellow of clouds, of Widmar's skin, of Rebecca's quilt, her gloves, her intestines; the blood red of mist, of Rebecca's dress and scarf, of Boruch's hair and of that of Isaac Gold, of the tiles falling from the roof in the high wind; the green of moonlight and the black of Angela's hair and kite, of Widmar's eyes and Tamten's hair; the lilacs and violets of dirty finger nails and intestines all seem to carry encoded but ultimately undecipherable messages. In fact, both the imperative desire that colors should have meaning and the suggestion that our interpretations of them are always askew are already implicit in the early, enigmatic reference to Gold's name: "The tailor was a very ugly old man with a heart of gold. At least that was the opinion all his customers had about him. But it turned out afterward to be quite different" (6). The falseness of interpretations based on visual perceptions is, perhaps, given its strongest expression in a passage where Widmar's belief is not only described by the narrative voice as illogical, but comes at a point toward the end of the novel where all the evidence makes such a belief untenable. Thinking of his wife, he asserts: "A woman with her eyes and legs couldn't possibly lie every day, every hour, every moment—because lying produces a physical distortion of a person's outward appearance" (124). The Cratylian desire for harmony between inner and outer, between name and object, is unrelentingly denied by this novel, as yet another form of the jealous mind's desire for a narration in complete harmony with its sexual longings.

Ironically, the only response to the "fog of jealousy" is to reject all external evidence and focus merely on the emotion without which life becomes intolerable, in Widmar's case, his love for Rebecca: "His personal life, his wife's betrayal, the extrauterine pregnancy, Tamten, the tailor, the window—all seemed to him completely nonexistent. Another reality had sprung up with an intense and irrefutable actuality. A man about to die sees the ordinary, everyday things around him with an implacable sharpness. A man near personal catastrophe experiences . . ." (158). The intensity of jealousy in this depiction is such that visual references alone are insufficient to carry forward the narrative: jealousy is so much a part of the individual's experience of external phenomena that all the senses come into play. The importance of hearing, as the jealous lover strains to overhear anything that might confirm what he or she fears to be the truth is evident in this novel from the beginning. The twin opening and closing scenes are filled with the noise of bells and sirens—the ambulance's siren and the bells in the hospital's emergency ward externalize the screams of fear, pain, and doubt in the jealous lover as he waits to learn the truth about his beloved, a truth he will, in fact, never discover, primarily because he does not want to do so. The city is full of other sounds, too: gunfire, dogs barking, patients crying out in fear or pain, doors banging, glasses shattering. And over it all, through the week in which these events take place, rages the tempest with its "cacophony of muttering, howling, thundering voices" (198), as though jealousy has bodied forth a pack of furies screaming for vengeance.

This cacophony suggests a parallel with the multiple clashing colors of a world whose principle seems to be, not the harmony the central characters long for, but chaos. And the parallel between sight and sound is strengthened by the ways in which information is gleaned from things overheard and only partially interpretable: just as Gold peers in at the lovers, so Rubinski eavesdrops on Tamten and his colleague discussing the operation, and snatches, during the operation itself, an expression that seems to hold the key to truth but that is in a foreign language, German: "Ein-ge-kap-selt!" (84). Later, the same phenomenon is evoked in Latin as "extra uterina" (102). While the meaning of these two terms gradually becomes clear to the figures in the narrative, the suggestion for the reader is that the inherent difficulties of interpreting the visual world have a close counterpart in the interpretation of the world of sounds.

Smell, too, provides a dominant series of allusions in the novel, reinforcing the strongly physical temper of jealousy and implying the way in which it reveals the animal forces in human nature. The mustiness of autumn leaves, the dankness of stale cellars, the smell of gasoline, and the aroma of death are all recurrent features of the protagonist's response to the claustrophobia of jealousy.

What becomes increasingly evident is that although these sensual impressions create a pattern, that pattern is merely the closed and constantly decreasing circle of jealousy itself: while Choromanski's jealous lover, in other words, longs to find patterns confirming his suspicions, all that is provided by the senses is the desire for pattern itself. Tamten, gazing blissfully into a brandy glass, offers the clearest image of this truth when he explains to Widmar that he adores Byzantine art and that "in the facets of the glass he [can] see something that [brings] a certain design to his mind" (48). Later, the text provides a sharp and cynical commentary on this passage by throwing the pattern into focus: what Tamten is seeing in his mind's eye is Widmar's naked wife. Pattern, it would seem, springs equally from desire and jealousy, making them appear mirror images of each other.

If both desire and jealousy distort the evidence of the senses, which is in any case unreliable, the narrative suggests that space is also open to distortion. Throughout the novel descriptions of place are unstable, and the links between the different rooms in which the characters meet are fraught with danger. The café and the hospital, the two main public spaces of the novel, are to a large extent interchangeable, Rebecca first contacting Dr. Tamten at the café, and Widmar continuing in the hospital meditations begun in the café. Rebecca's living room recalls the bedroom Tamten has rented, both being decorated in yellow. The only other private place we see is Gold's house, where the little girl's lies and the tailor's suspicions that his wife has betrayed him with his brother constantly cast reflections on the main story, making this house merely a further dimension of the smothering space of perfidy and jealousy. The way in which space offers an external manifestation of the emotions of rivalry is further emphasized by the dangers encountered in the streets. Attackers hide in dark alleyways, the wind wrenches tiles from roofs and hurls them on passersby, cars, seen by one of the minor characters as innately and inordinately menacing, thunder past at close range, and live electric wires dangle like hangman's nooses or spiders' webs. The movement between buildings, the movement that makes relationships possible, is thus presented as fraught with peril, just as relationships themselves are ultimately destructive.

The uncertainty that the senses create (imitated in the failure of instruments of measurement—watches and barometers) is intensified by the multiplicity of narrative voices and the unreliability of the narrators. Much of the story is told by one or the other of the characters, forcing the reader to question the validity, accuracy, and neutrality of that testament. Rubinski's account of the operation is skewed by our knowledge of Tamten's judgment of him as unreliable, both as a doctor and as a man; Sophia Dubilanka's given name may mean "wisdom, knowledge," but her diary is presented to us as that of a woman distorting truth, telling her own version of the tale because she has been abandoned by her lover in favor of the rival whose perjury Sophia claims to reveal. Moreover, the different narrators adopt different voices at various points—in letters or diaries, in talking to friend or foe—a change of style that suggests the shifting and uncertain nature of the evidence. A striking parallel for these changes of tone or rhetoric is provided by the scene in which Tamten first hears Rebecca's voice on the telephone:

> The receiver buzzed and he distinctly heard a kind of growl. It must be some old hag, he thought, croaking like that. Then suddenly the feminine voice on the wire changed and grew musical and lilting. It seemed as if another person were speaking. "Hello, hello!" cried the astonished doctor. For some unknown reason he experienced a sensual excitement. This new voice stirred up within him impressions which were erotic and voluptuous, almost morbid. She must be young, attractive, half-naked and lying in bed, he thought. He was sure of it. (66)

Underlying this richly suggestive passage with its implications that individuals read the world in the way that will offer them the most pleasure are the many stories in which the devil disguises himself as a seductive individual, and although he allows himself occasionally to be perceived as devil, nevertheless succeeds in arousing the desire of the person he wants to damn.[24] Passages like this, with its internal focalization, are balanced by passages of dialogue, by diary entries, by letters, by events narrated from the position of an omniscient narrator, setting up a constant train of questions about who speaks, who sees, how much of this is gossip, lies, fabrication. How much, in other words, is truth tailored and doctored to the needs of listener or teller?

Counterbalancing the weight of that unanswerable but central question is the series of maxims scattered through the text, lending it an equally suspect air of authority and reinforcing a political reading by the desire to condense irreducible reality to a few easily formulated laws. "Humiliation in love heightens the emotions of passion";[25] "The well-being of the human system is founded on a lie. The only real remedy [. . .] is self-delusion" (105); "The mind is a mechanism which justifies our feelings. A man deceived in love manages to enact a passable theory idealizing what has happened. The man who himself has betrayed can always prove to himself the morality of his actions" (135–36). What destabilizes these maxims is that occasionally they are followed by a narrative commentary throwing into doubt all the uncommented maxims as well. Widmar's long and apparently philosophical meditation on jealousy is powerfully undermined by statements such as the following: "The greatest crime is disloyalty to oneself, he thought with pathetic sophistry" (136).

The instability of the text is augmented by a complex web of metaphors in which both love and jealousy are depicted as madness, disease, addiction, drunkenness, epilepsy, sleepwalking, heart disease. Clarity, understanding, and knowledge are therefore incompatible with jealousy as Choromanski depicts it, the detective's longing for precise and incontrovertible evidence is constantly overthrown by the lover's inescapable mental precariousness. Gold's relentless pursuit of knowledge leads to his destruction in the web of electric lines (207), making him the spider caught by the trap he himself had spun for Rebecca.

24. A prime example is Jacques Cazotte's *Le Diable amoureux* (Paris: Le Terrain Vague, 1960).
25. Choromanski, *Jealousy and Medicine*, 104.

Equally destabilizing is the growing awareness of the extent to which the object of jealousy, like the focus of political repression, barely exists as an individual. Sexual desire, the novel insists, is no more than the impersonal desire for sex, and Rebecca, Tamten and Widmar are for each other merely elements of a vast impersonal paradigm. (Robbe-Grillet in *La Jalousie* conveys the same insight by designating his female character simply by the letter "A" and by depriving the jealous narrator of any appellation at all.) In many ways, Rebecca as individual does not exist, either for the male characters or for the reader. Choromanski's exploration of this phenomenon is worth quoting in full:

> Rebecca was sitting on the sofa. Yet her presence seemed something utterly unreal—Rebecca as such did not exist at all. Her thoughts and her psychic aura took up no place in space or time. The two men could look through her as through a glass or into a vacuum. Her existence was problematical, and the surgeon asked himself whether she were not a specter. This bodilessness, this wraithlike quality, was in the highest degree annoying, and Tamten despised himself for devoting so much time to a female phantom.
>
> But from another point of view, the fact that her very existence imposed its laws on everyone was undeniable. Although there seemed to be an empty place on the sofa, only a vacant seat, they knew—and there was absolute certainty in the knowledge—that a being without form was there, or rather an abstract sum of human properties. It was a kind of monster. It was made up of a strange combination of looks and smiles and moving arms, of woman's legs and breasts and thighs, and above all of sensual desires and scents. It filled the whole room, in which prevailed an atmosphere as absorbed as that at a séance.
>
> On the sofa sat a spirit who, from time to time, kept manifesting before their eyes. (49)

This highly original and chilling reinterpretation of the *ewig Weibliche* sharpens suggestions made elsewhere of Rebecca as harpy, Rebecca as devil, Rebecca as the incarnation of erotic

desire. In her presence, the men, reduced to a "slightly cata-
leptic" condition (49), can talk only of sex and are deprived of
any powers of intellectual reasoning. Summoned up by their
desire, as a spirit is called forth at a séance, she can be nothing
more than a glass or a vacuum, an empty space onto which the
men project their own sexual longings and are in turn doomed
to be no more than their own sexuality. Moreover, the narrative is punctuated by references to Tamten's scorn for women
as anything other than physical objects: "About women's
brains I'm not in the least concerned; I think a woman has
more interesting organs" (23); "The woman's role begins and
ends in bed. For me, at least" (75). In the crudest, but also in
the most profound of terms, she is no more and no less than a
hole, insatiably absorbing men's thoughts about her, and
thereby transforming them into mere void, too.

Yet Rebecca's absence as individual has another cause, and
one that forces us as readers to share that perception of absence: descriptions of her are not only rare but always in dis-
agreement with each other. Gold wants his son to confirm that
the woman he saw in the window the second time had Rebecca's black hair, but Boruch insists that this time the woman
was blonde. Rubinski reports that Tamten described Rebecca
in the following terms: "She wasn't pretty. She had a swarthy
complexion, strangely dark. It even occurred to me that this
was a peculiar pigmentation of the skin. As for her eyes, I really
can't tell you what color they were. They were enormous and
so dazzling that their flashing brilliance blinded me. I tell you
again, she seemed to me positively ugly rather than pretty"
(70). Rubinski's own impressions are significantly different: "I
had expected to see a vamp, but I found only a calm, attractive
young woman. I thought the superintendent had spoken of a
brunette, but I must have been mistaken, for your wife's hair
is light chestnut. She was in bed, rosy and smiling" (72). While
Tamten's description of Rebecca as dark coincides with Boruch's first vision, the reference to rosiness echoes the child's
second sighting of her. Sophia Dubilanka provides yet another
glimpse of Rebecca when she recounts in her diary the first
meeting of Widmar and his future wife: "This woman was almost ugly, and old-looking, too, without any charm. But I

guessed she might be attractive to men" (109). Rebecca, therefore, seems all things to all people.

It would be a misreading of the text to suggest here that Choromanski is merely giving voice to misogyny: although his narrative uses a woman as the space around which jealousy forms, it is also made clear that a parallel text could be written from the women's point of view and that in it the male object of desire would be just as much a vacuum as Rebecca is for Widmar and Tamten.[26] At one point, for instance, Rebecca, lulled into carelessness by familiarity, uses the expression she has employed before to convince her lovers of the depth of her emotions: "I'm a coward, perhaps, when I risk having a child by you?"[27] In this case she forgets that Tamten's scalpel has rendered her incapable of having children and has thereby sliced all meaning from that particular protestation. Tamten's resultant fury is a product of his awareness that he is merely one in the paradigmatic series of lovers, shorn of his individuality in the same way that he stripped Rebecca of hers.

If Widmar finds happiness at the end of this tale of deception and fabrication, it is only by accepting as lies, gossip, and blackmail the stories woven around the empty space designated "Rebecca." The only cure for a jealous sense of being deceived, *Jealousy and Medicine* seems to suggest, is the acceptance of self-deception. For all his efforts, the jealous detective cannot bring his fragmentary knowledge together to form a whole, because that knowledge focuses on something conceived of merely as a hole. In this case, jealousy cannot, or will not, read what it most dreads, and all its reading cannot decipher a mere cipher. If love has acquired any knowledge here, it is, as in *Un Amour de Swann*, that love's ignorance is preferable to love's knowledge.

The countless ways in which jealousy in this novel tropes the suspicions of totalitarian powers, its ambivalent and disturbing image of the suffering Jew, and its powerful figure of

26. There are numerous suggestions of homosexuality scattered in the text, particularly in the form of offers of cigarettes to Tamten. In a different context, *Jealousy and Medicine* could certainly be deconstructed in entirely different ways.
27. Choromanski, *Jealousy and Medicine*, 181, 195.

the hospital as a central image of contemporary society also make of Choromanski's novel not merely a uniquely unsettling portrait of sexual passion, but also an acid but ultimately ambiguous political statement.

Jealousy as distorting glass, a theme that lies close to the heart of the imagery dominating *Jealousy and Medicine*, is even more consciously spotlighted in Musil's *novella*, *Tonka*, written a decade earlier than Choromanski's novel at a time when Germany was suffering severe economic crises and when the imprisoned Hitler was drafting *Mein Kampf*.[28] Musil, ever fascinated by humanity's tendency to forge imaginary worlds that corrupt both memory and the evidence of the senses, creates a poetic prose of singular beauty and luminosity that intensifies the destructive potential of jealousy to transform that imaginary framework into a torture chamber. In his hands the crystallization process explored by Stendhal is transposed into a negative mode through the lover's constant distortion of the other.

Jealousy's power to throw into doubt even the clearest of memories is revealed in the novella's opening passages, where the idyllic opening scene is followed by the negating questions prompted by suspicion: "But had it really been like that at all? No, that was only what he had worked it up into later. That was the fairy tale, but he could no longer tell the difference."[29] The inability to tell truth from fabrication stems above all, in Musil's depiction, from the narrator's desire for Tonka to be other than she is, as Choromanski's male characters seek to deny Rebecca's personality. Because she fails to mirror his own emotions, he sees her as stupid and deceptive, yet finds himself forced to acknowledge that the failure may indeed be his: "Those were all very slight experiences, of course, but the remarkable thing was that they happened all over again, exactly the same. Actually, they were always there. And, even more remarkably, later they had meant the very opposite of what they had meant at the beginning. Tonka always remained so

28. See also Chardin, "La Jalousie sans qualités," in *L'Amour dans la haine*, 173–206.
29. Robert Musil, *Tonka and Other Stories*, trans. Eithne Wilkins and Ernst Kaiser (London: Panther, 1969), 132.

simply and transparently the same thing that it was almost like having an hallucination, seeing the most incredible things" (141). Those hallucinations, the inability to discriminate between truth and fabrication, arise in large part from the protagonist's constant projection of himself on to the outside world, and in particular on Tonka herself. The text records their promise to belong completely to each other, but adds, with a sardonic humor typical of Musil: "That is to say, he had talked and Tonka had listened in silence" (150). Such a projection of inner hopes on to outer realities makes it impossible to separate truth from dream: "These certainties of Tonka's infidelity had, indeed, something of the quality of dreams" (161).

Karl Eibl, in commenting on the central themes of *Tonka*, is only partly right when he argues that jealousy plays a secondary role to the problem of truth.[30] It would be even more accurate to say that jealousy provides the distorting glass through which the protagonist looks at the truth about existence and that the way in which jealousy chains him to memory supplies the spiraling structures that contrast so clearly with the forward thrust of Tonka's pregnancy to create much of the text's dynamics: "Amid all these uncertainties," Musil remarks with understated irony, "Tonka's pregnancy took its course, revealing the harshness of reality."[31]

However diverse their provenance, however differently conceived their political or social agenda, these passages, therefore, provide windows on jealousy by manipulating narrative focus, by weaving a web of images that reveal the nature of the individual's concept of the other, and by exploring the transformation of space, time, and personality under the influence of that passion. In addition, they examine the many ways in which reading the other leads to a state of knowledge that the protagonists might initially have desired but either lose interest in or thrust back into ignorance. Their use of jealousy as a trigger for seeking out information or for attempting to conceal, distort, or fabricate information invites readings that are at once timeless (in which jealousy and passion are seen as uni-

30. In Robert Musil, *Drei Frauen* (Munich: Carl Hauser Verlag, 1978), 152.
31. Musil, *Tonka*, 167.

versal givens) and specific to the moment in which they are written, creating allegories or symbols of a specific political, social, or personal moment. As interpreters of a particular text—whether accurate or mere fabrication, fantastic, or drawn from the very stuff of everyday existence—these protagonists supply us, the readers of their stories, with techniques of decoding, interpreting, and assessing the information available to us. As tellers of tales, whether in the role of deceitful lovers covering their tracks or in that of the suspicious lover attempting to uncover what is hidden, they are also paradigm figures of the writer, and their techniques and responses reflect back on those of the text itself. What is more, they suggest certain differences in the spatial and temporal images associated with male and female senses of betrayal. My next chapter, therefore, focuses on the ways in which literature engenders jealousy.

2 Engendering Jealousy: Revealing Differences

> We may not know exactly what sex is; but we do know that it
> is mutable, with the possibility of one sex being changed into
> the other sex, that its frontiers are often uncertain, and that
> there are many stages between a complete male and a complete
> female.
>
> Havelock Ellis, *The Psychology of Sex*

Literature has, of course, long depicted men as wanting both
the right to cause jealousy with impunity and to be free of any
cause of jealousy themselves, a desire encapsulated most tell-
ingly in the High Romantic figure of Gilda in Verdi's *Rigoletto*,
betrayed and abandoned but still willing to give her life to save
her seducer as he wanders off into the night with another
woman, singing of woman's infidelity. Though Romanticism
had dwindled into the constraints of Victorian morality by the
time Trollope wrote his novella *Kept in the Dark*, he nevertheless has his Lady Grant make a similar point when she asks
Cecilia: "Do you measure the one thing by the other [. . .] a
man's desires by a woman's, a man's sense of honor by what a
woman is supposed to feel? Though a man keep such secrets
deep in his bosom through long years of married life, the
woman is not supposed to be injured. She may know, or may
not know, and may hear the tale at any period of her married
life, and no harm will follow. But a man expects to see every
thought in the breast of the woman to whose love he trusts,
as though it were all written there for him in the clear light,

but written in letters which no one else shall read."[1] And yet, "Heaven," so Congreve had announced some hundred and fifty years before, "has no rage like love to hatred turned, / Nor hell a fury like a woman scorned."[2] Although the injunction "Always historicize" reminds us of profound social shifts between Congreve and Trollope, any reading of the visual arts reveals the extent to which these two images of woman coexisted not merely at least into the early decades of the twentieth century, but also in both protestant and catholic countries. The dichotomy between woman as Medea, vengefully destroying the perfidious man's trace through the murder of her children and woman with transparent breast, passively offering herself as text while she herself demurely declines to read, is yet another manifestation of the double standard used to justify the discrepancy between what phallocratic society decreed to be female morals and what it accepted as male morals. Hildegard Baumgart, in her psychological study of jealousy, argues, indeed, that: "One must understand many myths about violent and fearsome women, sorceresses and witches, Medea, Circe, Clytemnestra, the Sphinx, and the Amazons, or even Jocasta, in a new light, as figures of the protective defence of a male-dominated society that justifies itself through this depiction: women must be tamed and subordinated to a patriarchal culture, for if one gave them free rein, then they would be *like that!*"[3] Phallocracy and misogyny combine, then, to delineate the most common features of what Verdi's count di Luna refers to as the fiery serpent of jealousy.

Nevertheless, such duality is often paired not only with the simultaneously repugnant and enticing image of the enraged jealous woman, but also with the awareness, brought so compellingly into focus by Tolstoy's *Kreutzer Sonata*, that jealousy ostensibly caused by women may be a manifestation of repressed homosexuality. As Freud pointed out in his reading of

1. Anthony Trollope, *Kept in the Dark* (Oxford: Oxford University Press, 1991), 75.
2. Congreve, *The Mourning Bride,* 3.7.
3. Hildegard Baumgart, *Jealousy: Experiences and Solutions,* trans. Manfred Jacobson and Evelyn Jacobson (Chicago: University of Chicago Press, 1990), 222. See also Mary Daly's ferocious reading of such terminology in her *Pure Lust* (London: Women's Press, 1984).

the situation,[4] the husband allows himself to give vent to his feelings of jealous desire because he convinces himself that he does not desire the other man; it is the other man who desires his wife. In many texts, jealousy accordingly becomes a particularly potent means of exploring what is demanded of each gender and how individuals manipulate such demands in their projection of themselves, their desires, and their image of the other.[5]

Because of the very nature of the icons habitually associated with such expectations, representations of jealousy also allow for explorations of the function of those same icons, and in particular of such rhetorical devices as metonymy, when the individual is reduced to a mere part of his or her whole self or seen as representative of stereotypical characteristics identified (however arbitrarily) with male or female behavior in general.

What is even more central to our purposes is that the exploration of engendered jealousy also questions the engendering of the implied reader and, I would contend, creates a space in which we can begin to respond to Ross Chambers' urgent question: "what are we to make of the split that produces us in relation to [misogynistic and more generally ideologically unacceptable texts]: must it trap us in an endless replication of the discourse of power, or can it, and if so *how* can it, be made to yield the potential it contains for changing the world?"[6] Although Virginia Woolf may well be right when she argues in *A Room of One's Own* that "it is fatal for anyone who writes to think of their sex. It is fatal to be a man or a woman pure and simple; one must be woman-manly or man-womanly,"[7]

4. Sigmund Freud, *Gesammelte Werke* (London: Imago, 1940), 13: 195–207, especially 198.
5. It is a notable fact that many recent lesbian novels eschew the theme of jealousy altogether, turning away from Radclyffe Hall's tragic image of the impossibility of lesbian happiness to produce far more optimistic novels. Even Marie-Claire Blais's *Les Nuits de l'underground* (Ottawa: Stanké, 1978), which contains images of violent jealousy in the account of the protagonist's affair with Lali Dorman, turns toward a far happier vision in its second half and closes on a note of quiet joy. See my article "Marie-Claire Blais," in *Beyond the Nouveau Roman*, ed. Michael Tilby (London: Berg, 1990), 123–50.
6. Ross Chambers, "Irony and Misogyny: Authority and the Homosocial in Baudelaire and Flaubert," *Australian Journal of French Studies* 26, 3 (1989): 287.
7. Virginia Woolf, *A Room of One's Own* (London: Grafton, 1977), 99.

the fact remains that many male writers have spoken of their emotions while writing (and, indeed, while reading) in terms that are explicitly and profoundly sexual.[8] Jealousy, because of its potential for chaos, can be seen as a disruptive force that yields exceptional power despite a writer's apparent physical inscription within the perspective of a particular sex. The literary devices used to engender jealousy, both in the sense of bringing it to life and in that of fleshing it out according to the expectations made of each sex, within and outside the diegetic space, invite particular attention in any examination of the ways in which men and women are depicted as responding to jealousy in female- and male-authored texts.

Analyses of structural strategies often uncover unstated expectations and convictions while enabling, and even empowering, the reader's protest. Thus, even though jealousy may be relegated to a secondary theme in the main plot or rendered with a particular subtlety of shading that blurs the assumptions underpinning it, the depiction of gender-based differences in the experience of jealousy is often sharpened by situations paralleling the main plot, but stripped of the delicacy, nuances, calls for sympathy, and psychological complications associated with the presentation of the central protagonists. Such subplots can provide somewhat dog-eared, but nevertheless useful, codes for interpreting and reading the central images.

Kept in the Dark, for instance, offers, in a constant filigree running through the main tale, a coarsely drawn and overtly prejudiced study of the personality of Francesca Altifiorla, whose jilting by the ever-resourceful Francis Geraldine is treated in a way that highlights (and makes light of) both the double sexual standard of the time and the general scorn with which men regarded women. What is particularly pertinent for our study is the importance placed on reading in the episode in which, as the chapter heading aggressively and manipulatively puts it, Sir Francis "escapes." Not only does the letter in which he breaks the engagement deconstruct itself through a jarring juxtaposition of styles that exposes the insincerity of the message, but it is also subjected to close critical scrutiny

8. Flaubert's letters, for instance, abound in such references.

within the text, both by the letter writer and his friend, and by Miss Altifiorla herself. Geraldine, reading his letter, affirms: "I think I am bound in honor without a moment's delay to make you aware of the condition of my mind in regard to marriage. I ain't quite sure but what I shall be better without it alto-gether.—'I'd rather marry her twice over than let my cousin have the title and the property,' said the Baronet with energy. 'You needn't tell her that,' said McCollop. 'Of course when you've cleared the ground in this quarter you can begin again with another lady.' "[9] McCollop's unvarnished comment, of course, externalizes the unexpressed intentions of this slippery letter writer, but its complacency also appears to exact com-plicity from us, to line us up with the masculine power struc-tures, unless one argues that that very complacency triggers the reader's resistance.

If the unraveling of Geraldine's nature and motives through the written and spoken messages calls for no direct narrative intervention, the constantly changing focal positions adopted in the depiction of Miss Altifiorla's response to it suggest a narrative ambiguity as deep, and apparently as unquestioned, as the double standard itself. "Who shall picture the rage of Miss Altifiorla when she received this letter?" (208–9), asks the narrative voice, in a question that both assumes the passivity of a reader who waits for such challenges and invitations and evokes through the word "rage" images of Medea that have little to do with the pain in which we were invited to share when Western was jilted by his fiancée. The shifting narrative position, rocking from a form of free indirect discourse to im-plicit external judgment, ensures that sympathy with this woman's predicament is not perceived as a desirable response. "To whom should she go for succor?," the narrative voice asks, here briefly sharing her perspective before continuing with a xenophobic and snobbish sarcasm that is clearly both external and antagonistic: "Though her ancestors had been so noble, she had no one near her to take up the cudgels on her behalf" (209). That very xenophobia and misogyny, however, render the nar-rative voice at this point so repugnant as to precipitate the

9. Trollope, *Kept in the Dark*, 208.

reader into a sense of outrage. The narrator's jealous desire to force his reading on the reader, in other words, facilitates the possibility of rival interpretations, just as, in Trollope's *He Knew He Was Right*, it is the husband's jealous demands that push the wife into provoking jealousy.

Francesca's frenetic reading and rereading of this letter, and of every other "scrap of letter that she had received from the man" (209), reveals the impossibility of bringing her case to any court of law, including, apparently, the informal one of the narrator's (though not necessarily the text's) audience. Indirectly, moreover, it throws into sharp relief that manipulation of written language in which both Francesca and Geraldine have indulged, simultaneously revealing that the scales are heavily tipped in favor of the male and indicating the extent to which jealousy triggers in the reader a desire for other, more harmonious, narratives.

Whether misread or misreading, whether they are victims of jealousy or sufferers of jealousy, women in this novella are shown as manipulated by readings in which language itself apparently endorses the male. Here, in Lacan's terms, everything reiterates "le nom du père," but it does so in such trumpet calls as to alert the audience to the fact that the orchestra has other instruments apart from the brass.

Other novels by Trollope give more open expression to the duality of responses that are depicted in men and women as products of jealousy. *He Knew He Was Right*, the novelist's acerbic study of the corrosive effects less of jealousy than of a man's desperate desire to humiliate and triumph over his innocent wife, contains the following revealing passage, where the somewhat lumbering attempts at humor betray both a sense of barely repressed unease and a degree of paradoxical complacency:

> It is to be feared that men in general do not regret as they should do any temporary ill-feeling, or irritating jealousy between husbands and wives, of which they themselves have been the cause. The author is not speaking now of actual love-makings, of intrigues and devilish villainy, either perpetrated or imagined; but rather of those passing gusts of short-lived

and unfounded suspicion to which, as to other accidents, very well-regulated families may occasionally be liable. When such suspicion rises in the bosom of a wife, some woman intervening or being believed to intervene between her and the man who is her own, that woman who has intervened or supposed to intervene, will either glory in her position or bewail it bitterly, according to the circumstances of the case. [. . .] But when such painful jealous doubts annoy the husband, the man who is in the way will almost always feel himself justified in extracting a slightly pleasurable sensation from the transaction. [. . .] Terrible things now and again do occur, even here in England; but women, with us, are slow to burn their household gods.[10]

The suggestive clash here between the humor of the first half of the last sentence and the wish-fulfillment of the second half indicates an unwillingness to read reality that parallels and thereby highlights that of the text's protagonist. Indeed, in this novel, the jealous husband, Louis Trevelyan, is shown to be as incapable of reading his wife's character as he is unable to gauge the violence of the letters he writes her:

He hardly recognized the force of the language which he used when he told her conduct was disgraceful, and that she had disgraced his name. He was quite unable to look at the question between him and his wife from her point of view.
[. . .] There be men, and not bad men either, and men neither uneducated, or unintelligent, or irrational in ordinary matters, who seem to be absolutely unfitted by nature to have the custody or guardianship of others. A woman in the hands of such a man can hardly save herself or him from endless trouble. (257)

The inability to read the other, or to adopt a different point of view, the state, in other words, of being locked within a single perspective, is a characteristic of representations of jealousy

10. Anthony Trollope, *He Knew He Was Right* (London: Oxford University Press, 1948), 86–87.

brilliantly exploited by writers such as Choromanski and Robbe-Grillet, who are, perhaps, more narratologically sophisticated than Trollope himself. Yet, despite the heavy-handedness of the voice-over commentary in the quoted passage, Trollope's technique of slowly accumulating layer on layer of doubt, suspicion, or unease does make possible a particularly potent representation of the engendering of jealousy. Moreover, through the constant suggestion of the presence of a third party in the novel's numerous relationships (Dorothy and Brook threatened by the aunt, Mr. Gibson oscillating unhappily between the two Misses French, the detective Bozzle producing tiny scraps of possible evidence to widen the gap between Louis and Emily, the intrusive narrative voice coming between the reader and the plot), *He Knew He Was Right*, whose very title intrudes the third instance of irony, enacts the triangulation both of jealousy and of narration. And it is precisely in the mobility and instability of that triangulation that lies the potential for a disruptive reader response refusing the assumptions and conclusions Trollope's text apparently demands.

While Trollope's morality is stamped, at least on the surface, with the mid-Victorian seal, his techniques of doubling and triangulation thus set in train a disruptive static enabling the reader to superimpose his or her own narrative. This disjunction is similar to that used by the far more cynical, far more libertine Benjamin Constant, whose novel, *Adolphe*, both reflects the sexual libertinism of the late eighteenth century and adumbrates the changing moral codes of the early nineteenth century. Here, the jealousy described as located in Ellénore is reinforced, expanded, and transformed to a different plane by the static hum of the older narrator's explicit or implicit questioning of his younger self. Moreover, that questioning is shown to contain moments of reticence and aporia that in themselves set off the static interference of the reader's own disorderly response. And nowhere is that reticence so telling as in the area of gender.

The claustrophobia Adolphe professes to feel in Ellénore's company, once he has succeeded in seducing her, is reproduced for the reader by the oppressive nature of the narration itself, where the older narrator's reading of his younger self fragments any sympathetic rapport between reader and hero and also oppressively seeks to dominate the reader's own assessment of that character. Because this is a first-person narrative, in which Ellénore is allowed direct communication with the reader only through her death-bed letter, she becomes a mere extension, or even an alter ego, of Adolphe, a voice whose reported questioning of motives and behavior parallels in a more explicit and less subtle manner those of the older narrator himself.

As a result, here even more clearly than in Trollope's text, sexual jealousy appears as a metaphor for the narrative's jealousy of the reader, for its determination to drive out the disruptive outside voices and to enchain the reader, as Ellénore is accused of enchaining Adolphe himself. This metaphor can function so well only because of the extraordinary—and notorious—disparity the young Adolphe believed existed between men and women. His father, steeped in the cynicism of eighteenth-century France, holds women in contempt: "It seemed to him that all women, so long as it was not a question of marrying them, could, without any inconvenience, be taken and then abandoned; and I have seen him smile with a form of approval at this parody of a well-known saying: 'It causes them so little harm and brings us so much pleasure'."[11] And just as this attitude denies women rights and feelings, so the very structures of the narrative deny Ellénore a right to speak, and when that right is, apparently, at last allowed, it occurs only as a result of a further denial of rights, since she speaks through a letter she had made Adolphe promise to burn unread. Faced with that letter, Adolphe, who hitherto had presented himself as the cause rather than the sufferer of jealousy, shows the compulsion to look that is typical of the jealous lover: "In especially jealous individuals, the desire to look is simultaneously extremely seductive and extremely forbidden," Baumgart notes, in her exploration of this visual imperative.[12] Significantly, Ellénore's letter contains no trace of the jealousy for which Adolphe had criticized her, no hint of the devouring

11. Benjamin Constant, *Adolphe* (Paris: Société Les Belles Lettres, 1946), 19.
12. Baumgart, *Jealousy*, 206.

woman who had made it impossible for him to break free from her. Clearly, it is Adolphe himself who has clung to and enchained the other, as here he attempts to cling to and control his reader.

What seems to be offered here, therefore, is a curious example of Freud's category of projected jealousy, in which Adolphe's need to hold the attention of a father much loved, but perceived as cold and remote, drives him to choose precisely that form of liaison that, because it cannot earn him his father's approval, will succeed in fixing his father's gaze on him. Were he to contract a suitable marriage and embark on a successful career, he would no longer be of such pressing interest to his father. The compulsion to look, in other words, is also a need to be looked at.

The narcissism that marks the narrating Adolphe's painful and lingering exploration of his younger self is echoed by the longing for affection that cannot simply accept Ellénore's affection, since as a woman what she has to offer is perceived as paltry, but that cries out for the affection of the father. Adolphe's predicament stems from the fact that by engendering himself in this way, by feminizing himself to seize his father's attention, he equates himself with the unimportant, a spiritual castration that, within the conditions of this particular narrative, can lead only to death. The destructive force of jealousy is used both in Trollope's *He Knew He Was Right* and in Constant's *Adolphe*, therefore, to shatter their society's shackling image of gender and to divert the explosive energy of jealousy into the channels that surreptitiously but inexorably shape the individual.

In the wake of the highly ambivalent morality of Napoleon's regime and in face of the powerful social changes that made the mentality and morality of the Second Empire possible, Balzac's *Comédie humaine* suggests a world in flux, where only two driving forces remain constant: money and pleasure. In such a narrative, the explosive force of jealousy and the engendering power of the narrative voice attain a particular power, especially as the creative force is frequently figured by the great counterfeiter Vautrin, the homosexual who was first sent to the galleys for falsely confessing to a crime of forgery that he himself did not commit. More than devil's advocate, he, like Satan, builds a counterfeit world, one that illustrates Hans Andersen's parable of the Snow Queen, in which fragments of the devil's mirror lodged in the eye make good seem evil, vice virtue, and, most important for our purposes, constantly throw out of focus and into question distinctions between what society decrees as male and female. Here, for all the apparent cynicism of Balzac's *Physiologie du mariage*, the narrative voices are at once more aware and more sympathetic than either those of Constant or those of Trollope in regard to the position of women.[13] This does not, of course, preclude the presence of the dual image of woman as jealous Medea and self-sacrificing Gilda, an image in any case so deeply encrusted in French Romanticism that Balzac could hardly have offered his *études de mœurs* and left it out, but it does mean that a wider range of narrative perspectives is used in the depiction of female jealousy, and that the implied reader is frequently figured as female.

Béatrix, for example, a *roman à clés* that offers numerous studies of responses to the apparent loss of love, makes an explicit statement through the voice of the omniscient narrator concerning the difference between society's treatment of men and of women, and, where Trollope's narrative voice is marked by a barely-contained jocularity, Balzac's is, at least overtly, far more sympathetic:

> The reader will by now have understood perfectly well the enormous difference in the demands our laws and customs make, in the same circumstances, of the two sexes. Everything that turns to misfortune for a woman who has been abandoned is changed into good fortune for a man who has been abandoned. This striking contrast will perhaps inspire in more than one young woman the resolve to remain in her marital home, and to struggle there as Sabine de Guénic did,

13. This is not, need I say, a statement about the relative positions of the writers as social beings, but on the contrary a judgment concentrating on particular narrative strategies.

carrying out her own choice of the most murderous or the most inoffensive virtues.[14]

At all levels, from the overturning of Dante's image of a celestial Beatrice to the sly use of the epithets here attached to "virtues," Balzac's baggy monster of a novel questions established values and ingrained prejudices (while inevitably offering footholds to deconstructive readings revealing further, unquestioned, prejudices).

Female submission to, and acceptance of, male philandering is certainly not a response favored either by the language or the plots of the novels in *La Comédie humaine*: Adeline, in *La Cousine Bette*, is implicitly castigated for her ostensibly angelic acceptance of Hulot's adulterous affairs, and her daughter's refusal to submit to being similarly treated is portrayed not merely as the result of generation differences, but also, and more centrally, of a firmer character, and one in which family values and, more banally, family finances, are ultimately far safer. A woman's ability to fight for her man despite an appearance of fragility is deeply ingrained in the iconography of Romanticism and is effortlessly carried over into Balzac's own brand of realism, as *Béatrix* makes abundantly clear, when Béatrix and Camille Maupin, exploring their own responses to the young hero, Calyste, indulge in a display of metaphysical daggers reminiscent of the fulvous world of Delacroix's fighting animals:

"If I cannot be his wife," asserts Béatrix, "I shall not be his mistress. He has made me. . . .You won't laugh at me? No. Well! His adorable love has purified me."

Camille directed at Béatrix the wildest, most ferocious glance that ever a jealous woman directed at her rival. "On that score," she said, "I thought I stood alone. Béatrix, that statement separates us forever, we are friends no more. We are entering on a horrible struggle. Now, let me tell you: you will either succumb or you will flee. . . ."

Félicité [i.e., Camille] flung herself into her room after

14. Honoré de Balzac, *Béatrix* (Paris: Flammarion, 1979), 315.

having revealed to the stupefied Béatrix the face of a lioness in a towering rage. (218)

The violence of the glance exchanged, the contortion of features, the rush of blood to or from the face, are all presented as aspects of female jealousy, transforming the body into a manuscript in which traces of jealousy are easily legible for the rival gaze and therefore instantly decodable for a focalization that both uses that gaze and carries an overlay of omniscient commentary. Another passage in *Béatrix* further illustrates this particular narrative technique:

> "What will become of Calyste?" said the marquise with admirably naive vanity.
>
> "So Conti is taking you away?" asked Camille. . . .
>
> "Ah! You think you're going to win?" exclaimed Béatrix.
>
> It was with fury and her lovely face contorted that the marquise pronounced these dreadful words to Camille who tried to hide her joy through a false expression of sorrow; but the gleam in her eyes belied the spasm that crossed her mask, and Béatrix was an expert in grimaces. (240)

Reading grimaces, penetrating masks, deciphering gestures are all part of the complex demands made by the trope of jealousy in *La Comédie humaine*; demands, moreover, that are made not merely of lovers, actual or potential, but also of readers. Doubly addressed, open to multiple decodings, this flotsam left behind by jealousy posits a doubly gendered reader, resisting the limitations of a male reader only, that a Rougemont or a Girard, among others, might seek to impose.

Female jealousy can, of course, also be presented through the naive viewpoint of an ingénu male observer, as is the case with the young Eugène de Rastignac in the passage in *Le Père Goriot* where the duchesse de Langeais reveals to her "dear friend," madame de Beauséant, that the latter's lover is about to contract a marriage. The play of gestures and masks is explored here both from the viewpoint of the narcissistic Rastignac, who is as deeply deceived as the players would have him be, and by the cynical voice of the external narrator:

"These two women are good friends," Rastignac said to himself.

"From now on I'll have two protectors; each of these women must have the same feelings as the other, and so this new one will surely take an interest in me."

"To what happy thought do I owe the joy of seeing you, my dear Antoinette?" asked Madame de Beauséant.

"Well, I saw Monsieur d'Ajuda-Pinto going into Monsieur de Rochefide's house, and so I thought you'd be alone."

Madame de Beauséant did not contract her lips, she did not blush, her expression remained unchanged, her brow even seemed to lighten as the duchess pronounced these fatal words. [. . .]

"Do you have any news of General Montriveau?" she asked. "Sérisy mentioned to me yesterday that no one sees him these days. Did he visit you today?"

The duchess, who was thought to have been abandoned by the Monsieur de Montriveau, with whom she was wildly in love, felt the blade of this question penetrate her heart, and she blushed. [. . .]

"Clara, I'm sure you know," the duchess said, her eyes darting poisonous arrows, "that tomorrow the marriage banns of Monsieur d'Ajuda-Pinto and Mademoiselle de Rochefide are being read?"

This blow was too violent. Madame de Beauséant turned pale and replied with a laugh: "One of those pieces of gossip that fools find amusing."[15]

Jealousy here is made legible for the novel's reader if not for Eugène both by what the faces reveal, however overlaid they may be with a palimpsest of socially required responses, and by the relentless extended metaphor that depicts the women's friendship as being structured like a duel. Even when the women are not rivals for one man's love, therefore, Balzac chooses to depict them as being at daggers drawn, thrust into a situation of constant antagonism in which the emotion revealed by the eyes is incessantly and aggressively subjected to

15. Honoré de Balzac, *Le Père Goriot* (Paris: Garnier Flammarion, 1966), 82.

society's gaze. What is equally aggressive is that both Eugène and we, as readers, are also propelled into the role of antagonistic voyeur, even though the narrative slant is ostensibly sympathetic to Mme de Beauséant. Proust, moreover, in his pastiche of Balzac, brilliantly captures this ambiguity and the social violence set in train by the novelist's use of the disruptive force of jealousy: "Athénaïs could not contain her joy when she saw returning to her the lover that she had good hopes of stealing from her best friend. So she squeezed the princess's hand, as she maintained the impenetrable calm that women of high society possess at the very moment when they drive a dagger into your heart."[16] Here both the narrator and the sentence structure of the narration force the reader willy-nilly both to penetrate that impenetrable calm and to receive the dagger in the heart, and by making of us both aggressor and victim, Baudelaire's "Héautontimoroumenos," constrain us to participate in the experience of both genders.

The removal of almost all elements of narrative sympathy in presenting female jealousy is a technique Balzac uses in his portrayal of the spinster Lisbeth in *La Cousine Bette*, with the result that, while a reading that is antagonistic to Bette is greatly facilitated because we are not burdened with any sense of amiability in the jealous woman, the constant hostility of the narrative focus offered to us nevertheless makes such a reading become increasingly difficult to accept. Resisting the reading of female jealousy that the text apparently presents us with becomes, therefore, the natural course to follow: here, jealousy's chaotic energies are once again channeled to lead us in unexpected directions. The unscrupulous and unforgiving mockery of Bette's misfortune, the malevolence of the male onlooker's response to her refusal to conform to what society demanded of an unmarried woman, and the unstated but evident sense of fear at the woman's manipulative abilities, all invite other voices to start speaking on the party line, creating an incessant interference between reader and narrative voice that finds its parallel in the nature of jealousy itself.

The suggestion of parallels between textual strategies and

16. Marcel Proust, *Contre Sainte-Beuve* (Paris: Pléiade, 1971), 8.

narrative peripeteia is reinforced when Bette falls fatally ill at the shock of seeing the family survive the scandals and ructions she has set in motion: "Her condition worsened so much [*empira si bien*] that she was condemned by Bianchon to die a week later, defeated at the end of that long struggle marked by so many victories she had won. She kept the secret of her hatred in the midst of the terrible death throes of pulmonary consumption. Moreover, she had the supreme satisfaction of seeing Adeline, Hulot, Victorin, Steinbock, Célestine and their children all in tears around her bed, lamenting the passing of the one they saw as the family's good angel."[17] Irony is marked here both linguistically, by the jarring combinations of *"empira si bien"* and "defeated . . . by so many victories," and dramatically, by what the reader is encouraged to see as the inappropriateness of the appellation "angel" for what the text has presented as this diabolically malicious woman. That irony thrusts into prominence the play on words in the phrase "condemned by Bianchon," for clearly here Doctor Bianchon stands for the novelist himself, with his power of life and death over the creatures of his texts. But irony is like quicksand: once embarked on it, there is no telling how deep one may sink. If we know the family to be wrong in their reading of Bette, and if the text so pointedly mocks them for being so, is it not also possible that it surreptitiously mocks us for our own misreadings, suggesting, therefore, that we are as manipulated by narrative strategies and as overpowered by narrative focus as the family is by Bette and as Bette is by jealousy and envy?

Reading gestures and reading behavior, manipulation by characters and control by narrative focus are only some of the ways in which male writers engender female jealousy. In his novella *La Fanfarlo*, which is almost exactly contemporaneous with *La Cousine Bette*, the young Baudelaire plays brilliantly and wittily on expectations and prejudices in exploring the ways in which women, even the apparently meek and mild bourgeois wife, maneuver men, and it does so in ways that make nonsense of simplistic accusations of misogyny leveled at the author of *Les Fleurs du mal*. Moreover, in examining the

17. Honoré de Balzac, *La Cousine Bette* (Paris: Folio, 1978), 458.

creative force of jealousy and its power to transform the individual, *La Fanfarlo* draws inventively on the old chestnut of the letter sent to the wrong recipient and therefore read by an unintended reader, in ways that reflect on the reception of the tale itself and underscore the polygonal nature of narrative.

Begged by a childhood sweetheart, Mme Cosmelly, to seduce a dancer who is currently seducing Mme Cosmelly's husband, Samuel Cramer, budding poet and philanderer who publishes under the feminine pseudonym of Manuela de Monteverde, hopes to be rewarded by two conquests. However, the fiery sonnet he composes to excite the dancer ends up in an envelope addressed to the wife, and the pious platitudes written for Mme Cosmelly are sent to the uncomprehending ballerina. Rarely have the dual demands placed on women been more economically and comically laid bare. Mme Cosmelly laughs, reads Cramer's intentions correctly where she is concerned, and writes her own alternative script, well enough to recapture her husband without having to yield to her rescuer, while Samuel finds himself snared in all too bourgeois concubinage with La Fanfarlo. Here the role of the unintended reader is not only essential to the plot, but also reflects the hero's failure to reach his intended audience either as writer or as lover, for while he might believe he has succeeded in making the dancer his own, she very quickly reveals that she has taken possession of him, changing him from potential poet to actual pater familias and almost certainly engendering him as cuckold, too.

While for the main part the text adopts the narrative focus of Cramer (overlaid with a tongue-in-cheek commentary mocking his pretentiousness) and apparently espouses the opportunistic sexism of his character, with his desire to make love not to the woman, but to the actress with her costume and her rouge, the puns and irony of the conclusion deconstruct the apparent positions of men and women in society and throw trenchantly into question the engendering of power:

> As for La Fanfarlo, she grows fatter by the day; she has become a plump, clean, gleaming and cunning beauty, a kind of ministerial call girl.—One of these days she'll fast for Lent and give alms to her parish. Perhaps at that stage, Samuel, having

died in harness, will be *pushing up the daisies*, as he used to say in the good old days, and La Fanfarlo, with her canoness's bearing, will turn a young heir's head.—Meanwhile, she's learning how to make children: she has just been delivered of a pair of healthy twins. Samuel has given birth to four learned books. [. . .] La Fanfarlo wants her lover to be a member of the Institute and is scheming at the ministry to get him a gong.

Poor singer of *Ospreys*! Poor Manuela de Monteverde![18]

Steering a shrewd course between Medusa and Madonna, feint and sincerity, *La Fanfarlo* depicts both the gust of rage in the woman who, realizing she has been treated as a mere pawn, swears revenge:

"What are you muttering there? What is all this? I want to see," said La Fanfarlo.

"Oh, nothing," replied Samuel. "A letter from an honest woman to whom I'd given a promise to make you love me."

"You'll pay me for that," she muttered under her breath. (579)

and the contained violence of the middle-class housewife's jealousy, which threatens the whole fabric of her existence:

I spend most painful nights, deeply disturbed periods of insomnia; I pray, I curse, I blaspheme. The priest told me that one must bear one's cross with resignation; but maddened love and shaken faith do not know resignation. My confessor is not a woman, and I love my husband, I love him with all the passion and all the grief of a mistress who has been beaten and trampled under foot. (567)

With particularly biting irony, moreover, Cramer is shown, immediately after this quite extraordinary confession she has made to him, composing for Mme de Cosmelly the sonnet in

18. Charles Baudelaire, *La Fanfarlo*, in *Œuvres complètes* (Paris: Pléiade, 1975), 1: 580.

which "in mystical terms he praised her Beatrice-like beauty, her voice, the angelic purity of her eyes, the chasteness of her gait etc." (569). His failure to readjust his stereotypical images of woman in face of the evidence set before him, his unconscious determination to cling to Romantic dichotomies, lead, predictably enough, to punishment in the form of jealousy: "Samuel learnt all the tortures of jealousy, and the humiliation and sadness into which we are thrown by the awareness of an incurable and constitutional evil—in a word, all the horrors of that vicious marriage known as concubinage" (580). Here, the inability to read correctly the power and intensity of female jealousy condemns the misreader to that constant and compulsive attempt to read the mystery of the other that is the true nature of jealousy.

However varied these representations of jealousy may be, and however complex their depictions of female jealousy in particular, all these texts, although they may from time to time adopt a female narrative focus, are, of course, written by men. It is at least worth raising the question of whether texts written by women adopt different strategies and provide distinctive images in their representations of jealousy in women and in their engendering of the implied reader, however artificial, however socially determined, the terms "male" and "female" undoubtedly are.[19]

One of the most limpid female-authored accounts of jealousy dates from the late seventeenth century, at a time when women could not openly admit authorship: the need to hide becomes both a social and an emotional necessity in a work where the interplay of passion and politics is not only central but also extremely dangerous. Given so volatile and so male-dominated an age, responses of female writers and of female characters were severely limited. Certainly the dominant image provided by Mme de Lafayette's *La Princesse de Clèves* is one of woman's dignity, of her determination not to risk the suffering of jealousy even if avoiding it means forgoing possible

---

19. See Sandra Gilbert and Susan Gubar, *No Man's Land: Sexchanges* (New Haven: Yale University Press, 1989), xv–xvi. Need I add that I do not intend to give here anything like a full survey of female-authored strategies of presenting jealousy? I hope merely to sketch in a few general outlines.

pleasures, the decision, that is, to remain in charge of the narrative whatever the cost. This dignity stands out all the more sharply against the violent irrationality of the men, for from the moment when the princess confesses that she loves another man, a sentiment beyond her power to control, but asserts that she will not give her husband any cause for offense or grief, the prince's prior claims of self-control and promises of dignified behavior are swept away by a tide of furious and ultimately mortal jealousy. For the princess, love is a state that need not imply a deed: for her husband, this distinction has no meaning, love being a sign whose signified is an action. The ever-present threat of such violence means that the need to prevent others from reading one's personal truth in the malevolent microcosm of the court is a constant motif. The subtlety of analysis, and particularly of self-analysis, that marks this finely wrought exploration of male and female jealousy can be illustrated in the following quotation which comes from a point in the narrative where the princess is barely beginning to recognize her feelings for M. de Nemours: "It caused her deep pain to see that she was no longer able to master and hide her emotions and that she had let the chevalier de Guise know what she was feeling. She was also greatly distressed that M. de Nemours should know them; but this last grief was not as complete as the earlier one and was mingled with a kind of sweetness."[20] Transparency and legibility may always be negative characteristics in this society of compulsive readers, but allowing the beloved to decode at least some of one's feelings retains a certain charm.

The problem is that misreadings—of oneself, of the other, of situations—are presented as far more common than correct interpretations. Faced with a letter she believes Nemours wrote to another woman, who is clearly a long-established mistress, the princess finds herself incapable of reading at all: "Mme de Clèves read and reread this letter several times, yet without knowing what she had read. All she saw was that M. de Nemours did not love her as she had thought and that he loved

20. Madame de La Fayette, *La Princesse de Clèves* (Paris: Livre de Poche, 1958), 114–15.

others whom he deceived as he deceived her" (118). The deception is, however, far more profound than she imagines, for not only is this letter being read by unintended readers, but furthermore it was not written by Nemours at all. The opacity and duplicity of human features are reflected here in a letter that appears perfectly legible but that cannot be read correctly using the code the princess is currently applying.

The series of intercepted messages continues, reinforced by the classic image of Nemours hearing, while in hiding, a conversation between the princess and her husband, in which she confesses that she loves someone else. Here the text provides a perfect figure for jealousy, when the message between lover and beloved (the prince and princess) is intercepted by the rival in a violation of privacy that apes the violation of the marriage bed and reflects the voyeuristic act of reading. Here, the compulsion to look, which has been emblematized by the mythical character Gyges and so grossly ridiculed in the figure of Bozzle, the detective of *He Knew He Was Right*, merely intensifies Nemours's jealousy without allowing him to read the name of the man the princess loves, a name she keeps hidden both from her husband and from her lover. And the image of him as voyeur, and voyeur, moreover, through whose eyes we are obliged to look, thrusts us, too, into a position of questionable morality.

Although the princess does experience that same desire to look, she is consistently presented as having a stronger desire still: that of avoiding pain, and it is this longing that drives her eventually to seek the feminine safety of the convent, rather than take the gamble of accepting Nemours's love and thereby risking its loss. The court's masculine principles of violence, espionage, egotism, and passion are explicitly rejected here in favor of a feminine society of quiescence, self-control, communalism, and self-denial. The masculine power figures of the novel—husband, king, lover—subject the individual, or at least the individual woman, to the kind of diminution of self-control that is central to jealousy. As a result, the figure to whom the princess turns for guidance is the mother, whose philosophy focuses on the kind of abnegation and self-discipline that offer self-possession.

La Princesse de Clèves may seem particularly imbued in the mentality of its time and place, yet there is also a sense in which this mentality is less that of the seventeenth-century court of France, than that of jealousy itself. Thus, that same sense of self-control and the kind of self-preservation that are predicated on self-denial are also important, if not the determining, factors in Charlotte Brontë's Lucy Snowe in a novel deeply concerned with the violation of the individual by the gaze of others and the profound risk to personal integrity participation in any social structure entails:

> "I shall share no man's or woman's life in this world, as you understand sharing. I think I have one friend of my own, but am not sure; and till I *am* sure, I live solitary."
> "But solitude is sadness."
> "Yes; it is sadness. Life, however, has worse than that. Deeper than melancholy, lies heartbreak."[21]

Lucy's world, like that of the Princesse de Clèves, is the claustrophobic, salon-de-glaces milieu of social espionage, where the compulsion to pry is outweighed only by the need to keep hidden, a need figured in the narration by Lucy's teasing reticence.[22] Here the Jesuit's vision of the teacher's role as encompassing control of everything from a pupil's shoelaces to her soul is expanded by Mme Beck to embrace her entire school, pupils and teachers alike. Lucy's own expressed position is unambiguous. Attacking Paul for snooping from his observation post in a lattice, she contends: "Every glance you cast from the lattice is wrong done to the best part of your own nature. To study the human heart thus is to banquet in secret and sacrilegiously on Eve's apples."[23] Nevertheless, through circumstance or design, she cannot avoid sharing this banquet, as surreptitious study of the human heart is part of her job both

21. Charlotte Brontë, *Villette* (Harmondsworth: Penguin, 1981), 520.
22. See Paul Wotipka's subtle study of what he terms "the subversive potential of the eye" in his article "Ocularity and Irony: Pictorialism in *Villette*," *Word and Image* 8, 2 (1992): 100–108. See also Keryn Carter's feminist reading, "The Blank Space of Lucy Snowe's Reflection," *AUMLA* 76 (1991): 1–12.
23. Brontë, *Villette*, 455–56.

as a teacher and as narrator of her novel and innate to her own personality. Within the constraints of the first-person narrative, moreover, Lucy is the figure through whom the reader explores a particular study of the human heart, a study rendered all the more vigorous because that figure is so frequently driven by jealousy.

What makes *Villette* so powerful a study of different kinds of jealousy is in part the sexual ambiguity of the characters, or more precisely the refusal to make them conform to standard sexual stereotypes, and in part the manipulation of a metaphor—the gaze—that plays on its associations with penetration and violation while breaking free from the convention that makes women the passive object of men's gaze, by relocating it in women themselves. The phallic penetration of the gaze is therefore differently engendered, becoming bisexual, a game of reflections and speculation intensified by the moments of self-scrutiny in physical mirrors or of self-analysis in mental mirrors.

That scrutiny of self and others, of inner world and of outer world, is predicated on a refusal of expectation and convention. "Checked, bridled, disciplined" (455–56) though she may claim to be, weak and sickly though she may occasionally be, Lucy Snowe possesses a power of feeling and emotion that reveals her to be as different from Romanticism's sugared madonna images as her pupils are different from "the novelist's or the poet's ideal 'jeune fille' " (142).

Similarly, even though the architectural space of *Villette* is in the main comfortably and protectively bourgeois, checked and disciplined, the network of images associated with individuals draws largely on the untamed animal world—spiders, tigers, vultures. And when, in the opium-induced state of heightened tension in which she sees Paul and his ward and imagines them engaged, she is suddenly seized by jealousy, there is nothing bridled or insignificant in her experience of it:

> something tore me so cruelly under my shawl, something so dug into my side, a vulture so strong in beak and talon, I must be alone to grapple with it. I think I never felt jealousy till now. [. . .] This was an outrage. The love, born of beauty,

was not mine; I had nothing in common with it: I could not
dare to meddle with it, but another love, venturing diffidently
into life after long acquaintance, furnace-tried by pain,
stamped by constancy, consolidated by affection's own tests,
and finally wrought up, by his own process, to his own un-
flawed completeness, this Love that laughed at Passion.
[. . .] in *this* Love I had a vested interest; and whatever
tended either to its culture or its destruction, I could not view
impassibly. (566–67)

Although Lucy might refuse not only to experience "the love
born of beauty" but even to look on Graham's beauty, as she
tells Pauline, and although here she resolutely rejects the compulsion to watch (a compulsion she nevertheless acknowledges), she is nonetheless swift to transform what she has so
briefly seen into a convincing narrative that penetrates and in-
vades her very being: "I hastened to accept the whole plan. I
extended my grasp and took it all in. I gathered it to me with
a sort of rage of haste, and folded it round me, as the soldier
struck on the field folds his colors about his breast. I invoked
Conviction to nail upon me the certainty, abhorred while em-
braced, to fix it with the strongest spikes her strongest strokes
could drive; and when the iron had entered well my soul, I
stood up, as I thought renovated" (566). Everything here, from
the heart-pounding rhythms, to the battlefield imagery, recasts
and transmutes the image of the passive, submissive Lucy
painstakingly engendered for us by the narrative voice to show
a Lucy possessed and invaded less by the truth she invokes
than by a truth she imagines, the truth of passionate jealousy.
The sense of death and rebirth, of a violent possession of the
mind that informs and transforms the individual, recurs in a
final moment of jealousy when Lucy's claim to bid farewell to
Paul seems on the point of being denied both by the jealous
Mme Beck and by the jealousy of the Catholic church: "Pierced
deeper than I could endure, made now to feel what defied suppression, I cried—'My heart will break' " (580). That acceptance of "what defied suppression" leads to the remodeling of
Lucy's life and image under the controlling, engendering hand
of Paul. Part of the "little puzzle" that *Villette* poses us (622),

part of the paradox we are invited to scout (593), lies in that essential, enigmatic contradiction between the overt acceptance of female inferiority (208, 282, 325, 428–29) and the depiction of male pettiness, not just in the more effeminate Paul, but also in the resolutely masculine Graham; between the sharply drawn differentiation of male and female roles and the disturbing androgyneity of the central characters; and between the independence of Lucy's nature and her final, complete submission to a male-engendered projection of her personality and function.[24] Somehow this contradiction is a riddle that can never be solved, unlike the deliberately, parodically simplistic riddle of the phantom nun: but for that very reason it sets in train that disjunction between reader and text, that sharp awareness of Lucy's needling understatements that enacts the emotions and responses of jealousy itself.

The paramount importance placed on the gaze in these texts, where jealousy is both thematically and strategically central, is represented thrugh judgmental societies, where espionage, both emotional and political, is not only an important theme, but also a reflection of the reader's own role. These images and structures transcend the geographical, temporal, and social frameworks in which they were written. They can, for instance, be found in writers as different as the retiring English woman Charlotte Brontë and the outgoing French woman Marie d'Agoult, however contrasting the goals and natures of their texts. Thus, whereas *Villette* gives free, romantic rein to what the very young Paulina described as the "dredful miz-er-y"[25] of jealousy, the comtesse d'Agoult's semiautobiographical *règlement de comptes*, *Nélida*, conveys an icier, more exalted image of female jealousy. Moreover, whereas Lucy's jealousy urged submission to Paul, Nélida's leads to independence. Here, too, the role of the gaze is privileged, as the space in which the emotions are played out is inescapably that of a society guided by espionage and motored by *Schadenfreude*. In this world

24. On the suggestions associated with space in Brontë's novels, see Nancy Armstrong, *Desire and Domestic Fiction* (Oxford: Oxford University Press, 1975), 207.
25. Brontë, *Villette*, 90.

where pride and disdain are valued far above sincerity and emotion, men are figured as the weak-willed, vacillating toys of
strong-minded women. And whereas confessional novels that
are narrated by men habitually close with the protagonist's
death, as the ultimate escape from jealousy, *Nélida* finds its
solution in allowing the heroine to survive and rancorously
killing off the erring male. In its exploration and reversal of
sexual stereotypes, this novel, despite, or perhaps because of, a
certain lack of subtlety, indicates the extent to which the depiction of jealousy, however original or rebellious its handling,
draws on stereotypical situations.

Three such situations are particularly arresting in this context. This first occurs when the artist Guermann, Nélida's unfaithful lover, responds to her accusations and to the revelation
of the jealousy he has inflicted on her, in terms that expose his
instant and inescapable restructuring of life as art, his inability
to see her response as other than a theatrical creation. A reverse Pygmalion, he conceives of women only as works of art,
and thus he attempts to petrify their personalities. For him, in
other words, Nélida engenders her passion and resentment as
a form of entertainment for him, as his comparison between
her and the great actress Malibran demonstrates. Such a response provides yet another variation on the figure of the visual
imperative, for here the object of jealousy finds pleasure in
watching the expression of that jealousy, as though he were
atthe theater or observing a trial in which he has no part to
play:

> She was great and beautiful, seen like that, in her resent-
> ment. Indignation lent a sinister glow to her pale cheeks; her
> eyes glittered; her voice throbbed, her gestures had suddenly
> taken on an extraordinary dominion. Guermann looked at
> her admiringly. Less moved by the underlying meaning of
> her words than struck, in his quality as an artist, by this
> new beauty that was revealed to him, he remained silent for
> some time, contemplating her. Then, carried away in his turn
> by the one form of enthusiasm of which he was capable, he
> exclaimed:

"You're sublime like that, Nélida. Malibran has never been
so striking."[26]

Here the disruption of jealousy is paralleled by the irruption of
a reading that refuses to see life in terms other than those of
art: small wonder that the scene gives birth to a sense of mutual hostility (173). For Guermann that hostility springs from
the sense of jealous rivalry provoked in him by the revelation
of Nélida's own artistry, while for Nélida, Guermann's response makes patent what until now has been partially con-
cealed: an egotism that will not conceive of the other as
anything but an extension of the self.

The exploration of jealousy in *Nélida* also contains a scene
in which beloved and rival are unwillingly observed by the protagonist, one of those archetypal scenes that trope the espionage of the reader. Praying (or perhaps prying) in the chapel,
Nélida is forced to overhear a lovers' quarrel between her husband, Timoléon, and her rival, Hortense. The improbability of
such a scene is ironically commented on by Timoléon himself:
"Where ever did you get this impractical impulse to talk to me
out in the open and in pitch darkness?," he asks, as indeed the
reader may ask, too. But what the scene exposes with particular
clarity is the impossibility of closure in jealousy: the lovers
wander off before their conversation is finished, leaving Nélida
with both the possibility of hope and the impossibility of complete knowledge.

Paralleling this scene of the unintended voyeur is one in
which Guermann, as possibly unintended reader, comes across
Nélida's journal and discovers as a result of reading it that "the
woman who had been his slave had freed herself, and if she
agreed to wear chains, she no longer did so blindly, but fully
conscious of what she was doing" (190). Rage, fury, hurt pride:
Guermann's emotions on reading this journal are those of a
jealous lover who finds that his rival is one he cannot defeat,
the woman's own pride. His failure to keep her bound within
the limits he believes suitable for her gender while maintaining

26. Marie d'Agoult (pseud. Daniel Stern), *Nélida* (Paris: Calmann-Lévy, 1987),
172–73.

his own liberty, his sudden awareness that he can no longer convince himself that she feigns passion for his entertainment, his realization, in other words, that Nélida is after all no Galatea summoned to life by his artistic genius (136), all force him to accept the fact that Nélida as self-engendered individual, initially liberated by jealousy and now free from jealousy, has escaped his domination.

Female-authored studies of jealousy thus draw much on the violation of the individual brought about through the gaze or more generally through the kind of espionage that attempts to ensure that the individual remain within bounds determined by the lover or by society. Although exploited by women, this device is not, of course, limited to women, since, for example, such a violation is emblematized by Trollope's detective Bozzle whose continued existence, like that of Scheherazade, depends on his ability to tell tales.

Male writers exploring male jealousy may often also use a further form of violation, which is the reduction of the beloved to an image or fetish incapable of escaping.[27] Conversely, they may draw on the resonances of cuckoldry to suggest that in allowing a woman to betray him, the lover has himself been reduced. Few texts reveal this fear more clearly and in many ways more despicably than Malraux's *La Condition humaine* in the passage exploring Kyo's reasons for feeling jealousy when May announces that she has acted on their pact of mutual freedom to make love to a male colleague. While Kyo's analysis is ostensibly based on his awareness of "the deep-seated misogyny of almost all men"[28] and his assumption that the rival will now despise May, it is only too evident that the subtext here concerns the rival's presumed scorn for Kyo himself: "would one ever be jealous of anything except of what one supposes the other supposes?" (47). The narrative and syntactical complexities of such a fear, the way in which the central message carries multiple addresses, and the constant need to decipher suppositions make this a paradigm statement for

27. For a psychoanalytical reading of this tendency, see Mellita Schmideberg, "Some Aspects of Jealousy and of Feeling Hurt," *Psychoanalytic Review* 40, 1 (1953): 5–6.
28. André Malraux, *La Condition humaine* (Paris: Gallimard, 1946), 47.

models of a multisided narratology. Fear of appearing ridiculous in the eyes of the (male) other, of being reduced to stereotypical jealous husband, of being locked in the endless mirrors of trying to imagine what the other imagines are common themes, particularly, although not exclusively, in depictions of male jealousy.

Marion Halligan, in her novel *Spidercup*, does however offer a female version of this tendency, but one that draws very much on the male-authored imagery of *A Winter's Tale*, to which the novel's title alludes. The deceived wife briefly indulges in just such a reductive reverie: "O viperous act. With the one-eyed trouser snake. Pity it couldn't bite. Samantha furry-legged would shrivel up and get swept out with the dust. No antidote for the bite of this viper. Shut that away in the fridge and lean against the door. Watching her shrivel up. Get the dustpan."[29] Indeed, some degree of reduction of the other (lover or rival) or reduction of the self seems central to both male and female portrayals. Hoffmann's Erasmus Spikher, deprived of his reflection in the mirror by his faithless mistress Giulietta, or his Giglio Fava reduced (temporarily) to marionette through his love for Princess Brambilla, or, more archetypally, Samson shorn of his hair by Delilah, are merely reverse images of, say, Fromentin's Dominique obsessed by Madeleine's portrait while incapable of either declaring or renouncing his adulterous love for her, the Princess de Clèves gazing at the portrait of Nemours, or Robbe-Grillet's narrator possessed by images of the main female character, "A," brushing her hair.

While fetishism has causes, forms, and manifestations the study of which would far exceed the bounds of this analysis, it is certainly the case that accounts of jealousy often include the transformation of the beloved into metonymical object, controllable, repressible, and incapable of self-defense. One of the most striking examples is Baudelaire's gothic poem, "A une Madone," the subtitle of which draws attention to the strategy of transformation that empowers it: "Ex-voto in the Spanish mode." The poem is thus presented as a votive offering, an

---

29. Marion Halligan, *Spidercup* (Ringwood, Victoria: Penguin, 1990), 20.

expression of religious fervor and gratitude, whereas its immediate impact is that of pagan love transformed into furious hatred. Here the principal rhetorical device is metaphor: the woman is transmuted into a statue, lines of poetry interweave to form a crown, rhymes become crystalline jewels, respect is transformed into slippers. Most importantly for our purposes, jealousy is depicted as a cloak, thick enough to hide the beloved's charms from prying eyes and heavy enough to act as a watch tower, imprisoning her:

> Et dans ma Jalousie, ô mortelle Madone,
> Je saurai te tailler un Manteau, de façon
> Barbare, roide et lourd, et doublé de soupçon,
> Qui, comme une guérite, enfermera tes charmes;
> Non de perles brodé, mais de toutes mes larmes!

[And from my Jealousy, oh mortal Madonna, / I will be able to fashion for you a cloak / in a barbaric mode / stiff and heavy, and lined with suspicion / in which, as in a watch tower, your charms will be enclosed / a cloak embroidered not with pearls but with all my tears.][30]

Baudelaire here plays so extravagantly with the rhetorical transformations of jealousy and passion and manipulates with such consummate skill the conflicts between secular and religious love that his poem leaves the realm of felt experience to enter that of poetic play. Since its main focus is that of rhetoric, however, it shows with particularly vivid clarity the stratagems of sexual reverie and illuminates the function of the fetish within the strategies of jealousy.

Whereas Baudelaire here uses jealousy's transformatory powers to trope the function of metaphor in poetry, Balzac in his *Physiologie du mariage* combines such tropes with a pitilessly witty analysis to make a similar point about the reductive nature of jealousy. Addressing the male reader who fears cuckoldry, he asks:

30. Baudelaire, *Œuvres complètes*, 1: 58.

Have you ever counted how many different shapes Arlequin and Pierrot give their little white hat? They twist it over and over so often that they make it by turns into a spinning-top, a boat, a drinking glass, a half-moon, a beret, a basket, a fish, a whip, a dagger, a child, a man's head, etc.

An exact image of the despotism with which you must manipulate and remanipulate your wife.

A woman is a piece of property one acquires by contract, she is transferable, for possession is nine-tenths of the law; finally, a woman, properly speaking, is merely an annex of a man; well, slice, cut, gnaw, you are her fully-qualified owner.[31]

Balzac is, of course, playing with sexual imagery, wittily reversing the usual phallic associations of hats and male annexes to suggest in this highly ironic series of recommendations the ways in which fear of being cuckolded—*minotaurized*, in the text's terminology—paradoxically reduces the jealous male to manipulated fragment. In both these cases, rhetoric becomes less the medium than the message, but for our purposes this metamorphosis merely serves to heighten an awareness of the rhetorical devices frequently associate with the trope of jealousy.

Thus, the synecdochal manipulation of the hat in Balzac's passage finds a more subtle, metonymical equivalent in Fromentin's novel, *Dominique*, in a passage in which the protagonist discovers a portrait of his beloved Madeleine in an exhibition of modern painting. This "portrait cut off at the waist,"[32] this "mute effigy" (223), imprisoned within the frame and within a single expression of melancholy by the "pitiless and canny burin" (223), provides Dominique with a safely reduced and confined receptacle for the outpourings of love, grief, and pride that he would not dare to make to her living counterpart, if only for fear she might accept him. The destructive nature of Dominique's passion with its potent combination of jealousy toward the husband seen as rival, its love predicated

31. Honoré de Balzac, *Physiologie du mariage* (Paris: Flammarion, 1968), 154.
32. Eugène Fromentin, *Dominique* (Paris: Garnier-Flammarion, 1967), 222.

on a sense of certainty that it will not be reciprocated, and its blindness to other expressions of suffering are finely encapsulated here, in a series of images crystallizing around the central motif of reduction.

Robbe-Grillet's *La Jalousie* also offers a brilliant representation of the timeless theme of the reductive force of jealousy while throwing into question sexual stereotypes. It reduces the protagonist to a narrative voice stripped of all identity except that which is engendered by jealousy, limits the existences of beloved and rival to a series of obsessively and repetitively narrated scenarios, and curtails the identity of the woman to a few central characteristics, a contraction emblematized by the device of referring to her merely by the initial "A."[33]

Balzac's longing for instantly decipherable facial features finds a clear echo in the evocation of one of the aspects of "A" that is so monomaniacally depicted, her hair: "A's chignon [. . .] seen from so close up, from behind, seems very complex. It is very hard to follow the different locks [*mèches*] in their interweavings; several solutions work, at certain points, but elsewhere no solution seems possible."[34] The semantic density of certain of these terms, particularly the word *mèche*, with its associations with such phrases as "être de mèche avec quelqu'un," to be in collusion with someone; "découvrir la mèche," to discover the plot; "vendre la mèche" to give the game away, and "solution," which suggests the desire to solve something more important than the structure of a hairdo, indicate the metonymical nature of the chignon. The fact that *chignon* is cognate with *enchaînement* [linking together] facilitates the transformation of the complicated structure of the hair into a trope for the nature of jealousy itself and its constant narration of the same themes, as the following quotation suggests: "It's probably still the same poem continuing. If at times the themes fade away, it's only to return a little later, strengthened, almost identical. Nevertheless, these repetitions, these minute variants, these cuts, these backturns, can give rise to modifica-

33. For a stimulating reading of this aspect of the novel, see Gale Maclachlan, "Reading in the Jealous Mode," *Australian Journal of French Studies* 27, 3 (1990): 291–301.
34. Alain Robbe-Grillet, *La Jalousie* (London: Methuen, 1967), 22.

tions—although they are almost imperceptible—eventually leading very far from the point of departure" (43–44). This constant replaying of the same internal film, to use an expression Robbe-Grillet coined for his introduction to *L'Année dernière à Marienbad*,[35] is what most clearly reduces the narrator to a mere figure of jealousy, refusing individuality to that voice, as the voice, in turn, seeks to deny it to "A" and Frank. Although it has become traditional to refer to the narrative focus here as "the husband," there is in fact nothing within the text that stamps it as male, apart from conventional readerly expectations.[36] Similarly, there is nothing here apart from conventions of reading that forces us to see "A" rather than Frank as the one the narrator loves: only a blindered and plot-centered reading of *La Jalousie* could limit this study to an evocation of the traditional triangle and deny it its function as a neutrally gendered evocation of the nature of jealousy in the abstract.

La Jalousie, in accord with the convictions of the *nouveaux romanciers*, leaves it open to the reader to impose on the text certain gender-based suppositions, yet other explorations are more explicit, and thus manipulate our reading more, in their use of jealousy to question the stability of gender. Dostoevsky's *Eternal Husband*, to offer a particularly clear example, is structured around a series of changing triangles whose dynamics combine with a focalization centered on the adulterous Veltchaninov rather than the "eternal husband" Pavel Pavlovitch to create in the reader a sense of unease similar to that both of the jealous husband and of the illicit lover nervous that he might have been found out. As René Girard puts it, Pavlovitch becomes a deforming mirror in which Veltchaninov is forced to contemplate his own philandering nature.[37] The triangle of Veltchaninov and Pavel Pavlovitch each vying for the attentions of the latter's wife (a triangle rendered polygonal by such mirroring) finds a parodic echo in the novel's final scenes when

35. Quoted in ibid., xxvi.
36. Robbe-Grillet's own blurb makes such a suggestion, but whether or not literature has no *hors-texte*, as Barthes has affirmed, this statement demands the same close critical scrutiny to which the rest of the novel, and its critical commentaries, are subjected. There is no need to submit to authorial tyranny merely because it appears on a dust jacket.
37. René Girard, *Dostoïevski: Du double à l'unité* (Paris: Plon, 1963), 42–43.

Veltchaninov watches "the eternal husband" mocked by his new wife and her drunken lover. The pattern encounters a far more disturbing and sinister reflection in the relationships between the two central characters and the little girl, Liza, who is at first presented as Pavel Pavlovitch's child, but who may well be Veltchaninov's daughter. Several other triangles intensify the reader's sense of constantly shifting ground, of unresolvable tensions, and, increasingly, of a temperament that seeks out such tensions and ambiguities in response to ambiguities in its own sexual nature. Moreover, the stronger Veltchaninov's sense that Pavel Pavlovitch is physically attracted to him, the more powerfully and disturbingly Veltchaninov feels drawn in turn: "This new terror came from the positive conviction [. . .] that he, Veltchaninov (a man of the world), would end it all that day by going of his own free will to Pavel Pavlovitch."[38] The deciphering needed to explain such an emotion is illustrated partly through a letter Pavel Pavlovitch gives Veltchaninov, which proves to be from the former's wife, claiming that the child she is carrying is Veltchaninov's; and partly through the scene in which Pavel Pavlovitch attempts to stab his rival to death. The sexual implications of this scene are so strong that they unleash in Veltchaninov equally strong senses of repulsion and attraction in ways that suggest that sexuality itself in this claustrophobic world is an affair between men, with the female characters serving only to release drives that are essentially homosexual.

The fundamental sexual ambiguity that frequently underlies jealousy, or rather that jealousy is used to unravel, is rendered even clearer in Tolstoy's *Kreutzer Sonata*. Here the narrative strategies employed to justify and construct the narration of a *crime passionnel* force into sharp relief what the narrator struggles to keep hidden. The enclosed space of the railway carriage in which the tale is recounted, the way in which the train journey re-creates the sense of inevitable and uncontrollable forward motion within a time span beyond the control of the central characters, the ambivalent but predominantly an-

---

38. Fyodor Dostoevsky, *The Eternal Husband*, trans. Constance Garnett (New York: Macmillan, 1923), 127.

tagonistic relationships between narrator and audience, the striking contrast between the "impressive and pleasant voice,"[39] and the growing horror of what the voice is saying, between text and subtext, in other terms, and the way in which the irrational violence of the main action is offered as an exemplum in a rational debate, all combine to shed considerable light on the nature of jealousy itself. Moreover, as jealousy is figured in the interpolated narrative as an obsessive need to decode the other (an obsession replicated in the obsessive need to narrate), so the narrative itself not merely invites, but demands, decoding, a decoding whose difficulty is suggested by the fact that the carriage is initially plunged in darkness.

The narrative begins by revealing the desire to impose on the essentially irrational act of murder a rational explanation and to force the shapelessness of jealousy into a neat pattern of cause and effect. What is presented as the initial trigger to subsequent events is an attitude of mind the speaker now presents as debauched: "Dissoluteness does not lie in anything physical—no kind of physical misconduct is debauchery; real debauchery lies precisely in freeing oneself from moral relationships with a woman with whom you have physical intimacy" (365). Yet it soon becomes clear that such conduct, which the narrator Pòzdnyshev considers universal among men of his class, is to be condemned less because it reduces women from individuals to a necessary appendage for male sexual drives than because it allows the married man no freedom from the jealous awareness that to other men his wife is perceived as yet another appendage for their use. Freedom from moral relationships with women, therefore, paradoxically leads to perpetual enslavement to suspicion. That suspicion, moreover, is to be seen as the correlative less of a compulsion to watch the rival than of a desire to watch, for the text soon reveals the homoerotic nature of Pòzdnyshev's relationship with his rival. Not only are his first sexual experiences associated with boys (367), but the text itself invites a form of decoding in which what is said is to be treated as the opposite of what is intended,

---

39. Leo Tolstoy, *Kreutzer Sonata*, in *Great Short Works*, trans. Louise Maude and Aylmer Maude (New York: Harper and Row, 1967), 365.

so that we are invited to read references to women as references to men: "A handsome woman talks nonsense, you listen and hear not nonsense but cleverness. She says and does horrid things, and you see only charm. And if a handsome woman does not say stupid or horrid things, you at once persuade yourself that she is wonderfully clever and moral" (369). Much of Pòzdnyshev's narrative is concerned with an evocation of the horrors of marriage, the sense of repulsion and addiction aroused in him by the act of physical, heterosexual love, and the endless and inevitable disparity between the needs and wants of men and those of women. Much of this, for all its intrinsic interest, is peripheral to our purposes, but the stress on the inversion of values offers a series of figures for the engendering of jealousy and contributes significantly to an understanding of the relationships between sexual jealousy and social power structures. Pòzdnyshev articulates those links through a comparison with Jews:

> The domination of women from which the world suffers all arises from this. [. . .] It explains the extraordinary phenomenon that on the one hand woman is reduced to the lowest stage of humiliation, while on the other she dominates. Just like the Jews: as they pay us back for their oppression by a financial domination, so it is with women. "Ah, you want us to be traders only—all right, as traders we will dominate you!" say the Jews. "Ah, you want us to be merely objects of sensuality—all right, as objects of sensuality we will enslave you," say the women. (374)

But whereas the Jews in this comparison are seen as active—traders—women are presented primarily as passive, mere projections of the man's own sensuality, so that they are defined not as individuals, but as creatures bodied forth by the gaze of men. Their enslavement of men is made possible only by male willingness to be enslaved, the text implies. What enslaves is clearly sensuality itself. The point is clarified later on, with the assertion that the majority of women are mentally diseased, hysterical, and lacking capacity for spiritual development. "High schools and universities cannot alter that. It can only be changed by a change in men's outlook on women and women's way of regarding themselves" (386). While women are, therefore, allowed some role in the alteration of their present nature, it is evident that for Pòzdnyshev they are mere extensions of male desire and that therefore his jealousy will also originate not in the woman herself but in the male rival.

There are further close links suggested in the text between the position of women in society and the nature and experience of jealousy. In other words, the strategies set in motion by the choice of jealousy as major theme allow a series of particularly telling parallels with a less obvious but unavoidable center of interest: the position and nature of women. The ostensible cause of jealousy in the central section of the narrative is the violinist with whom Pòzdnyshev's wife plays, so the making of music becomes a metaphor for sexual intercourse, and the role of the listener therefore offers analogies with the experience of the jealous voyeur. Moreover, as women are subjected to male domination, so, the text suggests, music subjects the listener to the domination of the composer: "Music carries me immediately and directly into the mental condition in which the man was who composed it. My soul merges with his and together with him I pass from one condition into another. [. . .] How can one allow anyone who pleases to hypnotize another, or many others, and do what he likes with them? And especially that this hypnotist should be the first immoral man who turns up?" (411). Reinforcement of this parallel is provided when Pòzdnyshev, rushing back from his meeting in the fear of finding his wife and the violinist together, reflects on his own desire to control his wife's body: "What was terrible, you know, was that I considered myself to have a complete right to her body as if it was my own, and yet at the same time I felt I could not control that body, that it was not mine and she could dispose of it as she pleased, and that she wanted to dispose of it not as I wished her to. And I could do nothing either to her or to him. [. . .] I wanted her not to desire that which she was bound to desire. It was utter insanity" (418). The inability or refusal to consider the two bodies as separate, the admission that, this being the case, she is bound to desire what in effect Pòzdnyshev desires but cannot admit he desires, combined with the growing torment the marriage has produced and the conflicts lived out through the children as extensions of the adults' personalities, unite to produce the explosive charge of murderous jealousy.

Yet, if jealousy has destroyed the woman in this tale, it has also, and just as surely, destroyed the protagonist himself, not merely by throwing into doubt his assessment of all relationships between men and women, but also and most powerfully by questioning his own sexuality. This deeply disturbing narrative ends with a pathetic plea for forgiveness, but the reader is left to decide what is to be forgiven: the murder, the mordantly cynical evocation of sexual and marital relationships, or the light shed on the shifting grounds of gender.

The protagonist's plea for his audience's forgiveness at the end of *The Kreutzer Sonata*, together with the setting of the narration in the framework of an exploration of marriage and morals more generally, make it a particularly powerful example of the split Ross Chambers refers to between reader and misogynistic text. Chambers's question—must this split "trap us in an endless replication of the discourse of power, or can it, and if so *how* can it, be made to yield the potential it contains for changing the world?"[40]—seems inescapable here, where responses—those of the other passengers at the beginning of the episode, those of society and the first person frame narrator, those of Pòzdnyshev himself—are so implacably judgmental. No judgment here appears either adequate or able to escape the reproduction of the images and prejudices of power.

At least one lesbian novel appears to accept quite openly the gauntlet this nasty study throws down. Traces of Tolstoy's exploration of jealousy as unacknowledged homoeroticism can be found in Elizabeth Jolley's *Palomino*, a novel of lesbian love that also sets itself, briefly and self-mockingly, in the tradition of Thomas Mann's *Death in Venice*. The first-person narrator of this lyrical novel represents her general sense of difference by depicting herself sitting between two German women, watching the film of *Death in Venice*:

40. Chambers, "Irony and Misogyny: Authority and the Homosocial in Baudelaire and Flaubert."

The yearning of the older man to feel seems to mean nothing to them, nor does the slow return of feeling over youth and the pattern of movement and color and the music of Mahler, although both exclaim with real pleasure every now and then.

"Vott a beautiful hett Irma!"

"Ach Ja! Und such dresses!"[41]

The analysis of the longing to regain the power of feeling, together with the conviction of being surrounded by at best incomprehension, and at worst hostility, is what makes Jolley's novel, with its refusal of jealousy and its rejection of the conviction that the other can or should be controlled or subjugated in any way, so clearly a response to Tolstoy's vision. Laura's reading of the sonata offers a telling contrast to Pòzdnyshev's:

For the Kreutzer Sonata the two players should have an emotional and spiritual closeness which is apparent in their playing. At one time in my life, before everything changed, I was studying carefully this possible closeness which human beings could explore and experience, something more than the perfect sexual relationship. The playing of the Kreutzer Sonata when I could not see the players made me aware of the depths of the possibilities, but the elderly violinist and his pale pianist had no relationship of this kind, this was evident. The Kreutzer Sonata rattled on in a kind of frenzy of failure. A desperation which held all the disappointment of being sleepless and having to understand that sensation is not always enough, even when there is response, to bring about the desired relief and satisfaction. (11)

And as if to underline that she is alluding here not merely to the music, but to Tolstoy's exploration of it as well, (hinted at in the term "rattled," which recalls Pòzdnyshev's train journey) she adds, a page later, that her farm, symbolically situated in the valley, "looks like Tolstoy country" (12). However her valley may look, not only it, but also her images of jealousy and her depiction of love, are at the very antipodes of those put

41. Elizabeth Jolley, *Palomino* (New York: Persea Books, 1987), 17.

forward by Tolstoy and thus propose a feminist, and a lesbian, rereading both of the sonata and of sexual relations.

Female readings of gender and of jealousy not infrequently set themselves deliberately against an intertext of a male reading or readings, as Elizabeth Jolley's does here. Virginia Woolf's *Orlando*—"the longest and most charming love letter in literature," as Nigel Nicolson calls it[42]—must surely also be one of the most original and enchanting revisions of history and of the debates lying at the heart of literature, art, and love. In place of the consecrated climactic moments in history, Woolf explores the changing forms of everyday life, from street lighting and transport to clothing, and in place of a protagonist of fixed gender, she illuminates the androgyny of the creative artist. As a man, Orlando fiercely loves the exotic beauty Sasha and dreams of "making her irrevocably and indissolubly his own."[43] His jealous rage at her refusal to accept such an enchaining love transforms the time and space in which he finds himself. The apparent timelessness of the great freeze comes to an abrupt end when Orlando waits for Sasha to join him in order to flee with him. The striking of the clocks that convinces him he is jilted not only ushers in the emotional time of jealousy, but sets free that chorus of alien voices that breaks the duet between lovers: "The whole world seemed to ring with the news of her deceit and his derision" (42). The parallel between his aroused suspicions and the river set free from the grip of the ice combines with the powerful eroticism of the water imagery to create a universe that assumes the forms of sexual jealousy:

> The old suspicions subterraneously at work in him rushed forth from concealment openly. [. . .] All was riot and confusion. The river was strewn with icebergs. Some of these were as broad as a bowling green and as high as a house; others no bigger than a man's hat, but most fantastically twisted. Now would come down a whole convoy of ice blocks sinking everything that stood in their way. Now, eddying and swirling

---

42. Nigel Nicolson, *Portrait of a Marriage* (New York: Athenaeum, 1973), 202.
43. Virginia Woolf, *Orlando* (Harmondsworth: Penguin, 1967), 35.

like a tortured serpent, the river would seem to be hurtling
itself between the fragments and tossing them from bank to
bank, so that they could be heard smashing against the piers
and the pillars. (43)

Transformed into a woman, aware of the weaknesses and secrets of each sex, Orlando at length overcomes the "bewilder-
ing and whirligig state of mind" attendant on such knowledge,
(112) and gradually reaches a different hour of midnight, one
in which she discovers the ecstasy not of making another person one's possession, but of allowing them the freedom to become fully themselves.

The complexity of the interwoven explorations of gender and
jealousy, of love and lust, of art and ambition refuses any kind
of simplifying unraveling. Even though *Orlando* has as its initial inspiration the love between two women, what it offers is
something far broader, a revisionist reading of human sexuality
and human history that gently, but unhesitatingly, refuses the
traditional and demeaning associations in numerous other attempts to engender jealousy.

Woolf's buoyant *Orlando*, in this one aspect like Tolstoy's
undeviatingly nasty *Kreutzer Sonata*, challenges its readers to
find a response to sexual jealousy that goes beyond the discourse of society, prejudice, and the assumptions based on conventional expectations of both gender and genre. The power of
that challenge feeds largely on the vigorous emotions created
by the depiction of jealousy and can be more closely analyzed
by exploring the ways in which literary texts have investigated
the desire to silence and control the other, whether that other
be the beloved or the rival, male or female. This will be the
subject of the next chapter.

3 Silencing Jealousy: Responding to Rivals

> If Cynthia crave her ring of me,
> I blot her name out of the tree.
>
> Fulke (Greville), Lord Brooke

>   She had
> A heart—how shall I say?—too soon made glad,
> Too easily impressed; she liked whate'er
> She looked on, and her looks went everywhere.
> Sir, t'was all one! My favour at her breast,
> The dropping of the daylight in the West,
> The bough of cherries some officious fool
> Broke in the orchard for her, the white mule
> She rode with round the terrace—all and each
> Would draw from her alike the approving speech,
> Or blush, at least. She thanked men,—good! but thanked
> Somehow—I know not how—as if she ranked
> My gift of a nine-hundred-years-old name
> With anybody's gift. Who'd stoop to blame
> This sort of trifling? Even had you skill
> In speech—(which I have not)—to make your will
> Quite clear to such an one, and say, "Just this
> Or that in you disgusts me; here you miss,
> Or there exceed the mark"—and if she let
> Herself be lessoned so, nor plainly set
> Her wits to yours, forsooth, and made excuse,
> —E'en then would be some stooping; and I choose
> Never to stoop. Oh sir, she smiled, no doubt,
> Whene'er I passed her; but who passed without
> Much the same smile? This grew; I gave commands;
> Then all smiles stopped together.
>
> Robert Browning, "My Last Duchess"

In this powerful and sinister evocation of jealousy, Browning's Duke is as much concerned with enforcing a reading of his own character as with displaying a reading of his wife's. The vision of himself as paramount, as never stooping, even to conquer, collides with his wife's apparently unreflecting refusal to reflect such primacy and finds itself thrust aside by rival images of himself and above all by the mere existence of the woman's own personality. Jealous both of his own self-esteem and of his wife's affection, the Duke finds himself surrounded by rivals, etymologically by challengers standing on the same river bank and using the same stream, whose conflicting interpretations of himself and his relationships set up a surge that threatens to muddy the waters and thus drown out his own reflected image. His inability to accept the existence of the other, emblematized in his imposition on the woman of his "nine-hundred-years-old name," carries with it a refusal to countenance the thought of being perceived otherwise, a narcissism that finds its solution only in destroying the other.

Silencing rival voices and rival interpretations, shouting above the static on the line between lover and beloved, text and reader, literature is frequently concerned less with communication than with excommunication. Within the text the dual longing to speak and the fear of not having "skill in speech" often represent a dual desire to know and a refusal to know, as when Germaine Greer, having presented her mother with the results of months of research into her father's real identity, refuses to deal with the disruptive rejoinder: "How do you know he's your father? You don't even know that!"[1] Reporting the comment, but refusing to react to it, Greer epitomizes the jealous lover, frenetically exploring the labyrinths of experience, but refusing to accept that Ariadne may not have the only thread. The search for truth combined with the refusal of truth, the longing for the other that leads to the destruction of the other, the silencing of voices alien to the self's own perceptions, in other words, are all reactions triggered off by the

---

1. Germaine Greer, *Daddy, We Hardly Knew You* (Harmondsworth: Penguin, 1989), 306.

presence, imagined or not, of rivals. And the reader who resists the consecrated or invited modes of reading also introduces further patterns of rivalry.

Many works of literature seek to examine the self through the twin truths of love and art, yet, as if each were jealous of the self's attention, such a search often leads to the suppression of one or the other. Thus, Romanticism's fascination with the artist torn among love, art, and madness frequently induces a depiction in which either the voice of art or that of the beloved must be silenced, and the artist must retreat into a refusal to acknowledge in one sphere that which he or she cannot ignore in another.[2] Balzac's early novella, *Le Chef-d'œuvre inconnu*, for instance, reflects many of Romanticism's central concerns when it emblematizes through its three central characters the intricate interrelationships of creative art, erotic attraction, and madness. Like a jealous lover, Frenhofer, that epitome of the Romantic artist, searches ever deeper for the truth about painting, but, as his colleague Pourbus puts it: "He has carried out so many investigations, that he has come to doubt the very object of those investigations,"[3] in much the same way that Choromanski's Rebecca becomes increasingly nebulous as Widmar attempts to learn more about her and that Proust's Odette cocoons herself in more and more half-truths as Swann seeks out the single whole-truth he does not want to accept.

The young Poussin, torn between his passion for art and his love for his mistress, Gillette, attempts to resolve his dilemma by asking her to pose for the older man's painting, thus transforming Gillette into the object of Frenhofer's research, and, by making her into the focus of the male gaze, denying her the right to maintain her own subjectivity. She becomes, in other words, the mere projection of male desire, the page on which he writes his own narrative, the canvas on which he paints his

2. While few female writers in the Romantic era attempted to explore the domain of art through a female protagonist, counterexamples would include Mme de Staël's *Corinne*, George Sand's *Consuelo*, and Marceline Desbordes-Valmore's *L'Atelier de l'artiste*.

3. Honoré de Balzac, *Le Chef-d'œuvre inconnu* (Paris: Livre de Poche, 1970), 42–43.

sexual drives.[4] Frenhofer's own response is much more that of lover than of artist: "what husband, what lover is vile enough to lead his beloved into dishonor? [. . .] Poetry and women give themselves naked only to their lovers!"[5] But when Gillette and Poussin come to Frenhofer's studio, despite all their hesitations, he, too, is seized with a kind of jealousy, a desire to prove that his artistic creation is worthy of comparison with the beauty of nature, and he uncovers his canvas. When Poussin lets slip the fact that there is almost nothing on a canvas that for Frenhofer depicts the most beautiful of women, the old painter dismisses his visitors and kills himself after destroying all his canvasses, a latter-day Sardanapolis ordering the murder of his female slaves before he himself commits suicide.

Even if we leave aside questions of artistic rivalry that the narrative voice carefully elides from the text, by giving us only the perspectives of Poussin and Pourbus, and not that of Frenhofer himself, Balzac's short story, with its disruptive triangular patterning, offers several models of jealousy: the sexual jealousy explored by the studies of Gillette and Poussin, on the one hand, and Frenhofer and his canvas on the other; and the jealousy that makes art and love rivals for Poussin's attention. Above all, through a series of sexual symbols based on the painters' brushes and knives, the text also suggests the way in which the beloved, in this case the painted figure, is gradually silenced, defaced, and destroyed by the artist/lover's unrelenting imposition on her of his layers of painting, the countless strata of his visions of her.[6] It is this, no doubt, that provokes

4. The question of the role played by the gaze in Western culture has been the focus of much feminist criticism. See in particular Laura Mulvey, "Visual Pleasure and Narrative Cinema," in *Art after Modernism: Rethinking Representation,* ed. Brian Wallis (Boston: Godine, 1984), 361–74, and Griselda Pollock, *Vision and Difference: Femininity, Feminism, and the Histories of Art* (New York: Routledge, 1988).

5. Balzac, *Le Chef-d'œuvre inconnu,* 50–51. Balzac's choice of verb—"se livrer"—is significant here, suggesting the same abandonment of self that we find in the equivalent English expression, one of many that are gender-specific: "she gave herself to her lover."

6. For valuable readings of this and related aspects of *Le Chef-d'œuvre inconnu,* see Claude Bernard, "La problématique d l'échange dans 'Le Chef d'œuvre inconnu,' " *L'Année Balzac* (1983): 201–13; Jean-Luc Filoche, "'Le Chef-d'œuvre inconnu' peinture et connaissance," *L'Année Balzac* (1980): 47–59; Chantal Massol-Bedoin, "L'artiste et l'imposture," *Romantisme* 54, 4 (1986): 44–57; and

Poussin's comment: "He is even more of a poet than a painter,"[7] implying the endless desire to retell her story, to embroider on the initial vision. Typically, and revealingly, Gillette's own response remains hidden from us, silenced by Frenhofer's ecstatic commentary and the laconic panning given by Poussin and Pourbus.

Roland Barthes, in his *A Lover's Discourse*, comments on a variant of this form of silencing, which he illustrates not with reference to Balzac, but through allusions to various other writers, especially Proust. In this case, it is not so much that the beloved is silenced as that he or she chooses to *fade out* of the lover's existence. The critic's choice of an English word rather than its French equivalent here is, of course, a subtly ironic reflection of the polyglossia that enables the rivals to silence the lover's voice. Barthes defines "fading" as a: "Painful ordeal in which the loved being appears to withdraw from all contact, without such enigmatic indifference even being directed against the loving subject or pronounced to the advantage of anyone else, world or rival."[8] In the case of *Le Chef-d'œuvre inconnu*, the beloved, here figured as the painted image of beauty, eludes the artist's grasp, fades from him through the very intensity of his search for her. A similar kind of fading can be perceived in the relationship between Poussin and Gillette when Gillette realizes that the very fact that her beloved has asked her to pose naked for Frenhofer reveals that his love for her is fading, painted over by other interests and other passions. Barthes, idiosyncratically and brilliantly finding a way of exteriorizing this sensation through a comparison with blue jeans, notes: "The loved being, in the same way, endlessly withdraws and pales: a feeling of madness, purer than if this madness were violent" (118). As the frequent washing of blue jeans makes them less blue, so, in tales of jealousy, does the frequent search for knowledge, the desire to purify the other of

---

Lawrence Schehr, "The Unknown Subject," *Nineteenth-Century French Studies* (Summer–Fall 1984): 58–69.

7. Balzac, *Le Chef-d'œuvre inconnu*, 59.

8. Roland Barthes, *A Lover's Discourse*, trans. Richard Howard (New York: Hill and Wang, 1978), 112.

suspicion, bleach all color from any discoveries that are made, rendering the truth less true.

The lover may conceive of the verb "to fade" in the active sense, but for the beloved that verb may be passive: do jeans fade, or are they faded? Does Gillette fade from Poussin, or is it his action of "lending" her to Frenhofer that forces her to fade? Nabokov's *Lolita* offers a brilliant, deeply disquieting, and frequently misread exploration of such active fading, where Lolita's initial crush on Humbert is presented by his relentlessly distorting narrative voice as withering over time, but where the reader cannot ignore the ways in which Humbert's fallacious theories of what he terms "nymphetry" constantly attempt to bleach all individuality from the child herself. Time, the force that traditionally strengthens and deepens true love, is presented in this novel as uniquely destructive, since nymphets exist as such for so brief a period: Humbert's solution to this predicament reveals with particularly distressing clarity the way in which he actively fades Lolita, in a vertiginous scene in which he imagines not merely fathering on her a future nymphet for his incestuous delectation but even the far-off existence of a granddaughter, a Lolita III to delight his dotage.

What is remarkable about the text is Lolita's refusal to be silenced, her ability not to have her individuality leached from her: for the alert reader, what remains are Lolita's tears in the night, her intelligent wit, and her inventively planned escape. What she cannot escape, of course, is the destruction of her innocence. When Humbert eventually rediscovers her, married, pregnant, "only the faint violet whiff and dead leaf echo of the nymphet,"[9] she struggles to give adequate expression to the difference between her relationship with him and the feelings she had for Quilty: "She groped for words. I supplied them mentally ('*He* broke my heart. *You* merely broke my life.')" (279). Even here, Lolita's voice is thrust under, faded out by the narrator's determination to provide only one narrative of the relationship, to supply the words he wants to believe she is struggling to express. Actually listening to her is beyond his

9. Vladimir Nabokov, *Lolita* (New York: Vintage, 1989), 277.

powers, although not necessarily beyond the capability of his readers. Here the complexity of address and the multiplicity of messages (her message to Humbert, his interpretation of her message for the reader's benefit, his message to the reader, her coded plea to the reader, the text's hint to the reader) are rendered possible by the chaotic force of jealousy, and they demand, yet again, a narratology that responds to such apparent chaos without imposing arbitrary patterns.

Humbert's murder of Quilty, his hypocrite brother, merely reconfirms in its pointless silencing of a past rival the constant silencing of Lolita's own individuality in a love affair that has been uniquely self-centered: "Lolita, light of my life, fire of my loins. My sin, my soul" (9). The possessives unravel to reveal the irremediable egotism of a narrator whose constant efforts to silence the alterity of the other ironically create a narrative that refuses to allow such silencing. Here the resisting reader is empowered by the complexities of the text itself, so that, at the same time that Lolita's individuality is being faded and crushed, the reader's anger is conjured into existence.

The desire to silence rival voices, together with the realization that the beloved voice is fading despite our desires (or because of our desires), are often two sides of the same coin. The longing to give artistic expression to that desire, even though doing so reinforces the silence and absence of the other, is frequently the metal of which that coin is made. As Barthes puts it, again in *A Lover's Discourse*: "To know that one does not write for the other, to know that these things I am going to write will never cause me to be loved by the one I love (the other), to know that writing compensates for nothing, sublimates nothing, that writing is precisely *there where you are not*—this is the beginning of writing."[10] To some extent, all first-person narratives, even those composed of numerous different first-person narrators (epistolary novels, for instance), operate in the domain of the other's absence and frequently do so in the hope of imposing a presence that silences all other voices (as Valmont and Merteuil dictate their words to Cécile and Danceny in *Les Liaisons dangereuses*). Recent novels have

---

10. Barthes, *A Lover's Discourse*, 100.

made considerable play of such presumed silence and have simultaneously manipulated the expected relationships between narrator and narratee, narrative and reader, breaking down the interface between created characters and flesh-and-blood readers.

Julian Barnes's *Talking It Over*, for instance, offers a playful exploration of the paradigms of sexual and textual jealousy. Here, the narrative viewpoint fragments into a kaleidoscope of images and a cacophony of voices, with not only the three main figures in the sexual triangle, but also numerous minor characters demanding their right to the first-person voice and, therefore, to the reader's ear. But the increasing democracy of the text unleashes a form of revolt on the part of the characters, unwilling merely to submit to the analytical gaze of the reader: "What?" barks one of them, indicated simply as "female, between 25 and 35." "You want my credentials. YOU want MY credentials? Look, if anyone's got to provide documentation it should be you. What have *you* done to qualify for *my* opinions? What's your authority, incidentally?"[11] The pun on "authority" also questions the active role frequently assumed by modern readers, who have grown used to being invited to choose their own endings, for instance, and suggests a jealous silencing by the text itself of all external voices. Bullying the reader, indeed, is part of a textual strategy that parallels and reinforces the models of sexual jealousy that the narrative provides. In the following quotation, for instance, the narrator speaks directly to the reader: "We're stuck with it. That's the long and the short of the matter. We're stuck in this car on this motorway, the three of us, and someone (the driver!—me!) has leant an elbow on the button of the central locking system. So the three of us are in here till it's resolved. *You're* in here too. Sorry, I've clunked the doors, you can't get out, we're all in this together" (80). But even though each voice wants to hold the reader's attention without pandering to the reader's wishes, the dual relationship thus initiated is constantly broken apart not merely by other voices within the novel, but by echoes and parallels with other texts. The most obvious of these in the

11. Julian Barnes, *Talking It Over* (London: Jonathan Cape, 1991), 181.

case of *Talking It Over* is Fromentin's novel *Dominique*, in which the eponymous hero realizes that he has fallen in love only when the beloved has accepted another's offer of marriage. The echoes with this text, and its suggestions of a kind of loving that requires jealousy in order to germinate and flourish, are reinforced by the fact that Dominique's best friend is called Olivier and offers various parallels with the Oliver of Barnes's text. The multiple codings such echoes reveal parallel the multiplicity of voices, and thus reconstruct one of jealousy's central torments: the individual's realization that the beloved refuses to acknowledge the lover's own sense of irreducible uniqueness.

Barnes's playful symmetry, his ludic manipulation of the role of the reader, who is at one point directly appealed to by one of the characters, seeking information the parameters of the plot will not give him, together with his parodic evocation of other texts make this a highly conscious literary construction, in which the critic joins the novelist to explore the trope of jealousy as a means of silencing voices while it simultaneously produces the plot.

A. S. Byatt's showy study of academic and sexual jealousy, *Possession*, also explores some of the ways in which writing and reading operate to silence other voices. The young textual critic, Roland Michel, at the point when he is reading a private correspondence miraculously rediscovered after the lapse of a hundred years, muses that letters "exclude not only the reader as co-writer, or predictor, or guesser, but they exclude the reader as reader, they are written, if they are true letters, for *a* reader."[12]

Byatt's lesbian character, Blanche Glover, expresses far more forcefully, because more personally, the power of letters to exclude, when she refers in her diary to the letters her lover Christabel Lamotte has begun receiving. Byatt's pastiche here brings out all the boiling bitterness of Blanche's emotions, while, largely through the fragmentary nature of Blanche's diary entries, and the equally fragmentary knowledge we have of Blanche as individual, keeping us at a distance from her, setting

12. A. S. Byatt, *Possession: A Romance* (London: Vintage, 1990), 131.

up a kind of static between us and her that echoes the static the letters create between Blanche and her lover Christabel: "Letters, letters, letters. Not for me. I am not meant to see or know. I am no blind mouldiwarp, my Lady, nor no well-trained lady's maid to turn my head and not see what is stated not to concern me. You need not hurry them away to lie in your sewing-basket or run upstairs to fold them under your handkerchiefs. I am no Sneak, no watcher, no Governess" (46). Part of Blanche's problem is that without Christabel she is without definition, able to list what she is not, but having no way of affirming herself as self. The sense of sexual betrayal associated with jealousy here is also concerned with sexual identity, as the powerfully erotic images Blanche uses reveal: "Where is our frankness of intercourse? Where the small, unspeakable things we used to share in quiet harmony? This Peeping Tom has put his eye to the nick or cranny in our walls and peers shamelessly in" (46). In retaliation for being thus silenced, both physically and metaphysically, since Ash's courtship of Christabel threatens Blanche's lesbian self-image, Blanche attempts to silence him, by the theft both of his letters and of the poem he sends. Christabel's letter of explanation to Ash captures in its breathless style the rage and shame experienced by both women: "Today I happened—to run a little faster to greet the Postman. There was almost a papery—Tussle. I *snatched*. To my shame—to our shame—we—snatched" (189). Blanche's struggle not to be silenced by the wolflike power of male sexuality is reduced in Christabel's eyes to "Veils and Whirligigs of hindrances" (191), her revelations to Ash's wife come too late for anything to be changed, and faced with the triple impossibility of a sexual personality that has apparently been rejected, an artistic gift that is unappreciated, and a gender that prevents her from earning enough to keep herself, she chooses suicide, that final silencing of the self.

In contrast to these gleeful postmodern explorations of polyphony, Ford Madox Ford's *The Good Soldier* offers a doggedly grim illustration of the tactics of silencing, with its first-person narrator determined from the outset to stifle all voices but his own and to lure the reader into accepting a pact whereby, if we receive passively what we are given, we will be told "the saddest story [. . .] ever heard."[13] The story evokes voices fading away from the central figure, but the underlying trope is that of voices reduced by jealousy to silence. The final image, indeed, is that of the narrator carrying a telegram message between a husband and wife, with the enigmatic, no doubt cynical comment: "She was quite pleased with it" (229). The model provided by this image is both complex and clear: the message, whose contents we are invited to infer from the text but which we can never reliably know, has to be relayed through a third person—or is it a fourth person, as the telegram comes from outside this particular triangle? That third person is the very one whose reliability we have most come to doubt.[14]

Throughout, the narrator is at pains to present himself merely as the vehicle through which the story is told, the passive watcher on the sidelines, the one from whom the others fade away. Moreover, that proclaimed passivity is also visited on the implied reader, who is summoned into the text to judge whether or not a certain passage is a digression or integral to the "tale of passion": "You, the listener, sit opposite me. But you are so silent. You don't tell me anything. I am, at any rate, trying to get you to see what sort of life it was I led with Florence and what Florence was like."[15] Even in the words "get you to see" lies a clue, for the phrase implies something much more loaded than the neutral "show you": the reader is to see only the patterns and hues the narrative voice wants to reveal, but under so much pressure the text constantly slips from his control and suggests what it does not state.

Attempting to get the reader to see involves introducing several words or expressions whose full meaning is exposed only as the story progresses: the term *heart*, for instance, in the phrase "one of us had, as the saying is, a 'heart' " or "Captain Ashburnam also had a heart" (11), gradually unravels to mean not just heart condition but also, and perhaps primarily, a pas-

13. Ford Madox Ford, *The Good Soldier* (Harmondsworth: Penguin, 1971), 11.
14. Suggestive readings of the novel can be found in Carol Jacobs, "The Too Good Soldier," *Glyph* 3 (1978): 32–51, and Frank Nigro, "Who Framed *The Good Soldier*? Dowell's Story in Search of a Form," *Studies in the Novel* 24, 4 (1992): 381–91.
15. Ford, *The Good Soldier*, 20–21.

sion for sexual adventures. The narrator's desire to dominate interpretations also forces him to throw into question habitual interpretations of social discourse, of language and gesture, cliché and convention: "If poor Edward was dangerous because of the chastity of his expressions—and they say that is always the hallmark of a libertine—what about myself? For I solemnly avow that not only have I never so much as hinted at an impropriety in my conversation in the whole of my days; and more than that, I will vouch for the cleanness of my thoughts and the absolute chastity of my life" (18). A narrator's unreliability is never so reliably indicated as in such protestations of innocence. "There is," as the narrator goes on to affirm, "nothing to guide us": if Edward's words reveal the libertine only because of their chastity, how are we to interpret the words of the narrator, how much value are we to place on his assertions of sexual and more general innocence? The minuet so delicately danced before our eyes traces patterns that have constantly to be interpreted in ways that run counter to the apparent, superficial meaning. When Edward's wife, Leonora, describes herself as an Irish Catholic, thus allowing the narrator to argue that it is Florence's "mere silly jibes at the Irish and the Catholics" that have caused her pain, the narrator seizes on her words to reassure and quash his growing suspicion that Leonora is jealous of Florence. "Jealousy," he confides, ostensibly referring to Leonora, "would have been incurable" (66). Because the narrator so frequently reinterprets what he hears, the reader, too, is encouraged, by the narration if not by the narrator, to reinterpret what is related: how, for example, can the narrator assert of Leonora: "She was thinking, as a matter of fact, of poor Maisie" (66)? What is "fact," what does the word mean, in such a sentence, given that the narrator can only guess at her hidden thoughts?

This also gives rise to an equally disturbing insistence on how the reader is to interpret certain information: "Do you understand," we are asked, point blank, "that, whilst [Florence] was Edward's mistress, she was perpetually trying to reunite him with his wife?" (69) Throughout the text, in other words, the narrator, etymologically the one who knows, reveals his ignorance, and jealously struggles to induce us to ignore any knowledge that runs counter to what he wishes to convey, while the narration just as jealously tugs at our sleeves and demands that we pay attention to those very aspects that the narrator tries to keep hidden.

If the narrator is so eager to silence other interpretations of events, it is above all because, as he suggests in a powerful image early in the tale, he feels he is a mere gelding in comparison with the neighing stallions other men represent. Dissuaded by Florence's apparent heart condition from what he coyly terms "manifestations of affection" with her (83), he finds that he has left the field open not only to Edward, but also, far more destructively for himself and for the others, to Florence's former lovers. It is the discovery of this truth that precipitates Florence's death, ostensibly as the result of a heart attack, although the narrator suggests the possibilities of suicide and the narration points to her murder by the narrator, with its reference to the empty phial that should have contained medicine. Part of the power of this silencing of other voices stems from how closely he sails to what he is obfuscating: "Well, there you have the position, as clear as I can make it—the husband an ignorant fool, the wife a cold sensualist with imbecile fears—for I was such a fool that I should never have known what she was or was not—and the blackmailing lover. And then the other lover came along" (89). But there are further twists to the tale, for, as the narrator goes on to say, there is the relationship between that "blackmailing lover" and the narrator himself. Although he may protest that he "doesn't know that analysis of [his] own psychology matters at all to this story" (99), his assertion that he liked Edward "so much—so infinitely much" (89) together with other clues in the text, cannot but suggest the homosexual elements of jealousy Freud reveals in his reading of *The Kreutzer Sonata*. The narrator's attraction for Nancy Rufford after Florence's death, for instance, seems closely connected to the fact that Edward also loves her.

All these powerful crosscurrents of jealousy, deception, and especially self-deception culminate in the final images in the stable, where the narrator claims to realize that Edward is going to kill himself. But as he is the only witness, and as he has proved so unreliable a witness in the past, the reader, left with the narrator's last judgment of himself—"I also am a sentimentalist" (229)—and the picture of him trotting off with the telegram, cannot help wondering if here, too, murder masquerades as suicide, with the self-styled gelding choosing to destroy the rival stallion in the stable.

The constant attempt to stifle other voices in this claustrophobic first-person narrative is emblematized by the predicament of Nancy Ruffles, driven insane by passion and guilt and able only to utter the word "shuttlecocks," with its image of the jealous mind tossed restlessly between rivals. The firm silencing of the intended reader is a central strategy here, one that paradoxically triggers the disruptive interpretations of the unintended reader.

However much the narration may invite unintended readings, the narrator's appeal to an intended reader who will condone the results of jealousy and commiserate with the sufferer rather than the victim of that passion implies a society that tolerates the *crime passionnel* and a priori denials of the personality of the other. Suppressing that alterity can, of course, take purely verbal form. In *La Peau de chagrin* Balzac's Foedora silences the outpourings of Raphaël's infatuation with the damning comment: "All men trot out for us, with greater or lesser skill, those classic lines,"[16] just as Flaubert's Rodolphe reduces Emma to banal mistress, indistinguishable from his other women: "Emma was like all mistresses; and the charm of novelty, falling little by little like parts of her clothing, revealed in all its nakedness the eternal monotony of passion."[17] The external narrative voice refuses such facile silencing, however, with its own condemnation of Rodolphe's position: "He did not distinguish, for all his experience, the different feelings that can be found within similar expressions" (196).

Silencing rival interpretations in a first- or third-person narrative often calls for strategies that reflect a political context of censorship and essentialist judgments (it is the essence of women to be like that, it is the essence of all men to say the

---

16. Honoré de Balzac, *La Peau de chagrin* (Paris: Flammarion, 1971), 210.
17. Gustave Flaubert, *Madame Bovary* (Paris, Garnier, 1971), 196.

same thing). Indeed, using sexual jealousy to suggest parallels with the workings of political power is a device exploited in such novels as Alas's *La Regenta*, where the central female character serves as a focus less of sexual desire, although that is the metaphor used, than of a longing for doctrinal domination.[18] The numerous intellectual debates ironically indicate not so much the power of the mind to convince, but rather the close interrelationship that is perceived between political power and sexual power. Ana's fainting fit at the novel's end offers a corporeal image of the extent to which she is a mere physical token, whose personality is constantly silenced by the drive to power of those who attempt to win her over.[19]

Achieving similar results in an epistolary novel, however, calls for strategies reminiscent of the secret police and brainwashing. The manipulations practiced by the marquise de Merteuil and the vicomte de Valmont in *Les Liaisons dangereuses* reveal just such techniques.[20] As Jean Rousset explains: "From the outset, and merely on the epistolary level, the mechanism of the private exchange has been corrupted: instead of being a tête à tête closed to the external world, the intimate dialogue has been shattered; the mail has been intercepted and secrecy violated by the addition of an external reader."[21] Here individuals are reduced to mere pawns on the chess board of power, and Valmont himself is willing to silence his love for Mme de Tourvel because narcissistic jealousy leads him to conform to a self-image fashioned in the past and to whose code of practice he no longer adheres. In this masterly novel, the epistolary format ensures that each voice is allowed to speak, but as those who wield power over the others gradually gain the upper hand,

18. Leopoldo Alas, *La Regenta*, trans. John Rutherford (Harmondsworth: Penguin, 1984).
19. For stimulating readings of this novel, see Jo Labanyi, "City, Country, and Adultery in *La Regenta*," *Bulletin of Hispanic Studies* 43 (1986): 53–66; Jan van Luxemburg, "Ana's Pedestal: A Counterreading of *La Regenta*," *Style* 22, 4 (Winter 1988): 559–75; John Rutherford, *Leopoldo Alas: "La Regenta"* (London: Grant and Cutler, 1974); and Alison Sinclair, "The Consuming Passion: Appetite and Hunger in *La Regenta*," *Bulletin of Hispanic Studies* 69 (1992): 245–61.
20. For a brilliant study of the narratological implications of these letters and their addressees, see Jean Rousset, *Le Lecteur intime: De Balzac au journal* (Paris: Corti, 1986), chap. 6.
21. Ibid., 86.

the individual voice of the weaker characters is subsumed into
that of the more powerful: Cécile adopts the writing style of
the vicomte, and Valmont, in his destructive letter to Mme de
Tourvel, disastrously apes the mannerisms of the marquise.
Here, the way in which jealousy seeks to stifle the static between lover and beloved is troped in the very texture of the
language, setting up a powerful and largely cynical dichotomy
between the narrative's moral conclusion, in which the vicomte is killed and the marquise ostracized, and the narration's
representation of power and its ability to silence the voices of
the weak. Society, one feels, may well condemn the individual
Merteuils, but not the manipulative practices they embody.

Whereas the novels of Byatt, Barnes, and Laclos draw on the
possibilities of multiple narrators, and Ford's allows other
voices to whisper their messages through the attempted dictatorship of the first-person narrator, lyric poetry tends, by its
very nature, to stifle all voices but that of the single subject of
the poem, with the inevitable result that much love poetry is
less a conversation than a monologue. Yet the very act of in-
scribing private emotion in published verse creates a splitting
of the narrating persona into the self who acts and the self who
tells: as Donne so memorably puts it:

> I am two fooles, I know,
> For loving, and for saying so
> In whining Poëtry.[22]

Baudelaire makes particularly potent use of this doubling in
his prose poems, where, as his analogy with the kaleidoscope
suggests, single themes are treated in different ways from poem
to poem, revealing the different patterns that can be wrought
from the same materials.[23] What unites many of these poems
is the narrators' desire to block out rival interpretations of reality, of gender, and of their own self-image. Yet the collection
includes a damning icon of the poet who does stifle protest in
the poem "The Wild Woman and the Little Sweetheart," where

22. John Donne, "The Triple Foole," in *Complete Poems* (Oxford: Oxford University Press, 1933).
23. Charles Baudelaire, *Œuvres complètes* (Paris: Pléiade, 1976), 2: 47.

the narrator is mirrored in the barbaric fairground entertainer who reduces his wife to the state of wild animal and puts her on show to the public (with the permission of the authorities, as Baudelaire sardonically informs us, in a cynical aside that aligns us as readers with those very authorities).[24] Even though the narrator's ostensible and civilizing aim is to stop his beloved from indulging in insincere complaints and to make her realize the folly of wanting more from love than it can offer (as *Madame Bovary*'s narrative voice claims Emma Bovary dries out all emotions by wanting them to be too great), his refusal to allow her the right of reply parallels the barker's brutish imprisonment of the wild woman. Moreover, the final image of the little sweetheart as a pond frog demanding a magnificent overlord provides a damning indictment of Romantic poetry's own longings for the sublime, rather than a specifically misogynistic attack, as has often been too hastily concluded.

Romantic poetry itself is subjected to a further mocking voice-over by the wonderfully down-to-earth "mad little beloved" of "Soup and Clouds," who translates into a practical sphere Baudelaire's own mockery of the Pagan school—"Can you eat ambrosia broth?"[25]—by capping the poet's pretty but unproductive comparison between the clouds and her eyes, with her own pragmatic and creative response: "Are you going to hurry up and eat your soup, or aren't you, you b . . . b . . . of a cloud merchant?"[26] Her jealous but witty response to his window-gawking doubly silences him by drowning out his poetic similes, and by deflating him from dreaming poet to impotent shopkeeper, hawking his still-unwritten poems about clouds.

"Which Is the Real Benedicta?" creates a punchy parable of male/female relations, when the narrator, having briefly loved a woman who seemed perfectly to embody his image of the ideal Romantic woman attends her funeral only to find, dancing on the grave, a prostitute who is the living image of the

24. Baudelaire's brilliant bracketing here of economics, power, voyeurism, and male sexuality offers further support to the theories of the gaze explored by such critics as Laura Mulvey, Dorothy Kelly, and John Berger.
25. Baudelaire, *Œuvres complètes,* 2: 47.
26. Ibid., 1: 350.

lost Benedicta and who demands that he love her as she truly is. Screaming his refusal, the narrator stamps his foot on the freshly dug earth and sinks in up to his knee, remaining forever trapped with one foot in the grave of the ideal, as the text wittily puts it. Benedicta, therefore, refuses to underwrite the poet's determination to preserve in death what he believes cannot last in life, the woman's function as the madonna whose eyes "radiate the desire for grandeur, beauty, glory, and all that makes us believe in immortality" (342). Insisting on her difference from the romantic and phallocentric stereotype of woman that the narrative voice has attempted to foist on her, Benedicta writes her own script, asserting: "It's me! one of the real riff-raff! And to punish you for your madness and your blindness, you're going to love me just as I am!" (342). Here the woman is not silenced, nor can it be argued that she has nothing to communicate, but the narrator refuses to be party to her statement, both transforming himself into a burlesque icon of man trapped in the grave of the ideal, as he says, and also converting himself, as the text reveals through its choice of the wolf image, into an illustration of the adage "homo feminae lupus est." Benedicta fulfills, moreover, the same function as the male narrator of "The Wild Woman and the Little Sweetheart" by forcing him to perceive himself "with his feet in the mud and his eyes turned swooningly skyward, as if to ask the heavens for [a queen]" (290). In these and other of the prose poems, the interplay of voices, the kaleidoscopic interplay of the separate poems, and the disruptive power of the text itself serve to reject that silencing of the beloved women's voice on which lyric poetry often depends.

Yet even in his verse poetry the highly conscious Baudelaire is quite capable of focusing on such a desire to silence rival interpretations. In his verse poem "Confessionnel du cœur [The Heart's Confessional]" the poet-narrator's unthinking image of beauty and love as spontaneous and natural collides with the woman's revelations about the difficulty of maintaining that impression of spontaneity:

> Que c'est un dur métier que d'être belle femme,
> Et que c'est le travail banal

De la danseuse folle et froide qui se pâme
  Dans un sourire machinal;

Que bâtir sur les cœurs est une chose sotte;
  Que tout craque, amour et beauté,
Jusqu'à ce que l'Oubli les jette dans sa hotte
  Pour les rendre à l'Eternité!

[How hard a task it is to be a beautiful woman, / and how trite the work / of the mad, frigid ballerina who swoons / with a mechanical smile.

How stupid it is to build on hearts; / everything falls apart, love and beauty, / until Oblivion throws them into his sack / to hand them over to Eternity!] (45–46)

The very voice in which this rejection of the poetic doxa is expressed is described as resembling "a sickly child, horrible, morose and indecent, / which would make its whole family blush," while the statement itself is evoked as a "horrible secret whispered / during the heart's confession" (46).

Many of Baudelaire's contemporaries, however, like Baudelaire himself in the majority of his verse poems, preferred to give voice to a general or personal misogyny in stifling the female voice out of their poems of wounded love or damaged sexual pride. Like Browning's distrustful duke, these lyric I's plead their own case against the woman with an intensity suggesting that only by silencing alternative views of their failed love affairs can they maintain their own sense of integrity. Thus, Gautier, in his poem "L'Impassible" takes up and overturns a theme Baudelaire explores in his "Sed non satiata" and that many other male poets also touch on: the fear of woman's insatiable urge for sexual satisfaction. In this case, the woman causes fear because of her apparent indifference to the desire of others and because of the lack of desire she herself appears to display:

La satiété dort au fond de vos grands yeux:
En eux plus de désirs, plus d'amour, plus d'envie;

Ils ont bu la lumière, ils ont tari la vie,
Comme une mer profonde où s'absorbent les cieux.

Sous leur bleu sombre on lit le vaste ennui des Dieux,
Pour qui toute chimère est d'avance assouvie,
Et qui, sachant l'effet dont la cause est suivie,
Mélangent au présent l'avenir déjà vieux.

L'infini s'est fondu dans vos larges prunelles,
Et devant ce miroir qui ne réfléchit rien,
L'amour découragé s'assoit, fermant ses ailes.

Vous, cependant, avec un calme olympien,
Comme la Mnémosyne, à son socle accoudée,
Vous poursuivez, rêveuse, une impossible idée.

[Fulfillment sleeps in the depths of your great eyes: / In them can be found no more desires, no more love, no more cravings; / They have drunk the light, they have dried up the springs of life, / Like a deep ocean that absorbs the sky.

Under their dark blue can be read the vast tedium of the Gods / For whom every caprice is always already satisfied / And who, knowing the effect that follows the cause, / Mingle with the present a future which is already old./

Infinity has vanished into your vast eyes, / And before this mirror which reflects nothing, / Love, discouraged, sits down and folds his wings./

You, meanwhile, with Olympian calm, / Like Mnemosyne leaning against her pedestal, / You pursue, musing, an impossible thought.][27]

Here the poet-narrator finds himself faced with a woman who in no way responds to him and whose indifference causes his love to wilt, folding its Cupid wings, as the metaphor coyly

27. In Luc Decaunes, *Poésie parnassienne* (Paris: Seghers, 1977), 50.

frames it. The only possible cause for this must be that the woman longs for something that is impossible: were it possible, the poet would, of course, have been able to provide it, or so the subtext implies. Memory, mother of the muses, refuses to offer the poet-narrator what he longs to find, himself and his past reflected in her eyes, and because she has chosen to silence him, to reject him as individual, he retaliates by silencing her and by reducing her to the role of unfeeling statue. Jealousy here springs less from a sense of rival lovers than from a realization that in the woman he has encountered a rival view of himself, as someone not worth noticing, and it is this belittling of his desire, this symbolic castration, that forces him into that bitter rejection of an ideal that, were he, rather than she, to have professed it, might have been designated unobtainable, but would not have been so demeaned.

The polyphonic power of the novel may be denied to the lyric: yet, as these examples suggest, messages do go astray, the lines between lyric and "I" and intended receiver may break and the woman's voice still be heard, if only in filigree or *en creux*. It is hardly surprising that it should be in the poems of jealousy that these oppressive messages are most likely to encounter resistance in the reader, since jealousy, as I have been arguing, provides its own model of triangularity or polygonality and therefore invites a similarly multiple reading. The desire to silence, like any other desire not only feeds on, but also feeds, resistance.

So far I have explored works that attempt to silence rival interpretations and rival voices mainly by narratological or linguistic means: but the silencing of the other, rival or beloved, is also frequently presented in the form of violent murder within the text. Even though *Othello* would be for many the paradigm example of the individual driven to murderous rage by jealousy, it nevertheless remains to some extent outside my scope here, in that what lies at the heart of this play is not the analysis of jealousy as such—seen, on the contrary, as puerile and even stupid within this particular context—but the ways in which jealousy enables Iago's logic to invade and transform Othello's logic: as so often in male depictions of jealousy, this is an affair between men, where the woman is forced into the most passive of roles, mere victim in a deadly mental game. Here the parasite on the line parasitizes Othello's lines. The very fact that the triangular pattern has been replaced by a binary one reproduces the structures of political reactionism and reveals the ways in which sexual jealousy can unleash political chaos.

In terms of literary strategies, however, it may be more productive to focus on the exploitation of jealousy in Théophile Gautier's short story *Le Roi Candaule,* which retells the mythical tale of Gyges's ring and recasts it to explore concepts of female integrity and purity set against images of male self-definition that demand validation by another male. Written in the aftermath of the 1830 revolution, which overthrew a monarch but failed to produce a republic, the fable hinges on the conflict between king Candaule's admiration for his bride's beauty, an admiration that yearns for reinforcement from another male gaze, and Nyssia's own self-image of purity and modesty:

> The barbarians do not share the ideas of the Greeks where modesty is concerned:—whereas the young people of Achaie make no bones about allowing their oil-polished torsos to gleam in the sun of the stadium, and the maidens of Sparta dance without veils before Diana's alter, those of Persepolis, Ecbatane and Bactres, attaching more value to physical than spiritual modesty, consider impure and reprehensible these freedoms that Greek customs allow for the eyes' delight, and believe that a woman is not respectable if she allows men to catch a glimpse of more than the tip of her foot, scarcely pushing back as she walks the discreet folds of a long tunic.[28]

Here there is a double scandal: that of the woman opposing the man's image of her as manifest projection of his own sexual desires; and that of the happy lover, who can convince himself of the full weight of that happiness only if he creates for himself someone who will see him as rival, someone who will be envious of him. The central couple in Candaule's conception

28. Théophile Gautier, *Nouvelles* (Paris: Charpentier, 1923), 363.

of love is not that formed by the lovers: indeed, how could it be, when the woman is conceived of merely as a projection of the male ego? For him, the couple is formed by the lover and the male other who confirms his happiness by envying it. It is as though Narcissus, not content with seeing himself perfectly reflected in the pool of a woman's eyes, needed a male version of Echo to authorize his pleasure. Yet it should be noted that while the king envisages envy as a necessary proof, he fails to allow for the possibility of jealousy, because jealousy in his eyes could only be felt by a true equal, and not a mere subordinate.

For Candaule the artist, even more than Candaule the king, beauty exists to be admired, and, because he regards Nyssia as his possession, he seeks to share her beauty with others, in a fruitless attempt to silence her own independent self. (It is not, of course, that sharing her beauty would bring with it a sharing of her body—that might give Nyssia pleasure and lead her to judge the king's performance against that of others.) Facilitating the gaze of others reifies not only that which is seen, but also that which sees. The transformation of Nyssia into objet d'art and Gygès into an extension of the king's own gaze is evident in Candaule's patronizing comment to Gygès: "I have allowed you to read a few verse of a fine poem of which I alone possess the manuscript, to have your opinion about it, that's all" (409). Here Gautier touches on questions of hierarchy and equality that were both central and dangerous at the time at which he was writing.

The problem for Candaule is that Nyssia does not regard herself as an object—or as anyone's possession. (Whether or not Gygès, for his part, would be willing to continue as the king's eye rather than his own person the text does not reveal.) As the text suggests, in a passage that offers a masterful depiction of her eyes in Gautier's most exuberant, virtuoso style, Candaule may have possessed her body, as masculine terminology curiously puts it, but he has not won her love: as Proust reminds us, in the act of possession, we possess nothing. Although her eyes sometimes seem to promise the possibility of ineffable happiness, and sometimes contain "such unctuous and persuasive languors, such penetrating exhalations and irradiations, that the ice of Nestor and Priam would have melted on seeing them" (377), their most common expression is "a chastity that filled one with despair, a sublime coldness, an ignorance of any possibility of human passion. [. . .] Their unconquerable virginity seemed to defy love" (377). Herein, of course, lies yet another clue to Candaule's behavior: his failure to win his wife's love stirs him to seek a different kind of victory over her, one he conceives of in terms of destroying her independence.

Yet human passion can be unleashed in Nyssia, as Candaule is to learn when, to satisfy his desire to see his happiness envied, and therefore validated, by another, he hides Gygès in the marital bedroom to witness Nyssia in all her naked radiance. The problem is that while for Candaule Nyssia's eyes are merely to be gazed upon, for her they serve another and more obvious purpose, and through the crack in the door she glimpses Gygès's eye, "gleaming like the carbuncle of Oriental legends"[29] and divines all that it implies. Moreover, Gygès himself, far from considering the king's sharing of his wife's beauty as a sign of high favour, is filled with uncontrollable jealousy and a rage that may have much to do with his relegation to a powerlessness and reification that are usually associated with women:

> Now he had seen Nyssia's fair head leaning like a flower near Candaule's brown head, and that thought roused his anger to the highest pitch, as if a moment's reflection should not have convinced him that things could not be otherwise, and he felt in his soul the germ of a most unjust sense of anger directed at his master. The act of making him witness the queen's unrobing seemed to him to be a burning irony, an odious refinement of cruelty. [. . .] When he thought that tomorrow the scene he had just witnessed in invisible silence would without fail be repeated, his tongue clove to the roof of his

---

29. Ibid., 400. The transformation of male and female associations here, with the woman's gaze penetrating the crack in which the male eye is located, suggests the extent to which, even in presenting an independent woman, Gautier's imagery remains locked in traditional patterns that associate power and action with the male.

mouth, his brow was covered with pearls of cold sweat, and his clenched hand reached for the pommel of his broad, double-edged sword. (402)

Throughout this passage, of course, Gautier's imagery is highly erotic, with a superabundance of signs that attempt to detract attention from the political implications of a piece written in times of conspicuous royal consumption, set before the populace for contemplation, but not for participation.

For Nyssia, too, the tenderness previously felt for her husband has been replaced by murderous fury: "She would have preferred death to one of his caresses. It was impossible to forgive such an affront, for, among the barbarians and especially among the Persians and Bactrians, it is a great dishonor to be seen without one's clothes, not merely for women but even for men" (404). Candaule, in attempting to reduce his wife and his friend to mere functions of his own desire, has set in motion, not the monotony of power, where the powerful individual subsumes those over whom he holds power ("La France, c'est moi"), but the plural and destructive force of jealousy. The attempted silencing of Nyssia's self-image, like the reduction of Gygès to mere mirror in which Candaule's own desire will be reflected but never satisfied, leads inevitably to his own destruction, as condign punishment for his attempted destruction of the alterity of the other.

Nyssia finds herself indistinguishable from the vilest courtesan, now that "two men have seen [her] naked and both enjoy the sun's sweet light" (405). But if her uniqueness has been destroyed by a double gaze that transforms her into yet another in the long lines of prostitutes, so too does Gygès—who, however, insists on Nyssia's uniqueness, protesting that "nothing alive is worthy to be compared to Nyssia" (409)—find himself stripped of all individuality to become a mere adjunct of the king. Candaule attempts to silence each, to reduce Nyssia to "a fine poem" (408), and to refashion Gygès as the cup into which he can pour the excess of his joy and happiness, as he puts it in yet another image that suggests homoerotic impulses (409). Thus, Candaule unwittingly places himself in the position of rival for each of them: rival reader of her personality for

Nyssia, rival lover for Gygès, and when Nyssia demands of the latter that he either kill himself or murder the king, all words of protest are silenced. Nyssia warns Gygès: "winged words could fly uninterrupted from your mouth through an entire olympiad but you could not change my resolve" (412). Misreading the other, so this tale suggests in its deliberate misreading of the legend, releases the surge of jealousy that reduces the mistaken reader to permanent silence and allows those who have been misread to reestablish their own identity.

Gautier's mid-nineteenth-century representation of the destructive forces at work in jealousy carefully softens the contours by placing the tale in a time and space remote from his reader's experience; it focuses on the picturesque and the beautiful while subtly inviting comparison with contemporary politics. Simone de Beauvoir's mid-twentieth-century evocation of murderous jealousy, however, for all her attempts to inscribe it within a philosophical framework, is physically and psychologically brutal.[30] *She Came to Stay*, written in the year that saw the publication of Sartre's *Being and Nothingness*, suggests from its initial epigraph that it will be an exploration in literary guise of Hegel's proposition: "Every consciousness pursues the death of the other." The story's roots in autobiographical reality need not concern us: what matters is the way in which sexual (and, more generally, intellectual) jealousy is exploited and represented in this existentialist analysis of human relationships.[31]

Beauvoir's novel presents a triangular relationship in ways that consistently attempt to overturn the clichés associated with such patterns. To insist on the difference between her ideal couple, falsely figured at the beginning of the novel as

30. For an imaginative and sympathetic reading of this novel in the broader context of Beauvoir's production, see Françoise Rétif, "Simone de Beauvoir et l'autre," *Les Temps modernes* 538 (May 1991): 76–95. Rétif argues that Beauvoir's vision of a masculine response to the other here (the murder of Xavière seen as an aping by the woman of male ways of dealing with problems) is merely a stage that carries within it the seeds of a more radical response. Further studies of the novel can be found in *Roman 20–50* 13 (1992), a special number devoted to *L'Invitée* and *Les Mandarins*.

31. For biographical background, see Deirdre Bair, *Simone de Beauvoir: A Biography* (New York: Summit, 1990), and Claude Francis and Fernande Gontier, *Simone de Beauvoir* (Paris: Librairie académique Perrin, 1985).

existing timelessly in a "radiant and cloudless happiness,"[32] and a couple likely to be torn asunder by a triangular relationship, Beauvoir provides an almost entirely unsympathetic picture of three minor characters, Claude, Elisabeth and Suzanne, whose jealous spats, presented through Françoise's external viewpoint, appear merely debasing. The central couple, Pierre and Françoise, whose code of conduct theoretically allows complete freedom to each partner, based on the conviction that love has little to do with ownership and petty jealousies, consciously invite into their circle a young woman whose constant presence and irreducible individuality, acting like grit in an oyster, produces the destructive pearl that throws into question not merely the harmony, but the basic premises of the couple's conception of themselves as couple and of Françoise's image of herself as individual. Whereas neither Françoise nor Pierre challenges the other's self-image, so close is their apparent harmony (or, rather, so willing is Françoise to accept Pierre's image not only of himself, but of her as well), the young woman they choose to support, Xavière, refuses to alter her own vision of herself to conform to their desires, and in so doing forces Françoise to perceive herself no longer as an existence *pour soi*, but as she is seen by others, the *être pour autrui* she cannot bear to be.

While Françoise and Pierre convince themselves that they are acting only in Xavière's interests in attempting to transform her negative view of herself, her conviction of her own worthlessness, and her refusal to make a success of her life, Beauvoir's novel reveals the extent to which this ostensible act of charity in fact denies the other's right to self-determination. However hostile Françoise may feel about the way in which Xavière is reduced to a merely reproductive role by her uncle's plans for her, she blinds herself to the fact that her own vision of the young woman's future is also an imposition on the freedom of another human being: "She's so spineless. She would never have the strength of mind to train for a profession. And the only prospect her uncle can think of for her is a devoted

---

32. Simone de Beauvoir, *She Came to Stay*, trans. Yvonne Moyse and Roger Senhouse (London: Fontana, 1984), 23.

husband and a lot of children" (15). Not only is this assessment
of Xavière shown to be tragically false, but also Pierre's solution, which merely gives expression to Françoise's own
thoughts, is just as reductive as the uncle's, although the terms
are less traditional: "Why don't you bring her to Paris? [. . .]
You could keep an eye on her, and make her work. Let her
learn to type, and we can easily find a job for her somewhere"
(68). Clues scattered through the novel about the folly of such
an undertaking are ignored. Françoise throws aside a manuscript that she has been asked to read and that is subtitled *The
Incomplete Metamorphosis* and deliberately misreads her own
disorderly response to the way in which Pierre treats Xavière
as a person in her own right:

> perhaps she ought to attribute her uneasiness of this evening
> to jealousy; she had not liked Pierre taking Xavière seriously,
> she had been worried by the smiles Xavière gave Pierre. It was
> a passing depression, cause largely by fatigue. If she spoke of
> it to Pierre, it would become a disquieting and gripping reality
> instead of a fleeting mood. Thenceforth, he would have to
> bear it in mind even when she herself attached no importance
> to it. No, there was nothing to it, she wasn't jealous.[33]

This passage reveals Françoise's fear of presenting to Pierre an
image of herself counter to the one that she wishes to offer and
that he is willing to impose. Moreover, the image of herself as
jealous is already rendered repulsive because it would mirror
her own vision of the jealous Elisabeth and would henceforth
color all Pierre's visions of her, making her a fixed subject
rather than one still in the process of forging itself. Such a
metamorphosis is unacceptable for her. Hence she chooses to
deny a truth evident to the reader and in so doing takes the
first clear step into an existence which is other-directed, the
être pour autrui of existentialist terminology.

Furthermore, Françoise's refusal or inability to take Xavière
seriously, to consider her as an *être pour soi et en soi* results

33. Ibid., 60. For Françoise, as for Flaubert, therefore, words are rolling-mills
that stretch emotions out.

in Françoise herself being reduced to silence, washed out of the picture: "Françoise heard Pierre's analysis with annoyance; she had never suggested anything but entertainment to Xavière. Once again she had not taken her seriously enough. And now Pierre was trying to reach an understanding with Xavière over her head" (104). As the plot unfolds, it is the initially characterless Xavière who assumes more and more identity, while Françoise herself fades into featurelessness, reduced to the pallor of an image: "With calm audacity, Xavière chose to assert herself. Her reward was that she had a definite place in the world and Pierre turned to her with passionate interest. Françoise had not dared to be herself, and she understood, in a passion of suffering, that this hypocritical cowardice had resulted in her being nothing at all" (288). Pierre, for all he is presented as treating Xavière seriously, is shown as essentially incapable of accepting her as an individual: "Pierre was so constituted that he did not take much pleasure nature in the moments when Xavière was pleasant to him; on the other hand, her slightest frown convulsed him with rage and remorse. To be at peace with hinself, he had to feel that she was in his power" (141–42). Torn by jealousy himself, he even descends to depths that erase our earlier image of him, an image carefully built up by Françoise to present him as hero: when, in Françoise's presence, he peers through Xavière's keyhole to see if she is with another man, he expunges both the happiness of the evening they have just spent and the picture she had scrupulously attempted to maintain of him. Here the static chatter of jealousy not only drowns out the present, but also distorts irremediably the memories of the past.

Xavière's reaction to the situation is powerful, often physical, and predominantly sexual. The burning cigarette butt she publicly plunges into her hand in punishment for failure is both a clear sexual symbol and an easily read rejection of the partnership between Françoise and Pierre (292). Even her room is transformed into a spatial symbol of self-affirmation, a refusal to be silenced by the imposition on her of identities created by others: "It was not only a sanctuary where Xavière celebrated her own worship; it was a hot-house in which flourished a luxuriant and poisonous vegetation" (274).

When Xavière discovers that Françoise has made love to Gerbert, with whom she herself is in love, she forces Françoise to see herself as others see her, a woman who would seek a petty revenge to salve her own pangs of jealousy. What Françoise had chosen to perceive as an "an innocent love" has become, indelibly, a "sordid betrayal" (406). Rather than acknowledge this image of herself and go beyond it, Françoise allows herself to become entirely other-directed, presenting herself as victim: "she was at the mercy of this voracious consciousness that had been waiting in the shadow for the moment to swallow her up" (406). This destruction of self can be solved only by destroying the other, and the novel concludes with Françoise turning on the gas jet while Xavière sleeps. Though Beauvoir chooses to conclude on an apparently triumphant note—"She had at last made a choice. She had chosen herself" (409)—an earlier statement belies such triumph in its pessimistic anguish: "how was a consciousness not her own capable of existing?" (408). Killing Xavière will not solve such a hydra-headed problem.

Jealousy is troped here as the force that reveals the existence of the other as irreducible other, a force that can be overpowered only by the definitive and physical silencing either of the self or of the other. Despite all its philosophical trappings, the story remains precisely what Pierre had hoped it would never become, ignoble, no doubt because the apparent sophistication of the pact of sexual freedom made no allowance for the crude intensity of sexual realities, attempting to silence a voice that ends by silencing the would be silencers.

Whereas *She Came to Stay* thus chooses to focus on a single other person to exploit the chaotic forces of jealousy, and thus reveal the disruptive power of passion in a world in which the other is quintessentially threatening, the self is frequently depicted as becoming suddenly aware of its own fragility through a rapidly increasing chorus of other voices, released, once again, by the emotion of jealousy. Colette's brief but powerful *Duo*, for instance, concentrates with particular intensity on the ways in which jealousy obliterates not merely the couple's union, but also the male protagonist's self-image. As the unintended reader of letters revealing that his wife has had a brief and purely physical affair with a colleague, he releases, and in turn becomes the victim of, a violent response that eventually leads to his suicide. From his initial discovery that his wife has lied to him, Michel's position is one of outrage, marked above all by a refusal to listen and a determination not merely to silence any attempt at explanation, but also to destroy the image of himself, of his wife, and of his rival that his reading has set in train:

> "Listen, Michel . . . you'll understand. . . ."
> He gave a twisted laugh, raising his hand: "Oh! come now . . . Not likely . . . That'd surprise me. . . ."[34]

Colette tightens the screws in this depiction of jealousy by presenting a couple whose social standing means that they are rarely alone, constantly risking being seen, heard, or otherwise interpreted by servants, whose views (real or imagined) of their masters add yet more static to the line. When Alice, attempting to convince Michel of the insignificance of what she has done, agrees to his imposition of the word *ignominy* to replace her term, *folly*, she finds him so eager to silence whatever else she might want to say that she is compelled to raise her voice, despite the presence of alien ears in a nearby room:

> "No, no, no! You won't interrupt me all the time!" she shouted, suddenly, opening eyes that were almost blue in the penumbra. "You'll let me say what I have to say! . . ."
> With a silent bound, he reached the half-closed door, shut it carefully and noiselessly, and said: "Are you out of your mind? They're there, having lunch, in the kitchen. . . . Anyone would say . . . really they'd say. . . . Well I never! And have you remembered the mail man must be on his way up the hill?" (49–50)

That sense of others interpreting, producing multiple images of a self that seeks to impose a single image, is, of course, an extension of the jealous lover's dread of how he will appear in

34. Colette, *Duo* (Paris: Hachette, 1985), 33.

the mind of his victorious rival. Michel's concept of love carries with it, in Colette's philosophy, the concomitant punishment: conceived in terms of battles and victories, it forces a corresponding series of terms that portray jealousy as defeat and rout.

Moreover, by constraining the jealous lover to see himself differently, Michel's personal image of love also obliges him to see the beloved differently: "In his misery he turned away from the feverish Alice, grown ugly and with her hair in disorder, because she no doubt looked like that Alice whom another man had defeated" (52). The choice of word, "defeated," given extra stress by its position at the end of the sentence, reveals that for Michel love is nothing but a play for power, in which Alice is condemned always to be the loser, but which he, too, loses if she is "defeated" by a man other than himself. That she herself might choose is not an option he is willing to entertain.

Colette also explores the gap between the responses of her male and female characters by depicting each listening, separately, to the calls of the nightingales. For Michel, the focus of attention is, first, the way in which one bird drowns out the voices of all the others, and, second, the possibility of silencing his own wild thoughts by concentrating mechanically on the rhythms of the song:

> A nightingale, the closest among all those who, day and night, were wasting away in melody around their full nests, covered all the other voices, and Michel concentrated on following the long, identical notes, each reinforcing the others. He noted the "tz, tz, tz," which he compared to the sound made by curtain rings sliding along a copper rod, the "coti, coti, coti" repeated up to twenty times without stopping or breathing. . . . He took no pleasure in this, but, as he measured his breathing against the duration of an inextinguishable song, it provoked a kind of suffocation that prevented him from thinking and he no longer felt anything but the need to drink. (64)

A comparison with Alice's reaction, although it is explored in lesser detail, corresponds to recent studies of ways in which men, at a meeting, seek to dominate, while women attempt to find a concordance of views: "Left on her own, [Alice] in her turn listened to the nearby nightingale's song, against a constant background of distant nightingales. The nearest one poured out his heart in an ample, flawless, virtuoso voice, a brilliance and elegance that distanced all emotion. But during the moments when this one fell silent, the softened choir of far-off singers came back to life, independent but in tune, scorning rest beside their incubating females" (68). Alice's tendency to react not just to the dominant voice but to the chorus as a whole symbolizes her complex response to a situation rendered increasingly violent by Michel's tendency to focus precisely on the loudest song. One might note, too, that whereas for Michel the female is seen as passive (as we have already noted, in imagining the adultery he sees Alice as *defeated*, and he alludes only metonymically to the female nightingales through the reference to *full nests*), Alice thinks of the female nightingales as actively at work, incubating the eggs.

Moreover, when Michel attempts to theorize about women in general, to make them all conform to a dominant model that corresponds not to any external truth but only to his own illusory hopes, Alice (and therefore the reader, given this particular focalization) hears his diatribe only in confused fragments, as uninterpretable as the song of the nightingale (172–73).

Michel's inability to listen to the voice of reason, his constant attempts to reduce Alice to silence, and the incessantly renewed fear of how he now appears to others, can lead only to a violent silencing of himself. The novel's final paragraph suggests, through the fierce dichotomy between style and content, the long series of disparities the narrative has been exploring—between husband and wife, between images of love and eroticism in the two sexes, between before and after, between Michel's self-image and the image he fears others will now have of him, between the beauty of nature and the ugliness of human relationships: "He threw himself down the slope, crossed the thicket where night still held sway, and felt under his feet, heavy, held back by its iron-bearing clay, the river that lapped gently and silently against the broken fence of the estate" (227). Once the enclosed world of the couple has been violated by the wild influx of water, the jealous lover heads down a slippery slope toward an ultimate silence.

While the silencing of self results here from the inability to overcome an image putatively produced by a rival, literary texts also draw on the possibilities of jealousy provoked by other avatars of the self. Gide's homosexual adolescent in *The Counterfeiters*, for instance, attempts suicide after his first night of love in the fear that no future moment will be so perfect and that he will be left with a constant nostalgia for his lost self, the one for whom such elation was possible. And Mallarmé's Hérodiade, gazing at the metallic perfection of her beauty in a fountain, becomes aware that her lips are transforming themselves into flowers: whether one sees her as female Narcissus on the brink of metamorphosis or as icy virgin about to enter sexual womanhood, she reveals a violent sense of jealousy in regard to her own purity, a zealous longing to stop the forward movement of time in order to preserve her own self-image intact.

A frequent paradigm of such silencing is that of the replacement of the beloved or the rival by a picture, or symbol, or token of his or her presence. This blatant reification of the other, which is one of the most habitually employed mechanisms of Ovid's *Metamorphoses*, is perhaps the area in which jealousy—whether it be a fear of losing self-identity or more generally the fear of losing primary place in another's affections—becomes most clearly associated with the desire to dominate and control the other. Pan, making do with the reeds into which Syrinx had been metamorphosed, remarks: *"This much I have,"*[35] as though the fact of possession counted for more than what was actually possessed and continues to name the reed pipes he fashions, *"syrinx,"* as if there were no difference between nymph and instrument, woman and object. Moreover, Mercury tells the tale of the pipes' invention to allay the fears of Argus, who has been set to watch over Io to assuage Juno's jealousy and who is, therefore, himself an archetypal icon of jealousy. Mercury's ploy works so well that Argus falls asleep and his hundred eyes fail to perform the service Juno

35. Ovid, *Metamorphoses*, 25.

has demanded of them. Jealousy, so the parable suggests, is overcome not merely by the telling of tales, but also by the transmutation of love to art and woman to object: both the tale of Syrinx's fate and the music Mercury plays on the pipes lull the normally unassailable representative of jealousy and thus bring about his destruction.

Choosing to give one's attention to a talismanic representation of the beloved rather than risk the dominance, mutability, and possible rejection of the beloved in person is a frequently exploited narrative device, and one that tropes the relationship of literature and life. The Princesse de Clèves gazing at the portrait of M. de Nemours while she ties ribbons, in the colors that betoken him, around a walking stick that had formerly belonged to him is clearly doing what male protagonists are so often depicted as doing, reducing the individual beloved to the form of a fetish that can be dealt with more conveniently and less dangerously. Dorothy Kelly, in her interesting series of psychoanalytical readings of voyeuristic scenes in novels, *Telling Glances*, is perhaps too eager in insisting that the princess as *voyeuse* is unusual in playing a game habitually limited to men. The princess, when she gazes at Nemours's portrait and later when she watches him without his knowing she is there, is employing a device literature and folklore frequently show to be exploited by both sexes alike: that of transferring to the inanimate those emotions that could be dangerous and destructive if revealed to the person the inanimate object betokens.

Nemours, for his part, has no need to behave in such a way, because he has no reason to fear either the princess or his own emotions. Jealousy is not a motivating force within him, because he is already convinced she loves him: "Let me see you love me, beautiful princess [. . .] let me see what you feel. If only I can learn the truth from you one single time in my life, I'll allow you to resume forever the harsh treatment with which you punish me."[36] Although no sense of jealousy may be aroused in him by the picture, the princess herself, jealously eager to retain her own self-image and her integrity in a society

36. Madame de La Fayette, *La Princesse de Clèves* (Paris: Livre de Poche, 1958), 205.

whose innate destructiveness we have already seen, knows
that she can survive only by such transference of emotions
from living individual to lifeless portrait.

The German Romantic writer E. T. A. Hoffmann, whose tale
The Sandman inspired much of Freud's *The Uncanny*, frequently has his characters resort to similar devices to protect
themselves from the ravages of jealousy, either their own, that
of their partner, or that of society itself. In *The Golden Pot*,
Anselmus, the student torn between the philistine attractions
of bourgeois existence exemplified in Veronica and the call of
art embodied in the beautiful emerald-green snake Serpentina,
finds himself reduced in size and imprisoned within one of the
crystal bottles in Archivist Lindhorst's library when a night of
punch-drinking has so traduced his artistic abilities as to make
him to drop a blot on the parchment from which he is copying.
While the miniature version of himself he perceives may or
may not be his reflection in the Elbe as he stands on the bridge,
it is certain that the small-minded vision of the *bürgerliche*
Philistines who surround him and who mock his artistic pre-
tensions and aims do threaten to cut him down and reproduce
themselves in him, whereas Lindhorst's artistic demands eventually transport him to that "manor in Atlantis" that is the
domain of "life in Poetry."[37] In other words, Anselmus's vision
of himself in miniature form, imprisoned in glass, represents a
sudden moment of awareness of the way in which accepting
society's demands of him and refusing the call of his artistic
vocation will reduce him to a mere object and strip him forever
of his inner identity. Here, it is the jealousy of the bourgeois
society that transforms him temporarily into object, and Anselmus's own jealous determination to preserve his ambitions
that allows him to see what others consistently misread.

A more modern and decidedly feminist version of this jealousy of the self-image under threat from external readings and
expectations is provided in Margaret Atwood's witty novel,
The Edible Woman. Marian, gradually reaching a realization
of what being a woman means in the society of her time and
place, symbolizes her rejection of that role by creating a cake

37. E. T. A. Hoffmann, *Fantasiestücke* (Munich: Winkler Verlag, 1967), 254.

in female form which she offers to her fiancé, Peter: " 'You've been trying to destroy me, haven't you,' she said. 'You've been trying to assimilate me. But I've made you a substitute, something you'll like much better. This is what you really wanted all along, isn't it.' "[38] When he leaves without tasting it, Marian starts on the cake herself, judging it with the acerbity it needs: "Not bad, she thought critically; needs a touch more lemon though" (285). And just to show how well she has learnt society's protective tricks, she herself imagines Peter in reductive form:

> Already the part of her not occupied with eating was having a wave of nostalgia for Peter, as though for a style that had gone out of fashion and was beginning to turn up on the sad Salvation Army clothes racks. She could see him in her mind, posed jauntily in the foreground of an elegant salon with chandeliers and draperies, impeccably dressed, a glass of scotch in one hand; his foot was on the head of a stuffed lion and he had an eye-patch over one eye. Beneath one arm was strapped a revolver. Around the margin was an edging of gold scrollwork and slightly above Peter's left ear was a thumbtack. (285)

The novel leaves open the possibility that her lover Duncan is correct when he tells her that it was she herself who was attempting to destroy Peter and not he who wanted to assimilate her: certainly this image of Peter hanging in the clothes-racks makes such a reading feasible. That ambiguity, of course, is part of what makes *The Edible Woman* so witty an evocation of the self's constant, jealous protection of itself within a society that constantly demands of women self-abnegation.

The shift of pronoun from first person in the first half of the novel to third in the second half exemplifies Blanchot's dictum: "Move from the I to the He, so that what happens to me, happens to no one."[39] But it also sets in train a mode of per-

---

38. Margaret Atwood, *The Edible Woman* (New York: Bantam, 1970), 284.
39. Maurice Blanchot, *L'Espace littéraire* (Paris: Gallimard, 1968), 27. See also Ellen Peel, "Subject, Object, and the Alternation of First- and Third-Person Narration in Novels by Alther, Atwood, and Drabble: Toward a Theory of Feminine

ception that reifies and alienates the other, much as Marion feels society alienates her, and much as she, too, can perceive in her work mates only that which is irreducibly other, rather than seeing how much their foibles are also hers. Certainly the final phrase, Duncan's comment: "It was delicious," where the "it" might be the cake, the situation, or the novel itself sets in train in the reader's mind a series of interpretations and sequels that refuse closure, and thus jealously guards against the death by silence that would otherwise be the end of the affair and the end of the text.

One final example will illustrate how jealousy crystallizes around itself images of silencing, fetishism, and the destruction of the other in ways that are not merely of psychological interest, but also suggest narrative strategies. Michel Tournier's series of tales *Le Médianoche amoureux* are told at a banquet, ostensibly to mark the end of a love affair. In fact, the stories provide the couple with "a house of words to live in together" as the woman puts it, or, as the man expresses it, transforms them from "two carp huddled in the mud of [their] every day lives" to "two trout trembling side by side in the water of a mountain torrent."[40] The way in which the two fields of metaphors remain so resolutely separate may well suggest, not that the couple can never find complete union, but that, unlike the sand-sculptured homogeneous lovers on the beach whose forms melted with the incoming tide, their acceptance of each other's differences and the ability of each to maintain their own identity within their union will guarantee its future. Set against this frame story, "Lucie ou la femme sans ombre" tells of multiple unhappy love stories, reinforcing by counterexample the need for lovers to keep alive to the voice of the other.

Ambroise, who tells the story, explains that he has given its heroine the name Lucie "because there is *Lucie* in *elucidate*, and because it is also the story of an elucidation which was, in a sense, catastrophic" (131). The ten-year-old Ambroise, whose schoolteacher Lucie is (and Tournier, with typically

---

Aesthetics," *Critique: Studies in Contemporary Fiction* 30, 2 (1989): 107–22. Peel argues that "in patriarchy, a woman may refer to herself as 'she' rather than 'I' because of alienation from herself rather than a healthy detachment."
40. Michel Tournier, *Le Médianoche amoureux* (Paris: Gallimard, 1989), 42.

heavy-footed humor, draws lengthy attention to the ambiguity of the word *maîtresse*, meaning both schoolmistress and lover), returns home one evening to learn that his mother has left his father. The latter, incapable no doubt of formulating the words: "My wife has left me," announces to their son: "Son, your mother has left you." Distraught, the boy seeks consolation in the arms and bed of Lucie. This precipitates in his father a surge of vindictive jealousy, which destroys not only whatever relationship existed between father and son, but also Lucy's marriage and much of her personality. Dismissed for corrupting a minor, as a result of the complaint made by Ambroise's father, Lucie loses her sense of self, a loss "cured" by the psychologist who encourages her to separate herself from the fetishistic doll who represents her dead sister as well as herself. But the loss of the doll, although it may improve Lucie's sanity in general, social terms, leads to the loss of her self-identity: the Lucie that Ambroise meets in adulthood bears little relationship to the schoolmistress he so loved.

The letter her husband writes to Ambroise in explanation both of her metamorphosis and of the disintegration of their marriage indicates that this loss of Lucie's shadow, this entry into the bright light of normality, has also made it impossible for him to paint, to capture what he calls Lucie's *irisation* of the world around her. Tournier here evokes through a brilliant and characteristic metaphor the way in which the dark force of jealousy, matched with the demands of convention, crushes the individuality of the other. Although he makes use of the traditional image of silencing, for Lucie does not tell her story directly, speaking instead through her husband and through Ambroise, Tournier transforms the conventional metaphor of noise and silence into one of color and darkness and overturns expectations by insisting on the need for shadows and colors as well as pure white light if the individual is to remain fully alive. Lucie's transmutation to pure light and the destruction of the shadow represented by the doll break the intertwining of her life and the being of her dead sister, destroys her powers of enriching life, and reduces her to a two-dimensional existence.

Ambroise's conclusion suggests, however, that jealousy's

power to silence is limited in that he himself refuses to obey it, to turn the page, as Lucie's husband enjoins him to do. "I have locked that shadow away forever in my heart," he insists (158): as so often, Tournier here takes familiar topoi—the reduction of the other to fetish, the image of the shadow as negative—and transforms them into powerful forces for good: the fetish is no longer reduction but a means of offering continuity to the dead, and the shadow, no longer associated with the dark, destructive face of existence, becomes that without which light is leached of color. Tournier's short story, the riches of which I have only touched on here, reveals that the etymological links between zealous and jealous can be renewed in ways that transform the silencing power of a destructive jealousy into the creative powers of a life-giving and life-affirming love.

Literature, therefore, depicts jealousy as frequently attempting to control the other—beloved, rival, or reader—by reducing him or her to controllable size or by silencing them, physically or figuratively, in order to deny their image of the self as other. In so doing, these texts reproduce images of the way in which they themselves strive to remove the interference of outside voices and to dominate the way in which the reader responds to them, making of jealousy itself a trope for a wide range of literary and readerly strategies. Yet there are moments when the response to jealousy is not to deny the alienation of the self from the beloved and the rival, but rather to see it as inevitable and to react to it not by imposing the self, but, on the contrary, by attempting to make oneself identical with the other. It is on this strategy, which touches on techniques of the fantastic and overlaps with pastiche, parody, and plagiarism, that my next chapter will concentrate.

4 Mirroring Jealousy: Avatars of Amphytrion

> Hitherto she had but beheld the feeling of jealousy, but now she witnessed the livid passion of jealousy writhing in every lineament of a human face. That terrible passion had transfigured its victim in a moment: the ruddy, genial, kindly Griffith, with his soft brown eyes, was gone; and in his place lowered a face, older and discolored, and convulsed, and almost demoniacal.
>
> Charles Reade, *Griffith Gaunt*

A. S. Byatt makes explicit what might seem to be a central element of the seduction and intimacy of reading when she invites us to "Think of this—the writer wrote alone, and the reader read alone, and they were alone with each other."[1] But with whom, precisely, is the reader alone? And with what reader is the writer alone? Between reader and writer surfaces, minimally, the third instance of the text, which, despite all the best efforts of both, is no mere mirror and certainly can never be a two-way mirror. As such, the situation of reading echoes the polygonal nature of jealousy and intensifies as much the aloneness as the togetherness of reader and writer, or, perhaps more accurately, it draws attention to the multiplicity of individuals present at this apparent tête-à-tête. Many writers have, therefore, chosen to exploit a situation they cannot avoid, knowing that their readers will escape textual tyranny by misreading what lies before them, as Nabokov's *Pale Fire*

---

1. A. S. Byatt, *Possession: A Romance* (London: Vintage, 1990), 471.

so amply illustrates. Intertextual references and postmodernism's delight in playing with allusions and echoes in part override the potential disruptions breaking the contact between writer and reader by incorporating other voices into the text and making them part of the writer's own voice, thus simultaneously subverting and exploiting the anxiety of influence. But what if the incorporator is in turn incorporated? Numerous basic scenarios in mythology and literature, from Oedipus to the body snatchers, suggest such a fear.

Giraudoux's play, *Amphytrion 38*, illustrates beautifully and at several levels the jealous lover's and the jealous writer's desire to replace the successful rival by becoming that rival. Alcmene, loving only her husband, Amphytrion, can be won by another, so it would seem, only if that other becomes Amphytrion himself. But if Jupiter makes himself into his rival's double, to what extent is he still Jupiter? How far, in other words, does he replace his rival? In Giraudoux's version of the myth, Alcmene forces Jupiter to recognize that she never saw through his disguise and indeed took him for Amphytrion. As a result, Jupiter has to acknowledge that Alcmene was victorious over him. The price of retaining his inner self, his instantly recognizable quiddity, would be the failure to seduce the beloved (or perhaps in this case merely the desired). And what, after all, is the point of completely usurping the identity of the other, when the self wants to be loved or desired for itself?

Giraudoux's finely witty play, moreover, moves that question into the domain of authorial as well as sexual jealousy through its very title. This, so its author claims, is the thirty-eighth version of the myth and therefore apparently a mere reworking of a well-known story. Giraudoux's image, however playful, touches here on the area of plagiarism and pastiche, so brilliantly and playfully explored by psychoanalyst Michel Schneider in *Voleurs de mots*. The very etymology of "plagiarism," as Schneider reminds us, suggests the theft not so much of an object as of a person. I, as writer, set out to seduce you, reader or audience, by presenting as mine an idea that belongs to someone else; I thus masquerade as another person. Usurping authority, as Jupiter attempts to usurp the husband's dominion, the writer hopes to gain what is otherwise denied him or her. But Giraudoux draws such obvious attention to this device and reveals Jupiter's failure so wittily that he seems cheerfully to acknowledge that such usurpation is doomed to miscarry, that plagiarism cannot deck itself out successfully as ownership and invention.

Yet here, of course, lies Giraudoux's own distortion of his manifest message: the apparent openness of the title, which draws our attention to the previous versions of the Amphytrion story, is less an acknowledgment of plagiarism than a challenge to us to see his play as more audacious, more imaginative, profounder, and wittier than its predecessors. Here, in other words, Giraudoux attempts to subsume all the previous versions into his own, to draw on them only in order to go beyond them and thus to defeat his rivals, while avoiding the need to appear, not as Alcmene's beloved, but as a mere simulacrum. Just as the protean nature of Jupiter is shown to be outweighed by the uniqueness of Amphytrion, so the myth's numerous incarnations are presented as being outshone by Giraudoux's re-creation.

Above all, Giraudoux relies on a subtle and typically Gallic piece of flattery: as decoders and manipulators of the plots (Jupiter's and Giraudoux's plots), we are figured in the text by Alcmene herself, since it is she who, by taking for granted Amphytrion's uniqueness, succeeds in forcing Jupiter to accept her as unique, when he had wanted to make her a mere simulacrum by adding her to his list of conquests. The intelligence, humor, and tact of Alcmene thus become our own if we are willing to enter into this game on Giraudoux's own terms and acknowledge essential difference masquerading as mere repetition.

While the frothy, bitter-sweet subtlety of Giraudoux's play has a seductive charm all its own, the questions it raises about the relationship between self and other, text and reader, jealousy and rivalry had already been treated, but in a very different manner, by Giraudoux's compatriot, Rostand. In his entertaining, if lightweight, play, *Cyrano de Bergerac*, he creates a poignant image of the relationship connecting voice, medium, and recipient as well as among actor, dramatist, and audience. Moreover, this highly self-reflective play introduces a variant on the more traditional image of substituting oneself for the rival, in that it is by combining their gifts that the rivals create a figure who can win the beloved. Rostand seems here to be creating a new model of desire and a new version of crystallization, because the two male lovers respond to the female lover's complex image of perfection by creating a third persona that is little more than crystallized perfection.

Cyrano belives himself too ugly ever to win women's affection. As he puts it: "I'm forbidden to dream even of being loved by an ugly woman, thanks to this nose that wherever I go gets there fifteen minutes before me."[2] Because Cyrano can pour out his words of love only on paper or in the dark, and only on behalf of another man, he becomes, therefore, the image of the dramatist, whose seduction of the audience can operate only in favor of the actor who mouths his words. Yet for the audience who first saw this play in the aftermath of the Franco-Prussian war, it carried other messages, too, since, as Willy de Spens argues, "the embodiment of the Gallic rooster, Cyrano, with his provocations, his panache could not fail to seduce an audience wounded in its patriotic feelings by the defeat of 1870 and longing to be revenged on the enemy" (9). To the composite lover who projects Roxane's sexual desire is added, in other words, the composite hero who responds to the audience's political desires. Generous and exuberant, Cyrano combines numerous archetypal heroes: Don Quixote, to whom the duc de Guiche sinisterly compares him; Braggadaccio, but a Braggadaccio whose deeds outstrip his boasting; Dumas's image of the perfect musketeer, Dartagnan. In making his character recall, but surpass, these figures, Rostand is offering a further, literary, dimension to the image of the combined suitor, with these echoes of other heroes giving further force to the play in its attempted seduction of the reader.

Yet what makes Cyrano unique is his delight in the creation of rhetoric and poetry and the moral importance he attaches to the ability to produce it. When he discovers that Roxane, whom he had believed was on the point of confessing her love

2. Edmond Rostand, *Cyrano de Bergerac*, ed. Willy de Spens (Paris: Garnier Flammarion, 1989), 85.

for *him*, is infatuated with Christian de Neuvillette, whom she has seen but never spoken to, Cyrano's pain and jealousy find expression in his questioning not of Neuvillette's character, but of his control of language:

> CYRANO: "My poor child, you who love only fine words, beautiful spirit,—what if he were wild and profane?"
> ROXANE: "No, his hair is like that of a d'Urfé hero!"
> CYRANO: "What if he spoke as poorly as his hair is well dressed?"
> ROXANE: "No, every word he pronounces is fine, I can foretell!" (121)

While Cyrano takes for granted that Roxane will value physical beauty, he makes clear that what would cause him most distress would be the discovery that Christian lacked Cyrano's own intellectual, and especially verbal, prowess. Jealousy in this case clearly concerns the individual's self-image, a point revealed by the need to feel that the rival is worthy to share the same riverbank as the jealous and unhappy lover. Rostand emphasizes the link between sexual jealousy and Cyrano's intellectual and rhetorical skills when the duc de Guiche intimates to him that Richelieu would make it possible for him to see his five-act tragedy *Agrippine* staged. While the thought of this possibility makes Cyrano, according to the stage instructions, feel "tempted and somewhat charmed" (132), de Guiche's qualification unleashes in Cyrano a sense of jealous pride in his own independence:

> DE GUICHE: "He is one of the most expert. He will merely correct the odd line for you. . . ."
> CYRANO, whose face has immediately assumed a scowl: "Impossible, sir! My blood runs cold [*se coagule*] at the thought that even a comma [*virgule*] might be changed" (132).

The virtuoso rhyming here (particularly "*coagule*" and "*virgule*") self-consciously and playfully underlines the central importance placed on the expression, as well as the emotion, of love.

Given Christian's inability to produce the kind of rhetoric Roxane admires, rival and lover must fuse to create the ideal partner for her, as actor and playwright fuse to create the stage or screen image that seduces the audience:

> CYRANO: Since you're afraid that if you're alone you'll cool down her heart, would you like us—and soon you will set her on fire!—to blend together a while your lips and my lines? (149).

The embrace that seals the pact between the two men underscores the fusion of the two identities into one. Yet it would surely be to misread and diminish the play to see it as suggesting that here jealousy is primarily an affair between men, with the woman the passive and largely undiscerning prize. It is of course true that, like Giraudoux's Alcmene, Roxane, for all her quick-wittedness, charm, and intrepidity, is not allowed to see through Christian's disguise, even when, in the balcony scene in which Cyrano plays the role of Christian, she comments that neither his voice nor his rhetoric sounds familiar. Nevertheless, she is far from being a mere passive object. On the contrary, she is the desiring subject who forces the amalgamation of her rivals and who denies each his right to individuality. Indeed, it would be more accurate to claim that here she behaves like so many male heroes in stripping the beloved of uniqueness, thus making him conform to a generalized image of the Beloved.

Nevertheless, the chaotic power of jealousy tears apart such a merger, refusing to allow so simplistic a message to prevail. Cyrano, for instance, is narcissistically aware that the intoxication his words inspire in her is indeed his creation, whether or not that intoxication is directed at him. Such awareness is almost sufficient for his complete happiness: "Then, let death come! This intoxication is caused by me. By me!" (185).

Moreover, if Roxane can find love only when the gifts of two men are combined, she herself forces her unwanted lover, de Guiche, to speak with two voices when she first reads his letter as he wrote it, then gives a revised version of its contents to the monk who has acted as messenger. The letter she reads *sotto voce* goes as follows:

> Mademoiselle, the drums / are beating; my regiment buckles on its armor plating; / it is setting out; as for me, every one thinks I have already left: but I am staying. / I am disobeying you. I am in this convent. / I shall come to you and am sending you prior word / by a monk as simple as a goat / who cannot understand a word of this. Your lips / smiled too much on me today: I wanted to see them once more. / My boldness already forgiven, I hope, / I sign this as your very etc. . . .

The letter she reads aloud, however, forces de Guiche to play a different role:

> Mademoiselle, you must obey the will / of the cardinal, however hard that might appear to you. / This is why I have chosen, to place / these lines in your charming hands, a very holy / very intelligent and very discreet capuchin; / we wish him to give you, in your own home, / the ceremony (*she turns the page*) of marriage immediately. / Christian must become your husband in secret; I am sending him to you. You like him not. Resign yourself. / Remember that heaven will bless your zeal / and that you can be assured, Mademoiselle, / of the respect of him who was and will be / always your very humble and very . . . etc." (193–94)

His jealousy is manipulated by Roxane to stimulate her zeal, forcing him to incorporate into his identity as lover the more powerful identity of the one who brings about her marriage.

This principle of doubling, which mirrors one of the main structures of jealousy, is indeed what lends the play its dynamism, and that dynamism is clearly generated neither by male love, represented by Cyrano, nor by male power, represented by de Guiche. Only at the end of the play, after Christian's death in battle, when the dying Cyrano reads aloud to Roxane the letter of adieu he had written on behalf of his rival, does she realize the identity of the voice she had so loved and thereby replace dualism with a unity doomed to ephemerality:

"I loved but one man and I am losing him for the second time" (299).

The ideal, so Rostand's play suggests, can continue to exist only if it is never put to the test of time: the discovery of Cyrano as lover must herald the end of the relationship between him and Roxane, as it heralds the end of the play, as it is to the tension between physical beauty and rhetorical beauty that the love affair, like the play, owes its existence. As such, *Cyrano de Bergerac* offers a provocative reversal of the usual image of the ideal woman as combining purity and sexuality: just as no one woman can meet Romantic man's aspirations, so here, no one man can satisfy Roxane. In addition to the constant overtones of Cervantes, Ariosto, Shakespeare, and Dumas, a further voice, that of female desire, thus enters this play where the true protagonist must be seen as voice itself.

The interference of one voice by another, the incorporation of one individual by a rival (who may, indeed, be the individual's earlier or later self), forms a paradigm that recurs in literature both at the level of the plot and at that of a work's reception. Critical reactions to a work of literature can certainly be perceived as additional static on the line, coming between writer and reader, and figuring further dimensions of the jealousy often explored within the text. Rostand incorporates this element in his text by means of Cyrano's witty criticisms of what purports to be Christian's, but is in reality his own, statement of love:

> ROXANE: "Just listen to a bit of this: *she recites:* / 'The more you take my heart, the more heart I have ... !' " *Triumphant.* "Well? What do you say?"
> CYRANO: "Bah!"
> ROXANE: "And this: 'So that I may suffer, since I need another if you keep my heart, send me your own!' "
> CYRANO: "Sometimes he has too much heart and sometimes not enough. / Just how much does he want, after all?"
> ROXANE, stamping her foot: "You're devoured by jealousy!"
> CYRANO: "What!"
> ROXANE: "An author's jealousy!" (161)

The intricate interweaving of literary and sexual jealousy and the attempt to defuse external criticism by incorporating criticism into the text itself are not uncommon devices in texts as self-conscious as Rostand's.

Nevertheless, the voice-over of external criticism cannot always be so easily conjured and counteracted. The novels of Christina Stead and the critical responses to them offer interesting and often ironic examples of this unpredictable and uncontrollable interference, especially because she drew so closely on personal experience and based her characters so precisely on people she had known. The resentment at finding her own social voice silenced, and the desire to extract revenge by speaking in a medium in which she could not be silenced, are dominant characteristics in her writing, as, of course, they are for many other writers. Stead's difficult, traumatic, and in many ways destructive relationship with her father during her childhood and adolescence informs and empowers much of her writing.

A love-hate relationship in which she constantly struggled to make her father love her for herself, rather than perceiving her as a mere extension or appendage of himself, it is transformed into the central element of her novel, *The Man Who Loved Children*. As her biographer Hazel Rowley points out, anger was an important element in Stead's inspiration, something that was catastrophic in social terms but creative in literary terms. The ambivalence of her relationship with her father and the channeling of anger into a creative form mingled to create *The Man Who Loved Children*. Sam Pollit, the man of the title, is closely based on Stead's own father, and to help build his image and recapture his personality and voice, she used, more or less verbatim, several of the letters he had written to her in her adolescence. The problem is immediately obvious: once again, almost in spite of herself, Stead is falling silent to allow her father to speak, in the very work that she wrote to free herself of his dominance and to let her own voice be heard. Moreover, that unacknowledged plagiarism was punished as if David Stead enjoyed divine protection, when the critic Clifton Fadiman asserted that although the novel as a whole did not succeed, the letters from Sam Pollit revealed "extraordinary writing."[3] It is as though Fadiman, a sharp-eyed Alcmene, saw in Sam Pollit merely Christina Stead but in the letters David Stead had written perceived his master's voice.

It is, therefore, not enough merely to seize on and mirror certain aspects of the sexual or textual rival in order to rise triumphant above him or her, as Stead attempts to do in this and other novels. Central to what one might call the Amphytrion complex is the need to be recognized through that disguise as oneself, and still triumph, as one might argue Borges's Pierre Menard does in his conscientious plagiarism of *Don Quixote*. While Giraudoux's Jupiter fails in this, it remains the case, of course, that mythology's Jupiter succeeded. Like him, writers of pastiche want not merely to emulate the rival, but to ensure that their own voice is not subsumed by the very mimicry they have created. Proust's pastiches depend on our recognizing them as such and not assuming they are, for instance, unpublished manuscripts of the writers themselves, and when Gérard Genette wrote his brilliant pastiche of *Madame Bovary* it would have failed, for all its brilliance, if it had merely been seen as yet another of Flaubert's countless drafts.

Parodists choose to avoid this danger by so exaggerating the characteristics of their model as to leave their audience in no doubt about who speaks here.[4] The German Romantic writer E. T. A. Hoffmann provides an intelligent and witty variant on the interplay of sexual and literary jealousy through the medium of parody in his novel *Prinzessin Brambilla*, a work that operates simultaneously on several levels. First, there is the love story, where each of the lovers needs to acquire not merely more knowledge of the other, but above all more insight into their own nature. Added to this element there is an exploration of two different forms of theater: tragedy, which has become stale and hackneyed; and comedy, which offers a means of infusing the theater with new vigor while allowing the crowd to

3. Clifton Fadiman, *New Yorker*, 19 October 1940, p. 84. Quoted in Hazel Rowley, *Christina Stead: A Biography* (Melbourne, Australia: Heinemann, 1993), 263.
4. See Linda Hutcheon, *A Theory of Parody: The Teachings of Twentieth-Century Art Forms* (New York: Methuen, 1985). This study also contains a very useful bibliography.

see itself mirrored in the play in ways no longer possible in traditional tragedy. Finally, Hoffmann incorporates into this double framework his myth of love and self-discovery, where the need for self-knowledge is exemplified by the story of King Ophioch and Queen Liris. At all these levels, there is an element of parody in that the love story, tragedy, and Romantic fairy tales are all treated with a degree of caricatural humor.

What is perhaps most arresting in this *capriccio* is Hoffmann's use of sexual jealousy to illuminate other forms of jealousy and particularly the jealous longing to hold power that tragedy reveals when confronted with the surge in popularity of comedy. Rich in carefully orchestrated dichotomies, the novel mirrors its own artistic subtext through a series of aesthetic conversations between the Italian charlatan and puppet player, Celionati, and a group of German artists whose emphasis on a particular kind of irony also provides the reader with a means to decode what might otherwise seem merely a love story. This internal critical commentary, together with various direct references to the reader's power, appears, at least in part, to be an attempt to hamstring or even to harness the force of external critical reaction. Thus, Celionati's parable of Ophioch and Liris is described within the text as both revealing, and figuring through the spring known as the Urdarquelle, the wonderful ability of the mind to create its own ironic double.[5] This kind of self-analysis, especially the ability to perceive the self as its opposite, is represented in the parable by the spring into which the depressive king and the inanely laughing queen gaze, with the result that the king discerns what is comic about his seriousness and the queen finds a seriousness to balance her levity.

More important, the spring is seen to be a metaphor for the theater, that, like the mirror windows on the coach that brings the comic actors into Rome, enables the audience to see themselves for what they are and for what they can be. This duality is not, however, restricted to the level of character, but also dominates the narration itself. Celionati's tale, for example, combines the lofty tone used for fairy stories with far more

5. E. T. A. Hoffmann, *Prinzessin Brambilla* (Oxford: Basil Blackwell, 1972), 50.

salty humor in order to suggest that the new form of theater he promotes and represents incorporates the intellectual demands of tragedy within the overriding tone of comedy.

Exemplary of this duality are the two central characters, the tragic actor Giglio Fava and his fiancée Giacinta Soardi. Because the novel's focalization, while constantly changing in accord with the demands of romantic irony, rarely enters Giacinta's mind, her duality remains merely sketched in, dependent to a large extent on the vivid opening image of her donning the elaborate and expensive dress she has just made for a rich client and imagining that she is the princess for whom the dress was ordered. While Giglio's illusions of grandeur, which are part of what Celionati describes as his chronic dualism, are presented as merely ridiculous delusions, there is a sense that Giacinta's awareness of herself as princess is based more on an understanding of her own artistic and personal potential, an acknowledgment of her own creative skills. Moreover, she is determined to be loved for herself, energetically refusing and ridiculing male Romanticism's demands that women act as mere screens for the man's projected ideal. When Giglio tells her of a dream in which he saw himself loved by a beautiful princess, instead of subsuming her identity into that of the princess, she flies into a fury:

> "What?" Giacinta angrily interrupted the entranced Giglio, "you take it on yourself to dream of another girl than me? You take it on yourself to fall in love as you look at a stupid old dream image?" (10)

Her jealous reaction here suggests that she will not accept any transformation of herself into princess that comes at the cost of losing her own identity as Giacinta.

The novel focuses above all, however, on the development of Giglio from a ham-actor in tragedies to a fine comic hero. One of the central factors that make this metamorphosis possible is jealousy, both sexual and professional. Giglio, convincing himself that he is the prince, Cornelio Chiapperi, whom princess Brambilla loves, decks himself out in comic clothes and enormous glasses, as Celionati advises him to do, and repeatedly encounters a clown figure who appears to be aping him and in whom, eventually, Giglio recognizes his "second ego," his mirror image. Here, as in the best parodies, the closest reflection is provided not by a normal mirror, but, ironically, by a mirror that distorts.

At one point in the novel, Giglio reaches a confused awareness that his jealousy is projected against himself: " 'Aha!' thought Giglio, 'I have only my Self to blame for the fact that I can't see my fiancée, my princess; I can't see through my Self and my damn Self wants to kill me with dangerous weapons, but I'll play and dance it to death and then at last I shall be myself' " (54). His tragedian self is discovered to be a puppet stuffed with rolls of paper (the tragic plays in which he has acted and whose words he often quotes in everyday life). His image of himself as Cornelio Chiapperi is, however, equally flawed, as is revealed when he dresses in the bright clothes he has been assured the princess loves. In this transformation can be heard an echo of Malvolio that incorporates Shakespeare's voice into Hoffmann's text, and just as Malvolio is imprisoned for his false reading both of what he assumes to be Olivia's letters and of his own position, so Giglio finds himself taken for a brightly colored bird and imprisoned in a cage in the Pistoia Palace. Giglio overcomes both forms of jealousy only when he accepts himself as comic actor, transforming his chronic dualism from illness into the very source of his Thespian genius, and when he accepts Giacinta for what she is, realizing that in her he finds all the riches he dreamed of in the princess.

Finally, *Prinzessin Brambilla* abounds in references to its own audience, comically aware that its voice can easily be silenced by a higher authority. The narrative voice frequently addresses the reader directly, attempting to seduce them into reading the work in its entirety before judging it. Thus, at the beginning of the second chapter, Hoffmann confronts and attempts to reduce the static that may have come between text and reader:

Dear Reader, don't be angry if the one who has taken it upon himself to tell you the adventurous story of Princess Brambilla, exactly as he found it indicated in the bold pen strokes of Master Callot, immediately insists that you lend yourself willingly to its marvels at least until the last word in this little book, and, indeed, that you believe even the slightest detail. But perhaps at the moment when the Fairy Tale checked in to the Pistoja Palace, or when the princess arose from the bluish vapor of the wine bottle, you already shouted out: "What stupid grotesque stuff!" and hurled the book away in annoyance, without a thought for the attractive copper plates? Then everything that I'm on the point of saying to you, in order to win you over to the strange magic of Callot's capriccios, would come too late and that would indeed be bad enough for me and for the princess Brambilla! (20–21)

This exclamation is particularly pertinent for our purposes in that it draws specific attention to the Callot plates that have inspired the tale, making the text into a kind of Cyrano de Bergerac, speaking for another, lending words to another. Jealousy here, like the characters of the commedia dell'arte themselves, hides behind a mask in order the better to seduce and appears in the guise of another the better to win the viewer.

The kind of jealousy the writer feels in regard to his or her text and to the reader's response is also revealed in the closing paragraphs, where the reader's skill as critic is thrown into serious doubt by the Fürst von Pistoja's assertion: "Someone, whom we all have greatly to fear, for he certainly expresses harsh criticism of us and may even deny that we exist, could perhaps say that I came here in the middle of the night without any other reason and purely on his behalf [. . .] The someone is wrong" (118). Yet if at the end of the novel the characters deny their absolute dependence on the reader, jealously asserting their own freedom, so also does Celionati throw into doubt the writer's omnipotence, when the German artists treat the charlatan as mere storyteller: "I tell you, when the writer created me, he had something quite different for me in mind, and if he were to see the careless way you so often treat me he'd scarcely believe I'd slipped out his hands in such a way" (102).

Prinzessin Brambilla, therefore, explores the nature of sexual and artistic jealousy, makes of its central tale a mirror for the kind of self-discovery that Romanticism saw as enabling true art, and frees that art from the demeaning restrictions of jealousy. Its incorporation of countless other voices—those of commedia dell'arte, that of Callot in his depiction of comic figures, that of Shakespeare, in whose plays the German and French Romantics found such a potent and inspiring mixture of comic and tragic—also suggests a creative response to textual jealousy, in which the rival is subsumed into the lover, the precursor into the successor.

The image of the writer and lover as actor, thus incorporating the role of the rival, also enables the text to raise questions about the way in which certain elements of society are perceived and to offer rival interpretations of those elements. The dual image of women, for instance, especially the Romantic demand that women be either pure or prurient, sugar-plum fairy or hot-house whore (when they cannot combine and control that dichotomy to become the golden-hearted whore of Hugo's *Marion Delorme* or Dumas's *La Dame aux camélias*) is explored in Balzac's examination of Adeline's jealousy in *La Cousine Bette*. The virtuous and forgiving wife, Adeline, finds that virtue and forgiveness cannot succeed in winning back the affections of her philandering husband, Hector. Driven to desperation by his extravagant spending on his mistresses, Adeline attempts to make herself into the mirror image of her rival, to incorporate within her image as wife that of courtesan. The scene in which she dresses to seduce is a potent depiction of this aspect of jealousy, and one that releases in Balzac's narrator a complex metaphor whose exuberance is matched only by its misogyny: "Woman is man's soup, Molière said jokingly through the mouth of the judicious Gros-René. This comparison presupposes a kind of culinary science in love. The virtuous and worthy woman would then be a Homeric meal, flesh thrown on glowing coals. The courtesan, on the other hand, would be the work of a cordon bleu cook with his condiments, his spices and his elegance."[6] In her longing to emulate the effect of those spices and condiments, Adeline asks Bette how Valérie Marneffe succeeds in her seductions only to receive the

---

6. Honoré de Balzac, *La Cousine Bette* (Paris: Folio, 1972), 316–17. One need hardly point out the crude pun in *culinaire*, which adds to the misogyny of this image.

malicious reply: "There isn't any theory, the only thing that counts in that career is practice." Balzac sums up the image of incorporating the rival and at the same time voices a common male fantasy (at least of the nineteenth century) when he asserts: "To be an honest and prudish woman for the world in general and to turn into a courtesan for her husband is to be a woman of genius, and they are few" (318).

Yet the image of incorporation as a response to jealousy, and particularly of individual women attempting to become both what society demands of women and what husbands or lovers expect them to be, takes on a far more satirical note in texts written by women for a post–women's-liberation audience, an audience, in other words, in which women may set other needs above that of existing in the gaze of men. Angela Carter's exuberant, witty, and frequently sardonic *Wise Children* gives a particular twist to the screw (in both the common and the vulgar sense of the term) by making her principal characters actors and by choosing the make-believe world of Hollywood for one of her settings.[7] Because not only several of the minor characters but also the two protagonists, Nora and the narrator Dora, are twins, the novel is studded with reflected and refracted images of the self, and the difficulty of determining relationships merely adds to the problematics of self-identity (hence the title, suggesting the child's difficulty in correctly and unambiguously identifying its own father and mother). At one point in the novel, the movie mogul known as Genghis Kahn seeks to marry Nora but has to accept her identical twin, Dora, as fiancée. Carter's point here, of course, is that the kind of male Genghis Kahn represents is interested only in physical forms and not in personality, but Carter gives her feminist message even greater force when Dora, wandering through the scene set known as the Forest of Arden (an incorporation of Shakespeare that enforces memories of substitute brides in *Measure for*

7. Angela Carter, *Wise Children* (London: Chatto and Windus, 1991). Although Carter has been accused of pandering to a misogynistic and voyeuristic audience, such attacks, which usually center on her early writing, misread the inherent irony of her texts and have little to do, in any case, with novels such as *Wise Children*. For a reaction to these attacks, see Elaine Jordan, "The Dangers of Angela Carter," in *New Feminist Discourses*, ed. Isobel Armstrong (London: Routledge, 1992), 119–31.

Measure and *All's Well That Ends Well*[8] encounters her *Doppelgänger*: "I saw my double. I saw myself, me, in my Peaseblossom costume, large as life, like looking in a mirror. First off, I thought it was Nora, up to something, but it put its finger to its lips, to shush me, and I got a whiff of Mitsouko and then I saw it was a replica. A hand-made, custom-built replica, a wonder of the plastic surgeon's art. [. . .] Before me stood the exxed Mrs Kahn, who loved her man so much she was prepared to turn herself into a rough copy of his beloved for his sake" (155). Divorced by her husband but still in love, this woman is prepared to suffer physically to change her form, to accept the indignity of being loved as another, merely to overcome her jealousy. With the betrothed Dora now subsumed into her phoney double, the real Dora hides in the costume of a drunken actor: "And so it came to pass that it was as Bottom the Weaver, in plus-fours and an ass's head, that I went to my own wedding. I was beginning to see the funny side. It isn't every day you see yourself get married" (157). The reference to human duality contained in the passing allusion to Bottom, the biblical parody in the telling of the episode (and so it came to pass . . .), and the numerous allusions to Shakespeare's use of mistaken identities for the purposes of plot, all intensify the suggestion that, for Carter, sexual jealousy and literary parody are closely allied. The exxed Mrs. Kahn's face-lift mirrors, therefore, the writer's transformation of self into myriad ancestors.

Jealousy in literature both triggers and tropes that division and multiplication of the self that reveals the fear the individual entertains—as sexual being and as writer—concerning the role of the other—as lover, as reader, as literary ancestor, or sexual successor. The other as both needed and feared can release in the jealous individual that overwhelming desire to subsume all that is exterior to it, hence, at one level at least, the repressive commands of patriarchy. The "all else confusion" that Tennyson's "hard old king" professed to fear, if man did not command and woman obey,[9] is often reflected in narratives

8. Carter, *Wise Children*, 149.
9. Alfred Lord Tennyson, "The Princess," V, lines 440–41, in *The Poems*, ed. Christopher Ricks (Berkeley: University of California Press, 1987), 2: 264.

of jealousy as a compulsive repetition of an original event. Thus, in Musset's *Confession*, the painful relationship between Octave and Brigitte is inescapably stamped with the experience of Octave's first affair. As Richard Terdiman so subtly puts it, the "figural connection between the successive love affairs [. . .] wavers uncertainly between metaphor (the second story is *like* the first) and tautology (the second story uncontrollably *repeats* the first)."[10] Structurally, at least, the exploration of jealousy in *A la recherche* reveals an identical compulsion, with Marcel's story repeating in essence that of Swann. Similarly, Trollope makes explicit in *Kept in the Dark* the repetition of scenarios that is so nearly catastrophic for Western and Cecilia. In this case, the male's sense of uniqueness is challenged both by the discovery that he had a predecessor and by the realization that his story of being jilted mirrors that of Cecilia's jilting of Sir Francis. Trollope's exploration in this novel suggests a form of patterning that sheds further light on the conclusion of *He Knew He Was Right*. Indeed, although the latter novel seems to set up as counterfoils for Trevelyan's mad tyranny, three men whose relationships with their wives apparently offer a more harmonious distribution of power, its underlying patterns imply that under pressure all three men would repeat Trevelyan's catastrophic urge to dominate. As Christopher Herbert argues, "[T]he suggestion keeps appearing that Trevelyan in fact has far deeper affiliations with these moderate, urbane, amiable, well-meaning gentlemen than they would ever admit."[11] Rival images of marital relationships, they are, so it seems, all potential Amphytrions.

Jealousy, whether seen as hunger for power or desire for happiness, forces the jealous lover into a mode of constant iteration of a situation that brought powerlessness or unhappiness. Whereas the forms subsequent love affairs take may seem profoundly different from the initial unhappy event, jealousy, like Celionati's special glasses, reveals that underneath the multi-

---

10. Richard Terdiman, "The Mnemonics of Musset's *Confession*," *Representations* 26 (1989): 39.
11. Anthony Trollope, *He Knew He Was Right* (London: Oxford University Press, 1948), 467.

plicity of different episodes and different beloveds lies the monotonous reality of deceit.

Iris Murdoch explores this compulsion to replicate the situation that initially caused jealousy in her novel *A Word Child*, where the narrator twice falls in love, disastrously, with successive wives of the same man. As Goethe notes in his maxims: "Our passions are true phoenixes. As the old one burns away, a new one arises immediately from the ashes."[12] In each episode the protagonist precipitates the death of the woman. The structural metaphor Murdoch uses is that of London's underground railway, linking apparently arbitrary points of the city, but also containing within it the vital Circle Line. Going round and round on the Inner Circle is a stratagem frequently adopted in times of depression by the ironically named narrator, Hilary. Added to that image is the careful division of the week into constantly repeated activities: friends and relatives are visited strictly on prearranged days of the week, always the same day every week. Each of these tactics suggests both a desire for repetition and an obsession with keeping such repetition under control (a favorite word of the narrator's). But destabilizing elements are potently present in this framework. Even the word *control*, as Hilary himself informs us, slides between English and French usage. That destabilization is even clearer in matters of gender. The bisexuality of the narrator's name, Hilary, adds to his ambiguous relationship with the homosexual Clifford Larr to unbalance strict gender delimitations. Second, the women in his life, his sister Crystal and his mistress Thomasina (again, in its abbreviation to Tommy, a sexually ambivalent name) gently but persistently undermine his desire for control and impose themselves as other, no mere extensions of himself.

The Freudian underpinnings of this iterative structure, while perhaps heavy-handed, locate the genesis of Hilary's reenactments of a single situation unequivocally in childhood, and above all in prerational childhood, so that the crises of jealousy are presented in this text as both always already

---

12. Johann W. von Goethe, "Maximen und Reflexionen," in *Werke* (Hamburg: Christian Wegner Verlag, 1953), 12: 534.

experienced and quintessentially irrational, uncontrollable.[13] Hilary's mother—described, in what can only be termed shudder marks as a "tart"—died when he was "nearly seven," leaving him with no memory of her other than as a "state of being loved, [...] an era of light before the darkness started."[14] The longing for her to have been pure is transposed onto his image of his sister, whose relations with men he regulates, and if necessary disrupts in order to preserve that longed-for purity. The desire for reunion with the era of light leads him in search of mother substitutes, and the urge for repetition drives him to identify that mother figure with the forbidden, with someone whom he must wrest from the clutches of a father-substitute. The father-substitute appears in the guise of one of his Oxford dons, Gunnar Jopling, and the mother is easily located as Gunnar's wife. Hilary's urge to control Anne Jopling leads to her death in a car accident, in a scenario that he will repeat twenty years later with Gunnar Jopling's second wife, Kitty. The second scenario, however, has the added weight of Hilary's belated and traumatizing discovery that, after Anne's death, Gunnar sought consolation in the arms of Crystal, thus destroying in Hilary's mythology the purity that liberated their mother from the world's view of her.

Murdoch's characteristically labyrinthine plot and her exploration of a Freudian paradigm not only find appropriate metaphors in the Underground's inner circle and the repetition of activities on particular days of the week, but also carry with

13. Jack Turner's simplistic analysis of Murdoch's response to Freud fails to read the multiple ironies of the text, or to separate out writer and character, leading Turner to make the ludicrous assertion that "had Hilary gone into analysis, he likely could have done away with, or learned to control, much of the pain and guilt which drive and plague him throughout the novel. [...] But then the book would be quite a different book, perhaps with more realism, but not enough Murdochian 'truth' " (Jack Turner, "Murdoch vs. Freud in *A Severed Head* and Other Novels," *Literature and Psychology* 36, 1–2 [1990]: 115). For other readings of the novel see Catherine E. Howard, " 'Only Connect': Logical Aesthetic of Fragmentation in *A Word Child*," *Twentieth-Century Literature* 38, 1 (1992): 54–65, and Barbara Stevens Heusel, "Iris Murdoch's *A Word Child*: Playing Games with Wittgenstein's Perspectives," *Studies in the Humanities* 13, 2 (December 1986): 81–92.
14. Iris Murdoch, *A Word Child* (London: Panther, 1976), 17.

them extraordinarily potent images of Dante's circles of hell, especially the circle of the adulterers, with the souls "thrashed by the black wind's flailing,"[15] whirled endlessly through space and time. After Kitty dies from exposure in the frozen mud of the river bank, Hilary himself is swept away by the current as he had been swept away by jealousy itself: "[T]he Thames rushed me onward, squeezing me with its icy coldness, squeezing the remaining warmth out of my body, whirling me about and hurrying me onward and trying to kill me, to crush me to death in its cold embrace."[16] In this cataclysmic image, the river assumes the features of desire itself, deconstructing the triangular forms of jealousy to reveal the linearity of solipsistic lust.

There is a further aspect to this novel, for whereas Hilary strives to generate those words whose study has enabled him to escape the prison of social destiny, his iterative jealousy leads him merely to repeat the words of others and ultimately condemns him to silence. In the newspaper item he reads after Kitty's death he finds that he "had dropped out of the story as if [he] had never existed" (377). But silence is also escapism for him, when he learns that Thomasina had alerted Gunnar to his meeting with Kitty and thus precipitated the disaster. Hilary yet again places on a woman the guilt for his loss of happiness, and, invoking the lost innocence of childhood, he blinds himself once more to the role of personal responsibility in this constantly repeating circle of desire. The Inner Circle, after all, appeals to him not merely for its womblike shape and its monotonous repetition of destinations, but because it offers two bars, twin Circes that promise oblivion. The patterns underlying Murdoch's gothic fantasy here combine echoes of Homer and Dante, Freud and the infrastructures of a modern city, but in a way that overturns the basic thrust toward harmony and unity apparent in those sources. Desire, her novel indicates, always compels the ancestral voices to prophesy war.

Similar forces are at work if a writer attempts to incorporate

---

15. Dante, *The Divine Comedy*, 1.98.
16. Murdoch, *A Word Child*, 376.

the voices not merely of ancestors but also of his or her own readers. Nabokov's glitteringly self-reflexive parody of the purposes and methods of literary criticism, *Pale Fire*, is a particularly illuminating example of the use of parody to interweave evocations of literary and sexual jealousy and to shift and elide the differences between creation and criticism, reading and writing, truth and fantasy, prose and poetry.[17] The choice of title itself, ostentatiously plagiarized from Shakespeare, suggests parallels not only between writers and their predecessors and writers and their critics, but also between literary creation and divine creation. Moreover, it playfully indicates that even such pale fire is enough to blind the critic, for the exegete Kinbote, although he quotes the "re-Englished" and appallingly banalized version of the relevant passage from Shakespeare, claims elsewhere that he does not know the exact location of the expression "pale fire."[18] Not only has his translation, as this *mise en abyme* passage suggests, stripped the original text of the essential point, but he also attempts to

17. For particularly useful critical studies of this work, see Julia Bader, *Crystal Land: Artifice in Nabokov's English Novels* (Berkeley: University of California Press, 1972), and Brian Boyd, *Vladimir Nabokov* (Princeton: Princeton University Press, 1990), vol. 2.

18. Vladimir Nabokov, *Pale Fire* (New York: Vintage, 1989), 285. The title is found in *Timon of Athens* (4.3.433–38):

> The sun's a thief, and with his great attraction
> Robs the vast sea; the moon's an arrant thief,
> And her pale fire she snatches from the sun;
> The sea's a thief, whose liquid surge resolves
> The moon into salt tears.

See also *Hamlet* 1.5.89.
Kinbote's version, translated back from the Zemblan, is:

> The sun is a thief; she lures the sea
> and robs it. The moon is a thief:
> he steals his silvery light from the sun.
> The sea is a thief: it dissolves the
> moon.
>
> (*Pale Fire*, 80)

In the entry immediately following that in which he quotes these lines, Kinbote contrasts the "pale and diaphanous phase" of Shade's poem with the "sunset glow" of his own story (*Pale Fire*, 81).

shrug off Shakespeare's authority by this disingenuous denial of knowledge.[19]

Kinbote, reading Shade's poem "Pale Fire" and later glossing it, constantly attempts to discover within it encoded echoes of his own "wild glorious romance,"[20] as a jealous lover constantly reexamines the beloved's words to find in them proof of love or evidence of treachery. In so doing, he rewrites Shade's work, instilling into it those "echoes and wavelets of fire, and pale phosphorescent hints" he had hoped to find there (297). "Writing, reading, I've never really seized the difference," asserts Michel Schneider. "By reading, readers become authors, taking up anew, completing and prolonging their readings."[21] And although Kinbote ironically affirms that he has "no desire to twist and batter an unambiguous *apparatus criticus* into the monstrous semblance of a novel,"[22] semblances are what he, as a self-proclaimed Zemblan, can never escape. Mirror images of each other, Shade, the poet-critic who produces the four cantos, and Kinbote, the critic-creator who produces the commentary, are, in the chess game to which Nabokov has given the collective title *Pale Fire*, both mere pawns, even if promoted to "ivory unicorns and ebon fauns."[23] It remains, of course, a fact of chess that even a mere pawn, slowly moving across the board as Gradus slowly travels to Shade, can become a king, a regicide, or both. As such, Gradus and Shade are, as their names suggest, reflections of each other: Gradus assassinates the poet-king; Shade excises the Zemblan king from his text. Kinbote himself, acknowledging that his name means "a king's destroyer" silently adds that "a king who sinks his identity in the mirror of exile is in a sense just that" (267).

19. The classic study of strategies using the *mise en abyme* is that of Lucien Dällenbach, *Le Récit spéculaire: Essai sur la mise en abyme* (Paris: Seuil, 1977).
20. Nabokov, *Pale Fire*, 296.
21. Michel Schneider, *Voleurs de mots: Essai sur le plagiat, la psychanalyse et la pensée* (Paris: Gallimard, 1985), 288.
22. Nabokov, *Pale Fire*, 86. Linda Maddox, in *Nabokov's Novels in English* (Athens: University of Georgia Press, 1983), is surely mistaken in arguing that here we can "take Kinbote at his word" (14). The protestation, after all, comes in the middle of one of the longest and least justified digressions in the commentary and strikes me, at least, as not merely comic, but a flagrant proof of Kinbote's duplicity.
23. Nabokov, *Pale Fire*, 63.

At the beginning of his commentary, Kinbote presents mirror images as the essence of happiness; he even chooses to cut short his first meeting with his admired Shade because he is about to have "a kind of little seminar at home followed by some table tennis, with two charming identical twins and another boy, another boy."[24] Such mirror images are also present in texts. Rereading his commentary, Kinbote claims to find in it reflections from his "poet's fiery orb" and acknowledges his own unconscious aping of Shade's critical prose (81). The Zemblan language, whose beauties he so admires without necessarily convincing his reader they exist, is, after all, "the tongue of the mirror" (242), and the name itself is said to be a corruption of "Semblerland, a land of reflections, of 'ressemblers'" (265). Of course, it also seems a corruption of Zenda, just as Kinbote's narrative recalls the wild romances and Doppelgängers of *The Prisoner of Zenda*, the name of whose villain, Rupert Hentzau, is suggested in that of Hentzner (in whose barn Hazel Shade believed she saw reflections of another world),[25] and the name of whose author, Hope, is punningly allowed to spring eternal in allusions to Shade's study of Pope.

Yet within the apparent perfection of mirror images lie the seeds of disaster, for such images deny the possibility of uniqueness. The alternate possibilities made feasible in the mirror are precisely what destroy Kinbote's desire for a unique form of doubling. However closely he may resemble portraits of Zembla's deposed king, the fact remains that in his narration the king escapes because so many of his loyal followers make themselves into mirror images of him. As a result, he can never prove his identity as king. Similarly, he claims as unique the coupling of his images and Shade's genius in the potential production of the great poem, *Solus Rex*, but the very formulas he uses bathetically recall another such combination, Holmes and Watson, mentioned a page or so earlier: "Surely, it would not be easy to discover in the history of poetry a similar case—that of two men, different in origin, upbringing, thought associations, spiritual intonation and mental mode, one a cosmopol-

24. Ibid., 23. Of course Kinbote's homosexuality is also presented as part of this desire, not for the self's other, but for the mirror of the self.
25. Ibid., 265.

itan scholar, the other a fireside poet, entering into a secret compact of this kind."[26] Even more obvious and equally clearly embedded in the text is the case of Boswell and Johnson, so brilliantly parodied at the point when Kinbote's identity with that of the deposed king seems on the point of being revealed: " 'Nay, sir' [said Shade, refolding a leg and slightly rolling in his armchair as wont to do when about to deliver a pronouncement] 'there is no resemblance at all. I have seen the King in newsreels, and there is no resemblance. Resemblances are the shadows of differences. Different people see different similarities and similar differences" (265). The disruptive nature of such multiple doubling is intensified by the triangularity, indeed multisidedness, of the relationships that Kinbote frantically attempts to reduce to his idealized dualism. Kinbote as critic attempting to set up a one-to-one relationship with the reader finds himself constantly battling not only with other readings of the poem, but also with the poem's own failure to provide the "direct echo" of his narrative. Kinbote as man attempts to create with Shade a binary relationship complete in itself, but finds himself constantly ousted not merely by the shade of the poet's dead daughter, Hazel, but also by his wife of forty years, Sybil. His response to the daughter's challenge is to claim resemblance with her (193). His reaction to Sybil is to accuse her of forcing Shade to remove all references to the Zembla theme, thus suggesting a will to silence that would indicate that she experiences feelings of jealousy that in turn might provide some proof of the value Shade placed on Kinbote. "Proof" of that silencing is provided by the variants Kinbote claims Shade did not consign to the "pale fire" of the incinerator. There is, of course, little doubt that the variants, with their banal sentiments and awkward prosodies, are to be read as Kinbote's own creations. Like Proust's Odette creating lies by recycling as much as possible of the truth, Kinbote himself acknowledges this imposition of his voice on Shade's, but claims to have tarried only once, as he puts it, "on the brink of falsification" (228), a typically Nabokovian wink to the

26. Ibid., 80. See also 78.

reader that on countless other occasions he simply stepped straight over.

The intricate interweaving of sexual and textual jealousy in this novel appears at its most intense in the many descriptions of Kinbote spying on the Shades. Jealousy transforms their house, in their neighbor's eyes, into nothing more than "peeps and glimpses, and window-framed opportunities" (86). "The urge to find out what he was doing," claims Kinbote, ostensibly in relation to Shade's writing, "proved to be utterly agonizing and uncontrollable and led me to indulge in an orgy of spying which no considerations of pride could stop" (87). As his notebook later reveals, that spying is accompanied by a detailed record of the frequency of the Shades' lovemaking. With a characteristic twist, Nabokov also makes all this gazing into, and out of, windows an explicit narrative strategy: "Windows, as well known, have been the solace of first-person literature throughout the ages" (87). Solace rex, indeed. Yet, as the initial line of the poem suggests and the critic's commentary reveals, what the jealous lover or jealous critic sees in a window or a poem is a mere reflection of his or her own face, not real sky but "false azure." Yet, Kinbote would protest, "*reality* is neither the subject nor the object of true art, which creates its own special reality having nothing to do with the average *reality* perceived by the communal eye" (130).

Kinbote's "reality" is nothing if not sexual: both what he describes as his friendship with Shade and his relation to Shade's poem are described in terms that are not merely sensual but also specifically and powerfully erotic. He speaks of his longing to inspire in his friend the desire to write the story of the King of Zembla, as something he had thrust upon Shade with "a lover's urge" (296); and he conveys his mixed sense of betrayal and continuing desire in an unambiguous metaphor: "I now felt a new, pitiful tenderness toward the poem as one has for a fickle young creature who has been stolen and brutally enjoyed by a black giant but now again is safe in our hall and park [. . .]. The spot still hurts, it must hurt, but with strange gratitude we kiss those heavy wet eyelids and caress that polluted flesh" (297). The same sexual imagery and the same jealousy are revealed in Kinbote's complex relationship with his reader. The ideal, implied reader is projected as a lover, sharing the writer's bed as well as his text, but even in that case the reader escapes Kinbote's control: "[W]e too might wish to cut short a reader's or bedfellow's questions by sinking back into oblivion's bliss" (189). Moreover, while Kinbote speaks directly to his implied reader, the thrust to multiplicity that he himself has instigated by demanding multiple levels of meaning within Shade's poem multiplies the reader, too.

Ironically, it is the constant desire to control his reader (as a jealous lover attempts to control the object of jealousy) that leads him at one point, in quoting a letter he as king had written to his wife, to invoke a second-level reader. Nabokov has teasingly inserted this letter under the lemma "address," thus focusing his reader's attention on the central narratological questions of who speaks and who listens. An allusion to a ginkgo tree prompts the command "see again [. . .] the note to line 49" and the clarification: "I mean the reader should see again," thus adding to the implied reader of the letter, that of the commentary (257). Such a multiplication of readers is also insinuated in a slightly earlier sentence, with its image of countless voices coming between speaker and hearer, lover and beloved: "Do not try to explain to me what your lawyer tells you but have him explain it to my lawyer, and *he* will explain it to me" (257). Everything is mediated—not in the Girardian sense, where mediation eventually leads to a cathartic conversion, but in a far more destructive sense, leading to solipsistic isolation.

The interweaving of sexual and textual jealousy is also evident in Nabokov's manipulation of time, for running disruptively against Kinbote's meticulous, cabalistic attention to dates—the desire to pin down and account for all moments of the past and to imbue certain combinations of numbers with special significance—is the commentary's demand that we replace linear reading with a form of simultaneity.[27] Even as Kinbote himself condemns Shade's use of "the synchronization device" as labored, and complains that it has been "worked to

27. For an exploration of the significance to Nabokov of some of these dates, see Boyd, *Vladimir Nabokov*, 2:456. Boyd devotes all of his chapter 18 to a reading of *Pale Fire*.

death by Flaubert and Joyce,"[28] he attempts to create a similar synchrony on the level of the plot in moving between Shade's activities and those Gradus was performing at the same time, whereas at the level of the commentary, he increasingly refers us back and forth among his notes, as his own mind moves between Zembla and New Wye, distant past and immediate past. Here, as so often, he incorporates into his own text, the voices of Flaubert and Joyce in an attempt to wrest the reader's attention back to himself.

Nabokov's intricate exploration of the critic's jealousy with regard both to the reader and the text, together with his embedded parodies and pastiches, thus create an interweaving of sexual and textual jealousy that projects light on both emotions. The jealous person's desire to supplant the rival, or more accurately to subsume the rival's supposed attractions while retaining his or her own identity, can be seen both at the level of what is told and at that of how it is told. The example of *Pale Fire* is, of course, only one of many such explorations. I have focused so closely on it here because of the way in which the roles of the implied readers are so consistently highlighted in this text. Nabokov's techniques, indeed, provide a grid through which the interplay of sexual and textual jealousy in James Joyce's *Ulysses* can more easily be traced.

While Homer's narration provides only one of the many threads woven into Joyce's complex web, its stark contrasts between masculine and feminine, doing and making, circling around a center and providing that center, reappear in *Ulysses* stripped of that elevation in tone and narrative viewpoint that establishes normality in Homer's phallocratic universe. Joyce, in juxtaposing the Mephistophelean spirit that negates and the flesh that affirms, refuses simplistic gender-based roles and uses jealousy as one of the instigators of his exploration of the Other, both sexually and textually. As Suzette Henke puts it in her study of desire in Joyce's work: "Polymorphous perversity, translated into the bisexual drives of the unconscious, yields a curious and perplexed dissemination of sexual signifiers that challenge culturally embedded scripts of Oedipal

28. Nabokov, *Pale Fire*, 196.

triangulation."[29] Joyce also challenges such dissemination through numerous other embedded scripts. Indeed, his inscription of Bloom as plagiarist[30] hints at the extent to which not only his characters but also his readers are both products and reproducers of what they have read. Molly in her lyrical and open-ended monologue shows how fully the web she weaves reproduces such shaping texts as the romances exemplified by *Sweets of Sin*. Yet where such works delineate woman as constantly molded and defined by the male other, Molly's desires refuse such circumscription and yearn for a personal satisfaction beyond that of merely satisfying the male. Bloom's own absence from home, set against the background of Ulysses' peregrinations, is seen in this context to be less his wandering around Dublin than his long failure to engage in full sexual relations with his wife. (The Freudian overtones of such an absence from home are evident, and closely associated with Joyce's frequently annotated obsession with mother figures and mother substitutes.) In both cases, that of Molly and that of Bloom, the shaping texts are incorporated only to be parodied and eventually transcended.

While the text's desire to incorporate numerous other texts is made immediately clear through its exuberant pastiches and parodies, Bloom's sexual jealousy is far less immediately obvious. The presence of this theme is at first merely hinted at, through allusive and incomplete thoughts, as the internal monologue touches on, and sheers away from Bloom's awareness that on this day Molly and Blazes Boylan are to meet: "Today. Today. Not think" (180). Elsewhere, slight slips of the tongue, that sexually and textually perfidious instrument in Joycean texts, point forward to Ithica's Rabelaisian list of suspected rivals:

—Well, that's a point, says Bloom, for the wife's admirers.
—Whose admirers? says Joe.
—The wife's advisers, I mean, says Bloom. (313)

29. Suzette Henke, *James Joyce and the Politics of Desire* (New York: Routledge, 1990), 6.
30. James Joyce, *Ulysses*, 491.

Boylan himself leaps momentarily and in sharp definition across the screen of Bloom's voyeuristic imagination, as if conjured up in brief acknowledgment of jealousy's compulsion to spy: "By the provost's wall came jauntily Blazes Boylan, stepping in tan shoes and socks with skyblue clocks to the refrain of *My Girl's a Yorkshire Girl*" (254). But Bloom's jealous doubts about Molly become a dominant theme only as the time of his homecoming approaches, and they are always associated with various forms of parody. As if the question of jealous suspicion is too painful to be addressed directly, the text reproduces the tangential nature of Bloom's thinking about Molly and Boylan by conveying it through a parallel story and telling it in a style of hackneyed banality:

> the simple fact of the case was it was simply a case of the husband not being up to scratch with nothing in common between them beyond the name and then a real man arriving on the scene, strong to the verge of weakness, falling a victim to her siren charms and forgetting home ties. The usual sequel, to bask in the loved one's smiles, the eternal question of the life connubial, needless to say, cropped up.[31]

This parodic refusal to confer on such a situation any sense of uniqueness, either as narrative or as narration, underpins Bloom's own sardonic recognition that "each one who enters imagines himself to be the first to enter whereas he is always the last term of a preceding series even if the first term of a succeeding one, each imagining himself to be first, last, only and alone" (731).

If Bloom eventually reaches a state of equanimity that overcomes his jealousy and points to a possible solution for both himself and Molly, it is through his parodistically reported reflections on "the inanity of extolled virtue: the lethargy of nescient matter: the apathy of the stars" (734).

By acknowledging so clearly, if so ironically, his own lack of uniqueness within the long and constantly recurring series of those who have written on adultery and married love and by

31. Ibid., 651. The pun on the French word *verge* (penis) is evident here.

incorporating into his text abundant thematic and stylistic evidence of that lack, Joyce does of course, like Bloom taking over but inverting Boylan's place in the bed, create his own unique position in the history of those who have linked sexual and textual jealousy.

In reading Joyce, as in reading so many of those who have chosen to exploit the strategies made available by jealousy, we are never alone with a single writer but in the very center of a bustling market place.

Conclusion

Like Walter Benjamin before him, Peter Brooks presents the reader of a novel as isolated, cut off, remote, engaged in an archetypally private experience. Brooks, for whom the desire for knowledge, and therefore the impetus to read, both spring directly and predominantly from a longing for specifically sexual knowledge, argues that "this solitude and isolation make the reading of a novel the most intimate of literary experiences, a transaction without the mediation of actors or speakers, in which one typically feels an empathetic closeness to characters and events."[1] Approaching the question from a different angle, A. S. Byatt, in her rich, provocative, and playful novel, *Possession*, exhorts us to "Think of this: the writer wrote alone, and the reader read alone, and they were alone together."[2] Neither the sophistication of Brooks's reading strategies nor the beauty of Byatt's formula should blind us, however, to the imperfections of an argument that, in any case, Byatt's thematics counter as her characters read their authors through a growing web of textual commentary, critical assessment, and personal memory. All of them also read, as Paul Valéry argued we

1. Peter Brooks, *Body Work: Objects of Desire in Modern Narrative* (Cambridge: Harvard University Press, 1993), 29. See also Walter Benjamin, *Illuminations*, trans. Harry Zohn (New York: Schocken, 1969), 100.
2. A. S. Byatt, *Possession: A Romance* (London: Vintage, 1990), 41.

should, over the author's shoulder.[3] Such a reading alerts us to the fact that neither the reader nor the writer (as both reader and creator) is alone. After all, what is happening when, for instance, reading *Three Men in a Boat* in apparent isolation we come across the following passage:

> The weather changed on the third day [. . .] and we started from Oxford upon our homeward journey in the midst of a steady drizzle.
>
> The river—with the sunlight flashing from its dancing wavelets, gilding gold the grey-green birch-trunks, glinting through the dark, cool wood paths, chasing shadows o'er the shallows, flinging diamonds from the mill-wheels, throwing kisses to the lilies, wantoning with the weirs' white waters, silvering moss-grown walls and bridges, brightening every tiny townlet, making sweet each lane and meadow, lying tangled in the rushes, peeping, laughing, from each inlet, gleaming gay on many a far sail, making soft the air with glory—is a golden fiery stream.[4]

Clearly we're no longer at home alone with Jerome K. Jerome, since Longfellow, Banjo Paterson, and goodness knows who else have penetrated our cozy isolation.

Whereas narratologists and Freudian or post-Freudian critics, among others, might urge us to accept that reading is structured like an intimate encounter with the novelist, Cervantes long ago made it clear that whenever we are one or two together, we are three or four or more: having lined up Don Quixote and the Gallant Basque in mortal combat, Cervantes abruptly announces that the tale's first narrator apparently abandoned the reader at that point, offering no clues as to the outcome of the mighty struggle. Only through the kind of good luck familiar no doubt to all of us involved in research did the Cervantes figure come across the documents needed to tell the rest of the story:

---

3. Paul Valéry, *Œuvres*, éd. établie et annotée par Jean Hytier (Paris: Pléiade, 1957–1960), 2: 626.

4. Jerome K. Jerome, *Three Men in a Boat* (London: J. M. Dent, 1950), 184.

One day I was in the Alcana at Toledo, when a lad came to sell some parchments and other papers to a silk merchant. Now as I have a taste for reading even torn papers lying in the streets, I was impelled by my natural inclination to take up one of the parchment books the lad was selling and saw in it characters which I recognized as Arabic. But though I could recognize them I could not read them, and looked around to see if there was not some Spanish-speaking Moor about, to read them to me; and it was not difficult to find such an interpreter there. For even if I had wanted one for a better and older language, I should have found one. In short, chance offered me one, to whom I explained what I wanted, placing the book in his hands. He opened it in the middle, and after reading a little began to laugh. I asked him what he was laughing at, and he answered that it was at something written in the margin of the book by way of a note. I asked him to tell me what it was and, still laughing, he answered: "This is what is written in the margin: 'They say that Dulcinea del Toboso, so often mentioned in this history, was the best hand at salting pork of any woman in all La Mancha.' "[5]

Realizing that the parchments recount the continuation of the Don's story, the narrator buys them all and hires the Moor to translate them for him. The tale is, moreover, illustrated: "On the first sheet was a very life-like picture of Don Quixote's fight with the Basque. Both were shown in the very postures the story describes, with swords aloft, the one covered by his shield, the other by his cushion, and the Basque's mule was so life-like that you could tell from a mile off that it was a hired one" (76). Discovering the story demands, it would seem, a series of intermediaries: the boy selling the parchments, the interpreter, the illustrator, the Arab who narrates the tale, and the unknown hand that added the marginal commentary, which in itself relies on other voices: "They say. . . ." Cervantes, who specializes, among other things, in the deferment of meaning and pleasure, here provides us with a witty and energetic picture of the necessarily deferred and multivocal pleas-

5. Miguel de Cervantes, *Don Quixote*, trans. J. M. Cohen (Harmondsworth: Penguin, 1950), 75.

ure of texts. His numerous digressions provide an obvious example of such pleasure. Multiple voices, whose veracity we're willing not to question too deeply because they tell a tale we want to hear, combine and contrast, contending for our attention, cutting across or interweaving with the main narrative.

What I have been arguing in this essay is that narrative (and frequently poetry, too) is not troped as a love scene in which two voices alone participate (that of the writer and that of the reader) but rather as jealousy and rivalry, in which multiple seducers stand on the river bank vying for our favors, telling tales to reveal a truth (not necessarily *the* truth) about the other, inventing scenarios to hide the truth about self or other, telling stories to silence the other, or taking over the voice of the other by parody and pastiche. Crossed wires may disrupt a two-way communication, but they may also offer us tales we would prefer to hear, told by voices we would rather listen to, in ways that stimulate us, too, to indulge in telling tales.

Medieval aubades frequently figure the stock character of the "gilous," not the husband, but the unfavored rival, who puts the couple at risk by threatening to tell the husband what is going on: jealousy is figured here, therefore, as a source of narrative that will in turn force the wife into further narratives, in which she tries to cover the traces of her actions (culpable or not) to prevent her husband from reading or misreading them. These are the sorts of tales that, as Byron puts it with typical slippery sexual ambiguity, "somehow lengthen when begun."[6] That such tales frequently carry overt or encrypted political messages is hardly surprising, because information about the other—regardless of the truth of that information— is a potential source of considerable power and because power of this sort lends itself to repayment in sexual favors. Jealousy is both a weapon used to manipulate the other, indeed to deny the independence of the other and a flaw in the individual's nature, a flaw that can in turn be exploited.

The way in which jealousy leads the lover to use his or her

6. Lord Byron, *Beppo*, XCIX, in *Complete Poetical Works*, ed. Jerome J. Mc-Gann (Oxford: Clarendon Press, 1980–1993), 4: 160.

power to suppress the individuality of the beloved, and to become in turn reduced to a mere expression of jealousy, is a central element in works depicting this passion. Jealousy's destabilizing effect on the lover's conception of the beloved inevitably tends also to destabilize the lover's self-image and that of his or her entire physical or societal context. For both reasons—the suppression of individuality and the instability thus produced—jealousy also becomes a potent metaphor for all forms of repression and offers a particularly formidable means of exploring the nature of political repression without necessarily incurring the wrath of the censor. Thus the Polish writer, Michal Choromanski, writing *Jealousy and Medicine* in 1932, in the particularly dark days of a Poland in the grip of a brutal military dictatorship, creates a setting in which space, time, even the weather, body forth the sense of helpless oppression suffered alike by the lover rent by doubts about the beloved, the beloved oppressed by such doubts, and by those living under regimes that thrive on suppression of the truth. This view of jealousy depends above all on the refusal to countenance the irreducible alterity of the other: the depiction of the woman around whom such jealousy crystallizes (to use Stendhal's term) reveals the extent to which she is merely a peg on which the lover hangs his ideals or his fears in a world in which the evidence of the senses is constantly being distorted.

As readers we are figured in Choromanski's text as voyeuristic outsiders, peering through nicks and crannies, given information not available to the jealous lover, yet it is also possible that we are being shown a series of imaginary vignettes produced by the suspicions of that same jealous lover. The supposed deception practiced by the beloved is indeed often troped and doubled in texts concerning jealousy by the narrator's deception of the reader, particularly in the case of first-person narratives. We have seen that works such as *Villette*, *Adolphe*, and *The Good Soldier* provide fine examples of a narrator's attempted deception of the reader within analytical studies of jealousy. Each sets us a riddle to solve, a paradox we are invited to scout,[7] and each offers us a series of clues meant

---

7. Charlotte Brontë, *Villette* (Harmondsworth: Penguin, 1981), 593.

to lead us toward a solution acceptable to the narrator, but it is a solution thrown into question by aspects of the narrative itself. If the first-person address used in these texts encourages a sense of closer intimacy between writer and reader, that intimacy is frequently exposed as false or at best misleading, as certain letters in *Les Liaisons dangereuses* most brilliantly reveal by reflecting a Valmont or a Merteuil reading (and indeed writing) over the shoulder of a Cécile and a Danceny.

I have argued, therefore, that deceptions practiced within the text and paralleled by the narrator's attempted deception of the reader offer a form of intellectual pleasure that can elevate a theme that might otherwise be merely banal or sordid. Yet jealousy can also be exploited as a metaphor for the desire for political control over the minds and bodies of a subject people. In this case, stories tend to be told with the aim not just of deceiving the other, but of silencing alternative versions, shouting down other voices, imposing barriers on communication. Victor Hugo, for instance, blends sexual and political repression in his novel *Notre-Dame de Paris*. Writing in the immediate aftermath of the revolution of 1830 and strongly affected by memories of the repressive mentality of the final stages of Charles X's rule, Hugo chooses to set a contemporary political commentary in what is only superficially a safely distant past. The oppression of the poor, of gypsies, and of the weak is tightly linked to the Church's desire to destroy the newly created printing presses. Even though that urge to suppress dissident voices is presented as historically specific, extrapolation into the reader's own society is facilitated both by the paradigmatic relationship between the powerful Frollo with the fragile Esmeralda and by the constant movement within the text between vertical and horizontal, inviting parallel readings that move between past and present.

Frollo, initially haunted by the alchemical secrets and their promises of power and subsequently by the equally deceptive lusts triggered by the sight of Esmeralda dancing in the sunlight, offers us a highly suggestive icon of multiple aspects of jealousy. In tracing the words of others on the wall of his cell, he transforms that architectural space into an encapsulation of a certain version of knowledge, surrounding himself with voices, none of which can in the end speak as loudly as Esmeralda's tambourine. In similar ways, the writer who is jealous of his or her reader's attention and haunted by a sense of other voices speaking more forcefully, more directly, above all more seductively may attempt to incorporate those other voices, to capture them within the cell of the text. Parody, pastiche, and plagiarism are all means whereby the haunted writer attempts not to exorcise the ghosts of rivals past or present, but to allow them to possess the text. Jealousy lends itself admirably as the thematic material for such tactics because the jealous lover is also haunted: by images of what is irremediably past, or never was, or might have been. Truffaut's disturbing image of the betrayed wife dressed as her rival in *Domicile conjugal* carries further resonances as an icon of Truffaut's own desire to incorporate into his films the devices, tricks, and voices of the American "B" series movies that so haunted at least part of his creative personality.

Jealousy thus enables a series of highly creative narrative strategies that have little to do with the negative and destructive sides of the emotion itself. The ways in which reading for the plot or remaining at the level of thematics can overlook the power of these strategies become obvious if we ask, for instance, the question of why characters become jealous. However much the response to that question might vary within the diegetic framework, it remains a constant that jealousy is introduced into a fictional relationship through an authorial *fiat*. Answering such a question by saying, for instance, that Othello is overwhelmed with jealousy because Desdemona has lost a handkerchief might be glib, but in the last analysis it is no more superficial than locating the source of Marcel's jealousy in the unknowable depths of Albertine's nature. Both responses, by remaining at the level of what is narrated, ignore the structural and narrational forces released and exploited by the initial choice of jealousy as a central passion.

Proust's focus on jealousy, for instance, enables and justifies that intense inspection of another person that simultaneously illuminates the narrator's own mentality. Moreover, the structures used for that exploration are those employed for the study of art or nature and thus establish patterns of analysis and perception that rise above the sordid raw material that has set them in train. Robbe-Grillet in *La Jalousie* allows the potentially explosive and corrosive force of the emotion to tear apart habitual modes of reading, to question the structures of personal relationships, and thereby to insinuate an equally explosive and corrosive interrogation of the politics of colonialism. Other writers use the distorting mirror of jealousy to replace habitual modes of representing and conceptualizing time and space or to reconsider societal preconceptions concerning gender. And for writers as diverse as James Joyce and Angela Carter, Virginia Woolf and E. T. A. Hoffmann, Rostand and Nabokov, jealousy of an individual merges with the jealous desire to capture and control the reader's attention, and thereby it instigates the rich interweaving of parodies and pastiches that allows the narrator to speak with multiple voices.

That multiplicity, with its seductive invitation to open the banal triangular model of jealousy into something far more multisided, parallels the multiple facets that jealousy, like Proust's vision of memory, discloses within an individual. Yes, Odette was a strumpet—but not the Odette Swann loved. The Desdemona Iago made Othello see in the arms of Cassio was as far removed from the Desdemona the reader sees and society sees as Odette the strumpet is from the Odette Swann so passionately desires. Crystallization in both cases has so transformed the original branch that the question of whether or not the jealous lover's suspicions are justified has no meaning. If lovers are deceived, it is never by the person they believed they loved.

Does it matter, then, whether or not the suspicions of jealousy are well founded? (Can murder ever be fully justified?) Would the child's family story, the tale in which he or she is the biological offspring of someone rich, famous, loving, and definitely different from the parents with which it finds itself, be changed in any way, gain or lose force, if the child found it did indeed have biological parents elsewhere? In extradiegetic terms, those of the child's future, possibly. But in terms of the child's tale itself? What seems to count above all is the narrative possibilities unleashed by the emotion or by the mere question of "what if"—what if I were the daughter of X, what if the person I love loved someone else. It is this "what if" and all that it entails that liberates the surge of energy, the influx of chaos, and in so doing lends so much of literature its dominant power. The chaos that jealousy releases within the individual and within society, like that of adultery, is, after all, what sets in motion the dynamics of the text.

Above all, the apparent triviality of jealousy as a theme is merely a deceptive mask: its power lies in the strategies the theme offers not merely the writer but also the reader. Jealousy as a literary strategy liberates in a text and in its readers energies that create new visions, new structures, new modes of discourse, and new ways of reading.

Bibliography

Primary Texts

Agoult, Marie d', pseud. Daniel Stern. *Nélida*. Paris: Calmann-Lévy, 1987.

Alas, Leopoldo. *La Regenta*. Trans. and with introduction by John Rutherford. Harmondsworth: Penguin, 1984.

Anon. *Les Mille et une nuits*. Trans. Galland. 2 vols. Paris: Garnier, 1988.

Ariosto. *Orlando furioso*. Trans. Barbara Reynolds. 2 vols. Penguin: Harmondsworth, 1975.

Atwood, Margaret. *The Edible Woman*. New York: Bantam, 1970.

Balzac, Honoré de. *Béatrix*. Paris: Flammarion, 1979.

——. *Le Chef-d'œuvre inconnu*. Paris: Livre de Poche, 1960.

——. *La Cousine Bette*. Paris: Folio, 1972.

——. *La Duchesse de Langeais, La Fille aux yeux d'or*. Paris: Livre de Poche, 1972.

——. *La Peau de chagrin*. Paris: Flammarion, 1971.

——. *Le Père Goriot*. Paris: Garnier Flammarion, 1966.

——. *Physiologie du mariage*. Paris: Flammarion, 1968.

Barnes, Julian. *Talking it Over*. London: Jonathan Cape, 1991.

Baudelaire, Charles. *Œuvres complètes*. Ed. établie et annotée par Claude Pichois. 2 vols. Paris: Pléiade, 1976.

Beauvoir, Simone de. *L'Invitée*. Paris: Folio, 1943.

——. *She Came to Stay*. Translated by Yvonne Moyse and Roger Senhouse. London: Fontana, 1984.

Blais, Marie-Claire. *Le Loup*. Ottawa: Stanké, 1980.

——. *Les Nuits de l'underground*. Ottawa: Stanké, 1978.
Borges, Jorge G. *Labyrinths*. Harmondsworth: Penguin, 1971.
Brontë, Charlotte. *Villette*. Harmondsworth: Penguin, 1981.
Byatt, A. S. *Possession: A Romance*. London: Vintage, 1990.
Byron, Lord George. *Complete Poetical Works*. Ed. Jerome J. McGann. Oxford: Clarendon Press, 1980–1993.
Carter, Angela. *Wise Children*. London: Chatto and Windus, 1991.
Cather, Willa. *O Pioneers!* New York: Viking Penguin, 1989.
Cazotte, Jacques. *Le Diable amoureux*. Paris: Le Terrain vague, 1960.
Cervantes, Miguel de. *Don Quixote*. Trans. J. M. Cohen. Harmondsworth: Penguin, 1950.
Choromanski, Michal. *Jealousy and Medicine*. Trans. Eileen Arthurton-Barker. Norfolk, Conn.: New Directions Books, 1964.
Colette. *Duo*. Paris: Hachette, 1985.
Constant, Benjamin. *Adolphe*. Paris: Société Les Belles Lettres, 1946.
Dante. *The Divine Comedy*. Trans. Dorothy L. Sayers. 3 vols. Harmondsworth: Penguin, 1949.
Decaunes, Luc. *Poésie parnassienne*. Paris: Seghers, 1977.
Donne, John. *Complete Poems*. Oxford: Oxford University Press, 1933.
Dostoevsky, Fyodor. *The Eternal Husband*. Trans. Constance Garnett. New York: Macmillan, 1923.
Duffy, Maureen. *The Microcosm*. Harmondsworth: Penguin, 1989.
Flaubert, Gustave. *Madame Bovary*. Paris: Garnier, 1971.
Ford, Ford Madox. *The Good Soldier*. Harmondsworth: Penguin, 1972.
Fromentin, Eugène. *Dominique*. Paris: Garnier-Flammarion, 1967.
Gautier, Théophile. *Nouvelles*. Paris: Charpentier, 1923.
Gilbert, W. S. "Utopia Limited." In *Original Plays*. Third series. London: Chatto and Windus, 1923.
Giraudoux, Jean. *Théâtre complet*. Ed. établie, présentée et annotée par Guy Teissier. Préface de Jean-Pierre Giraudoux. Paris: Livre de poche, 1991.
Goethe, Johann Wolfgang von. "Maximen und Reflexionen." In *Werke*, 12: 365–547. Hamburg: Christian Wegner Verlag, 1953.
Greer, Germaine. *Daddy, We Hardly Knew You*. Harmondsworth: Penguin, 1989.
Hall, Radclyffe. *The Well of Loneliness*. New York: Anchor, 1956.
Halligan, Marion. *Spidercup*. Ringwood, Victoria: Penguin, 1990.
Hazzard, Shirley. *The Bay of Noon*. Boston: Little, Brown, and Company, 1970.
——. *The Transit of Venus*. Harmondsworth: Penguin, 1980.

Hoffmann, E. T. A. *Fantasie- und Nachtstücke*. Munich: Winkler Verlag, 1967.
——. *Prinzessin Brambilla*. Oxford: Basil Blackwell, 1972.
Hugo, Victor. *Notre-Dame de Paris*. Paris: Garnier-Flammarion, 1967.
Jerome, Jerome K. *Three Men in a Boat*. London: J. M. Dent, 1950.
Jolley, Elizabeth. *Palomino*. New York, Persea Books, 1987.
Joyce, James. *Ulysses*. New York: Vintage, 1990.
La Fayette, Madame de. *La Princesse de Clèves*. Paris: Livre de Poche, 1958.
La Rochefoucauld, François de. *Maximes*. Paris: Larousse, 1975.
Malraux, André. *La Condition humaine*. Paris: Gallimard, 1946.
Meredith, George. *The Egoist*. Harmondsworth: Penguin, 1968.
Monési, Irène. *L'Amour et le dédain*. Paris: Mercure de France, 1974.
Murdoch, Iris. *A Word Child*. London: Panther, 1976.
Musil, Robert. *Drei Frauen*. Text, notes, and commentary by Karl Eibl. Munich: Carl Hanser Verlag, 1978.
——. *Tonka and Other Stories*. Trans. Eithne Wilkins and Ernst Kaiser. London: Panther, 1969.
Musset, Alfred de. *La Confession d'un enfant du siècle*. Paris: Gallimard Folio, 1973.
Nabokov, Vladimir. *Ada or Ardor: A Family Chronicle*. New York: Vintage, 1990.
——. *Lolita*. New York: Vintage, 1989.
——. *Pale Fire*. New York: Vintage, 1989.
Ovid. *Metamorphoses*. Trans. Rolfe Humphries and Winifred Davies. Bloomington: Indiana University Press, 1988.
Plato. *Phaedrus*. Trans. and with commentary by R. Hackforth. Cambridge: Cambridge University Press, 1972.
Proust, Marcel. *A la recherche du temps perdu* Ed. établie et présentée par Pierre Clarac et André Ferré. 3 vols. Paris: Pléiade, 1954.
——. *Contre Sainte-Beuve*. Paris: Pléiade, 1971.
Reade, Charles. *Griffith Gaunt: Or, Jealousy*. London: Chapman & Hall, 1867.
Robbe-Grillet, Alain. *La Jalousie*. London: Methuen, 1967.
Rostand, Edmond. *Cyrano de Bergerac* Ed. Willy de Spens. Paris: Garnier Flammarion, 1989.
Shakespeare, William. *The Complete Works* Ed. Peter Alexander. London: Collins, 1951.
Stead, Christina. *The Man Who Loved Children*. Harmondsworth: Penguin, 1970.
Stendhal. *De l'amour*. Paris: Garnier-Flammarion, 1965.

Svevo, Italo. *As a Man Grows Older*. Trans. Beryl de Zoete. London: Secker and Warburg, 1962.
——. *Confessions of Zeno*. Trans. Beryl de Zoete. Harmondsworth: Penguin, 1964.
Tennyson, Alfred Lord. *The Poems*. Ed. Christopher Ricks. 3 vols. Berkeley: University of California Press, 1987.
Tolstoy, Leo. *Anna Karenin*. Trans. Rosemary Edmonds. Harmondsworth: Penguin, 1954.
——. *Kreutzer Sonata*. In *Great Short Works*. Trans. Louise Maude and Aylmer Maude. New York: Harper and Row, 1967.
Tolstoy, Sophia. *The Diaries*. Trans. Cathy Porter. New York: Random House, 1985.
Tournier, Michel. *Le Medianoche amoureux*. Paris: Gallimard, 1989.
Trollope, Anthony. *He Knew He Was Right*. London: Oxford University Press, 1948.
——. *Kept in the Dark*. New York: Dover, 1978.
——. *Kept in the Dark*. Oxford: Oxford University Press, 1991.
Tusquet, Esther. *The Same Sea as Every Summer*. Trans. Margaret E. W. Jones. Lincoln. Nebraska: University of Nebraska Press, 1990.
Valéry, Paul. *Œuvres*. 2 vols. Ed. établie et annotée par Jean Hytier. Paris: Pléiade, 1957–1960.
Vallès, Jules. *L'Enfant*. Paris: Livre de Poche, 1985.
Wharton, Edith. *The Age of Innocence*. New York: Collier, 1968.
White, Patrick. *The Tree of Man*. Harmondsworth: Penguin, 1961.
Winterson, Jeanette. *Oranges Are Not the Only Fruit*. New York: Atlantic Monthly Press, 1987.
Woolf, Virginia. *A Room of One's Own*. London: Grafton, 1977.
——. *Orlando*. Harmondsworth: Penguin, 1967.

Critical Works

Ariès, Philippe. *L'Enfant et la vie familiale sous l'Ancien Régime*. Paris: Seuil, 1973.
Armstrong, Nancy. *Desire and Domestic Fiction*. Oxford: Oxford University Press, 1987.
Attridge, Derek. *The Cambridge Companion to James Joyce*. Cambridge: Cambridge University Press, 1990.
Auerbach, Erich. *Mimesis*. Trans. Willard R. Trask. Princeton: Princeton University Press, 1968.
Austin, John Langshaw. *How to Do Things with Words*. Oxford: Oxford University Press, 1975.

Bader, Julia. *Crystal Land: Artifice in Nabokov's English Novels.* Berkeley: University of California Press, 1972.

Bair, Deirdre. *Simone de Beauvoir: A Biography.* New York: Summit, 1990.

Bakhtin, Mikhail M. *The Dialogic Imagination: Four Essays.* Trans. Caryl Emerson and M. Holquist. Austin: University of Texas Press, 1981.

Bal, Mieke. *Narratologie: Essais sur la signification narrative dans quatre romans modernes.* Paris: Klincksieck, 1977.

Barthes, Roland. *Fragments d'un discours amoureux.* Paris: Seuil, 1977.

——. *A Lover's Discourse.* Trans. Richard Howard. New York: Hill and Wang, 1978.

——. *Le Plaisir du texte.* Paris: Seuil, 1973.

Baumgart, Hildegard. *Jealousy: Experiences and Solutions.* Trans. Manfred Jacobson and Evelyn Jacobson. Chicago: University of Chicago Press, 1990.

Bazin, Nancy Topping. *Virginia Woolf and the Androgynous Vision.* New Brunswick: Rutgers University Press, 1973.

Benjamin, Walter. *Illuminations.* Trans. Harry Zohn. New York: Schocken, 1969.

Berger, John. *Ways of Seeing.* London: Penguin, 1972.

Bernard, Claude. "La Problématique de l'échange dans 'Le Chef-d'œuvre inconnu.' " *L'Année Balzac* (1983): 201–13.

Berthaud, Madeleine. *Le Thème de la jalousie dans la littérature française à l'époque de Louis XIII.* Geneva: Droz, 1981.

Bettelheim, Bruno. *The Uses of Enchantment: The Meaning and Importance of Fairy Tales.* New York: Vintage, 1977.

Blanchot, Maurice. *L'Espace littéraire.* Paris: Gallimard, 1968.

Bloom, Harold. *The Anxiety of Influence: A Theory of Poetry.* New York: Oxford University Press, 1973.

——. "Introduction to Proust." In *Dilemmes du roman: Essays in Honor of Georges May,* ed. Catherine Lafarge, pp. 311–25. Saratoga, Calif: Anma Libri, 1990.

Boas, George. *The Cult of Childhood.* London: Warburg Institute, 1966.

Booth, Wayne. *The Company We Keep.* Berkeley: University of California Press, 1988.

——. *The Rhetoric of Fiction.* Chicago: University of Chicago Press, 1961.

——. *A Rhetoric of Irony.* Chicago: University of Chicago Press, 1974.

Boyd, Brian. *Vladimir Nabokov.* 2 vols. Princeton: Princeton University Press, 1990.

Brooks, Peter. *Body Work: Objects of Desire in Modern Narrative.* Cambridge: Harvard University Press, 1993.

——. *Reading for the Plot: Design and Intention in Narrative.* New York: Knopf, 1984.

Bryson, Norman. *Looking at the Overlooked: Four Essays on Still-Life Painting.* Cambridge: Harvard University Press, 1990.

Butler, Judith. *Gender Trouble: Feminism and the Subversion of Identity.* New York: Routledge, 1990.

Carter, Keryn. "The Blank Space of Lucy Snowe's Reflection." *AUMLA* 76 (1991): 1–12.

Chambers, Ross. "Irony and Misogyny: Authority and the Homosocial in Baudelaire and Flaubert." *Australian Journal of French Studies* 26, 3 (1989): 272–88.

——. *Mélancholie et opposition.* Paris: Corti, 1987.

——. "Narrative and Other Triangles." *Journal of Narrative Technique* 19 (1989): 31–48.

——. *Story and Situation. Narrative Seduction and the Power of Fiction.* Minneapolis: University of Minnesota Press, 1984.

Chardin, Philippe. *L'Amour dans la haine, ou la jalousie dans la littérature moderne.* Geneva: Droz, 1990.

——. "La Jalousie sans qualités." *Europe* 741–742 (Jan.–Feb. 1991): 36–44.

Charles, Michel. *Rhétorique de la lecture.* Paris: Seuil, 1977.

Clark, Kenneth. *Civilisation.* London: BBC and John Murray, 1969.

Cohn, Dorrit. *Transparent Minds.* Princeton: Princeton University Press, 1978.

Dällenbach, Lucien. *Le Récit spéculaire: Essai sur la mise en abyme.* Paris: Seuil, 1977.

Daly, Mary. *Pure Lust.* London: Women's Press, 1984.

De Man, Paul. *Allegories of Reading: Figural Language in Rousseau, Nietzsche, Rilke, and Proust.* New Haven: Yale University Press, 1989.

Dentan, Michel. *Le Texte et son lecteur.* Lausanne: L'Aire, 1983.

Eakin, Paul J. *Fictions in Autobiography: Studies in the Art of Self-Invention.* Princeton: Princeton University Press, 1985.

Ellmann, Richard. *James Joyce.* New York: Oxford University Press, 1959.

——. *Ulysses on the Liffey.* London: Faber and Faber, 1972.

Felski, Rita. *Beyond Feminist Aesthetics.* Cambridge: Harvard University Press, 1989.

Fetterley, Judith. *The Resisting Reader: A Feminist Approach to American Fiction.* Bloomington: Indiana University Press, 1978.

Filoche, Jean-Luc. " 'Le Chef-d'œuvre inconnu': Peinture et connaissance." *L'Année Balzac* (1980): 47–59.
Finkelstein, Joanne. *The Fashioned Self.* Philadelphia: Temple University Press, 1991.
Francis, Claude, and Fernande Gontier. *Simone de Beauvoir.* Paris: Librairie académique Perrin, 1985.
Freud, Sigmund. *Complete Works.* Ed. James Strachey. Vol. 18. London: Hogarth Press, 1974.
———. *Gesammelte Werke,* vol. 13. London: Imago, 1940.
Gallop, Jane. *The Daughter's Seduction.* Ithaca: Cornell University Press, 1982.
Genette, Gérard. *Figures I.* Paris: Seuil, 1966.
———. *Figures II.* Paris: Seuil, 1969.
———. *Figures III.* Paris: Seuil, 1972.
———. *Palimpsestes.* Paris: Seuil, 1982.
Gilbert, Sandra M., and Susan Gubar. *The Madwoman in the Attic.* New Haven: Yale University Press, 1979.
———. *No Man's Land: The Place of the Woman Writer in the Twentieth Century.* I: *The War of the Words.* New Haven: Yale University Press, 1988. II: *Sexchanges.* New Haven: Yale University Press, 1989.
Girard, René. *Dostoïevski: Du double à l'unité.* Paris: Plon, 1963.
———. "Jealousy in the *Winter's Tale.*" In *Alphonse Juilland: D'une passion l'autre,* ed. Brigitte Cazelles, pp. 39–62. Saratoga, Calif.: Anma Libri, 1987.
———. *Mensonge romantique et vérité romanesque.* Paris: Grasset, 1961.
———. *"To Double Business Bound": Essays on Literature, Mimesis, and Anthropology.* Baltimore: Johns Hopkins University Press, 1978.
Godard, Barbara. "Telling It Over Again: Atwood's Art of Parody." *Canadian Poetry* 21 (Fall–Winter 1987): 1–30.
Green, André. *Narcissisme de vie, narcissisme de mort.* Paris: Editions de Minuit, 1983.
Gregory, Stephen. "A Project for a Revolution in the Labyrinth, or Just Jealousy?" *AUMLA* 76 (1991): 22–38.
Grzywacz, Margot. *"Eifersucht" in den romanischen Sprachen.* Bochum-Langendreer, Germany: H. Pöppinghaus o. H.-G., 1937.
Gutwirth, Madelyn. *The Twilight of the Goddesses: Women and Representation in the French Revolutionary Era.* New Brunswick: Rutgers University Press, 1992.
Hart, Clive, and David Hayman, eds. *James Joyce's "Ulysses": Critical Essays.* Berkeley: University of California Press, 1974.
Heilbrun, Carolyn G., and Margaret Higonnet, eds. *The Represen-*

tation of Women in Fiction. Baltimore: Johns Hopkins University Press, 1983.

Henke, Suzette. *James Joyce and the Politics of Desire*. New York: Routledge, 1990.

Herbert, Christopher. *"He Knew He Was Right*, Mrs. Lynn Linton, and the Duplicities of Victorian Marriage." *Texas Studies in Literature and Language* 25, 3 (1983): 448–69.

Heusel, Barbara Stevens. "Iris Murdoch's *A Word Child*: Playing Games with Wittgenstein's Perspectives." *Studies in the Humanities* 13, 2 (December 1986): 81–92.

Howard, Catherine E. " 'Only Connect': Logical Aesthetic of Fragmentation in *A Word Child*." *Twentieth-Century Literature* 38, 1 (1992): 54–65.

Hunt, David. *Parents and Children in History: The Psychology of Family Life in Early Modern France*. New York: Basic Books, 1973.

Hutcheon, Linda. *Narcissistic Narrative: The Metafictional Paradox*. New York: Methuen, 1984.

———. *A Theory of Parody: The Teachings of Twentieth-Century Art Forms*. New York: Methuen, 1985.

Jacobs, Carol. "The Too Good Soldier." *Glyph* 3 (1978): 32–51.

Jameson, Fredric. *The Political Unconscious: Narrative as a Socially Symbolic Act*. Ithaca: Cornell University Press, 1981.

Jardine, Alice A. *Gynesis: Configurations of Woman and Modernity*. Ithaca: Cornell University Press, 1985.

Jean, Raymon. *Lectures du désir*. Paris: Seuil, 1977.

Jefferson, Ann. *"De l'amour* et le roman polyphonique." *Poétique* 13 (April 1983): 149–62.

Johnson, Barbara. *A World of Difference*. Baltimore: Johns Hopkins University Press, 1987.

Jordan, Elaine. "The Dangers of Angela Carter." In *New Feminist Discourses*, ed. Isobel Armstrong, pp. 119–31. London: Routledge, 1992.

Kelly, Dorothy. *Fictional Genders*. Lincoln: University of Nebraska Press, 1989.

———. *Telling Glances: Voyeurism in the French Novel*. New Brunswick: Rutgers University Press, 1992.

Kermode, Frank. *The Sense of an Ending*. New York: Oxford University Press, 1967.

Kern, Stephen. *The Culture of Love*. Cambridge: Harvard University Press, 1992.

Klein, Melanie. *Contributions to Psycho-Analysis, 1921–1945*. London: Hogarth Press, 1973.

Kristeva, Julia. *Histoires d'amour*. Paris: Denoël, 1983.

———. *Soleil noir: Dépression et mélancolie.* Paris: Gallimard, 1987.

Labanyi, Jo. "City, Country, and Adultery in *La Regenta.*" *Bulletin of Hispanic Studies* 63 (1986): 53–66.

Lee, Hermione. *The Novels of Virginia Woolf.* London: Methuen, 1977.

Leenhardt, Jacques. *Lecture politique du roman "La Jalousie" de Robbe-Grillet.* Paris: Minuit, 1973.

Lloyd, Rosemary. *The Land of Lost Content: Children and Childhood in Nineteenth-Century French Literature.* Oxford: Clarendon Press, 1992.

———. "Marie-Claire Blais." In *Beyond the Nouveau Roman,* ed. M. Tilby, pp. 123–50. London: Berg, 1990.

Luxemburg, Jan van. "Ana's Pedestal: A Counterreading of *La Regenta.*" *Style* 22, 4 (Winter 1988): 559–75.

Maclachlan, Gale. "Reading in the Jealous Mode." *Australian Journal of French Studies* 27, 3 (1990): 291–301.

Maddox, Lucy. *Nabokov's Novels in English.* Athens: University of Georgia Press, 1983.

Marin, Louis. *Le Récit est un piège.* Paris: Minuit, 1978.

Massol-Bedoin, Chantal. "L'Artiste et l'imposture." *Romantisme* 54, 4 (1986): 44–57.

McCarthy, Mary. "A Bolt from the Blue." *New Republic,* June 4, 1962.

McDonald, Christie. "Republications." Trans. G. Smolenski. In *Reading Plus,* ed. Mary Ann Caws and Eugene Nicole, pp. 197–222. New York: Peter Lang, 1990.

Miller, Joseph Hillis. *Ariadne's Thread.* New Haven: Yale University Press, 1992.

———. " 'Herself against Herself': The Clarification of Clara Middleton." In *The Representation of Women in Fiction,* ed. Carolyn G. Heilbrun and Margaret R. Higonnet, pp. 98–123. Baltimore: Johns Hopkins University Press, 1983.

Millet-Gérard, Dominique. "Review of Chardin, *L'Amour dans la haine.*" *Revue d'histoire littéraire de la France* 93, 2 (March–April 1993): 305–6.

Moi, Toril. "The Missing Mother: The Oedipal Rivalries of René Girard." *Diacritics* 12 (1982): 21–31.

———. *Sexual/Textual Politics: Feminist Literary Theory.* London: Methuen, 1985.

Mulvey, Laura. "Visual Pleasure and Narrative Cinema." In *Art after Modernism: Rethinking Representation,* ed. Brian Wallis, pp. 361–74. Boston: Godine, 1984.

Murdoch, Iris. *The Sovereignty of Good.* New York: Schocken, 1971.

Nardine, Jane. "Tragedy, Farce, and Comedy in Trollope." *Genre* 15, 3 (1982): 303–13.

Naremore, James. *The World without a Self: Virginia Woolf and the Novel.* New Haven: Yale University Press, 1973.

Nicolson, Nigel. *Portrait of a Marriage.* New York: Athenaeum, 1973.

Nigro, Frank. "Who Framed *The Good Soldier*? Dowell's Story in Search of a Form." *Studies in the Novel* 24, 4 (1992): 381–91.

Nussbaum, Martha. *Love's Knowledge.* Oxford: Oxford University Press, 1990.

Paulson, William R. *The Noise of Culture: Literary Texts in a World of Information.* Ithaca: Cornell University Press, 1988.

Peel, Ellen. "Subject, Object, and the Alternation of First- and Third-Person Narration in Novels by Alther, Atwood, and Drabble: Toward a Theory of Feminine Aesthetics." *Critique: Studies in Contemporary Fiction* 30, 2 (1989): 107–22.

Pollock, Griselda. *Vision and Difference: Femininity, Feminism, and the Histories of Art.* New York: Routledge, 1988.

Pollock, Linda. *Forgotten Children.* Cambridge: Cambridge University Press, 1983.

Prince, Gerald. *Narratology: The Form and Functioning of Narrative.* The Hague: Mouton, 1982.

Rabine, Leslie W. *Reading the Romantic Heroine: Text, History, Ideology.* Ann Arbor: University of Michigan Press, 1985.

Rétif, Françoise. "Simone de Beauvoir et l'autre." *Les Temps modernes* 538 (May 1991): 76–95.

Rougemont, Denis de. *L'Amour et l'occident.* Paris: Plon, 1939.

———. *Love in the Western World.* Trans. Montgomery Belgion. Rev. and augmented ed. New York: Pantheon, 1956.

Rousset, Jean. *Le Lecteur intime: De Balzac au Journal.* Paris: Corti, 1986.

———. *Leurs Yeux se rencontrèrent: La scène de première vue dans le roman.* Paris: Corti, 1981.

Rowley, Hazel. *Christina Stead: A Biography.* Melbourne, Australia: Heinemann, 1993.

Rutherford, John. *Leopoldo Alas: "La Regenta."* London: Grant and Cutler, 1974.

Schefski, Harold K. "Tolstoy and Jealousy." *Irish Slavonic Studies* 10 (1989): 17–30.

Schehr, Lawrence. "The Unknown Subject." *Nineteenth-Century French Studies* 12–13 (Summer–Fall 1984): 58–69.

Schlegel, Friedrich. *Lucinde and the Fragments.* Trans. Peter Firchow. Minneapolis: University of Minnesota Press, 1971.

Schmideberg, Mellita. "Some Aspects of Jealousy and of Feeling Hurt." *Psychoanalytic Review* 40, 1 (1953): 1–16.

Schneider, Michel. *Voleurs de mots: Essai sur le plagiat, la psychanalyse et la pensée.* Paris: Gallimard, 1985.

Schochet, Gordon. *Patriarchalism in Political Thought.* New York: Basic Books, 1975.

Schor, Naomi. *George Sand and Idealism.* New York: Columbia University Press, 1993.

Schultze, Sydney. "Choromanski's *Jealousy and Medicine.*" *International Fiction Review* 10, 1 (Winter 1983): 15–18.

Segal, Hanna. *Introduction to the Work of Melanie Klein.* London: Hogarth Press, 1973.

Segal, Naomi. *Narcissus and Echo.* Manchester, Eng.: Manchester University Press, 1988.

——. *The Unintended Reader: Feminism and "Manon Lescaut."* Cambridge: Cambridge University Press, 1986.

Segalen, Martine. *Love and Power in the Peasant Family: Rural France in the Nineteenth Century.* Trans. Sarah Mathews. Chicago: University of Chicago Press, 1983.

Serres, Michel. *Le Parasite.* Paris: Grasset, 1980.

Shorter, Edward. *The Making of the Modern Family.* London: Collins, 1976.

Showalter, Elaine. *Sexual Anarchy.* New York, Penguin, 1990.

Sinclair, Alison. "The Consuming Passion: Appetite and Hunger in *La Regenta.*" *Bulletin of Hispanic Studies* 69 (1992): 245–61.

Spacks, Patricia Meyer. *The Female Imagination.* New York: Avon, 1975.

Stanzel, Franz K. *A Theory of Narrative.* Trans. C. Goedsche. Cambridge: Cambridge University Press, 1984.

Stone, Lawrence. *The Family, Sex, and Marriage in England, 1500–1800.* London: Weidenfeld and Nicolson, 1977.

Suhamy, Henri. "Le Psychologisme contre la psychologie: Quelques remarques sur la jalousie de Leontes et de quelques autres." *Caliban* 21 (1984): 191–210.

Suleiman, Susan. *Subversive Intent: Gender, Politics, and the Avant-Garde.* Cambridge: Harvard University Press, 1990.

Suleiman, Susan, and Inge Crosman, eds. *The Reader in the Text: Essays on Audience and Interpretation.* Princeton: Princeton University Press, 1980.

Tanner, Tony. *Adultery in the Novel.* Baltimore: Johns Hopkins University Press, 1979.

Taylor, Charles. *Sources of the Self: The Making of the Modern Identity.* Cambridge: Harvard University Press, 1989.

Terdiman, Richard. *Discourse/Counter-Discourse.* Ithaca: Cornell University Press, 1985.
——. "The Mnemonics of Musset's *Confession.*" *Representations* 26 (1989): 26–48.
——. *Present Past: Modernity and the Memory Crisis.* Ithaca: Cornell University Press, 1993.
Turner, Jack. "Murdoch vs. Freud in *A Severed Head* and Other Novels." *Literature and Psychology* 36, 1–2 (1990): 110–21.
Van Sommers, Peter. *Jealousy.* Harmondsworth: Penguin, 1988.
Watt, Ian. *The Rise of the Novel.* London: Chatto and Windus, 1957.
Wolf, Naomi. *The Beauty Myth: How Images of Beauty Are Used against Women.* New York: Morrow, 1991.
Wotipka, Paul. "Ocularity and Irony: Pictorialism in *Villette.*" *Word and Image* 8, 2 (1992): 100–108.

Index